W9-BCU-391

EXPLORING LITERATURE

A Collaborative Approach

Kathleen Shine Cain

Albert C. DeCiccio

Michael J. Rossi

Merrimack College

NEW HANOVER COUNTY
PUBLIC LIBRARY
201 CHESTNUT STREET
WILMINGTON, N C 28401

Allyn and Bacon

Boston   London   Toronto   Sydney   Tokyo   Singapore

Editor in Chief, Humanities: Joseph Opiela
Series Editorial Assistant: Brenda Conaway
Production Administrator: Susan McIntyre
Editorial-Production Service: Kathy Smith
Text Designer: Susan McIntyre
Cover Administrator: Suzanne Harbison
Composition Buyer: Linda Cox
Manufacturing Buyer: Louise Richardson

Credits: pages 5 and 136, from *The Poetry of Robert Frost* edited by Edward Connery Latham.
Copyright 1930, 1934, 1939, © 1969 by Holt, Rinehart and Winston. Copyright © 1958, 1962 by
Robert Frost. Copyright © 1967 by Lesley Frost Ballantine. Henry Holt and Company, Inc. Publisher;
p. 88, Copyright © 1980 by The New York Times Company. Reprinted by permission; p. 191,
"Metaphors" by Sylvia Plath from *The Collected Poems of Sylvia Plath* edited by Ted Hughes. Copyright
© 1960 by Ted Hughes. Reprinted by permission of HarperCollins Publishers; p. 202, "Girl" from *At
the Bottom of the River*" by Jamaica Kincaid. Reprinted by permission of Farrar, Straus & Giroux, Inc.;
p. 203, ©The Executor of Henry Reed's Estate. Reprinted from Henry Reed's *Collected Poems* edited by
Jon Stallworthy (1991) by permission of Oxford University Press; p. 216, "Everyday Use" from *In Love
& Trouble,* copyright © 1973 by Alice Walker, reprinted by permission of Harcourt Brace Jovanovich,
Inc.; p. 222, Copyright © 1983 David Bottoms. From *In a U Haul North of Damascus* published by
William Morrow and Company, Inc., New York. Reprinted by permission of David Bottoms and Maria

Continued on page 263, which is to be considered an extension of the copyright page.

Copyright ©1993 by Allyn & Bacon
A Division of Simon & Schuster, Inc.
160 Gould Street
Needham Heights, MA 02194

All rights reserved. No part of the material protected by this copyright notice may be reproduced or
utilized in any form or by any means, electronic or mechanical, including photocopying, recording, or
by any information storage and retrieval system, without the written permission of the copyright owner.

Library of Congress Cataloging-in-Publication Data

Cain, Kathleen Shine.
    Exploring literature : a collaborative approach / Kathleen Shine
Cain, Albert C. DeCiccio, Michael J. Rossi.
      p.   cm.
    Includes index.
    ISBN 0-205-13919-1
    1. Reader-response criticism. 2. Literature—Study and teaching
(Higher) I. DeCiccio, Albert C. II. Rossi, Michael John.
III. Title.
PN98.R38C345 1993
807'.71'1—dc20   92-26590
                                                 CIP

Printed in the United States of America
10 9 8 7 6 5 4 3 2 1   96 95 94 93 92

Contents

PART II   FROM EXPLORATION TO COMMUNICATION: MAKING FORMAL PRESENTATIONS

Preface

We are the inheritors, neither of an inquiry about ourselves and the world, nor of an accumulating body of information, but of a conversation, begun in the primeval forests and extended and made more articulate in the course of centuries. It is a conversation which goes on both in public and within each of ourselves. . . . And it is this conversation which, in the end, gives place and character to every human activity and utterance.

—Michael Oakeshott

COLLABORATIVE THEORY

As its title indicates, this book is based on the theory of **collaborative learning**. Like Michael Oakeshott, we believe that reading and writing are social, collaborative acts, and that literature itself is a product of such acts. Like those who produce literature, those who read and write about it are participants in a collaborative process—to a great extent, they are all participants in the ongoing conversation of humankind.

In the traditional literature classroom, this conversation is less dialogue than monologue: Instructors hand down to students the "accumulating body of information" generated by literary critics, sometimes creating the impression that literary works have an indisputable meaning and that absorbing information about the works is more important than experiencing the works firsthand. While this approach has its merits, it does not reveal the route taken by critics and professors in formulating their responses to literary works—namely conversation and, in some cases, healthy argument.

In the collaborative classroom, a real dialogue takes place, with students actively engaging in exploring literary works. Students begin to practice what critics and professors do when they make meaning of a work: read, ask questions, discuss, write, read again, ask more questions, discuss again, write again, and so on. Engaging in this process not only helps students understand how meaning is made, but it also provides them with the confidence to begin questioning the *experts* as well as their peers. Students in the collaborative classroom find their own meaning in literary works, recognizing that meaning is not the sole property of critics or professors.

One of the major premises of this book is that a literary work is always in the process of coming into being—that authors write to engage their readers in a conversation that extends beyond the limits of place, time, and even culture. Readers participate in that conversation when they take up a poem, a story, a play, or an essay. Both as individuals and as members of a community of readers, they *negotiate* meaning by responding to the written words and by seeking understanding. *Negotiation* here refers to the active give-and-take that readers engage in, trying to reconcile their responses to the work itself and to the responses of others.

Every work is constantly renewed and recreated by each new reader who experiences it and who engages actively in thinking about its significance. In this sense, meaning is *made* rather than *found*. Readers make meaning partly as the artistry of the author directs them and partly as their own social and intellectual environment and values direct them. In the end, what a literary work *means*, or what a reader who speaks or writes about literature can comfortably and confidently *say* about a literary work, will probably differ to some extent from age to age, community to community, and person to person. As they negotiate the meaning of a work in conversation—trying to reconcile different responses—readers seldom achieve consensus, but they do succeed in recognizing the richness of response possible for a work. As readers test and develop their ideas collaboratively, they come to see the meaning of a work as an outgrowth of their shared experience of it.

This book offers students and instructors an invitation to join in the conversation both within the classroom and within the wider communities of readers. Within the classroom that conversation is usually informal, whether oral or written; within wider communities, however, readers usually rely on more formal—usually written—means of communicating ideas about literary works. This book encourages readers to become comfortable with talking informally about literature, and it provides strategies to assist in communicating formally about literature. We hope that as students read, respond to, and write about literary works using this text, they will grow comfortable with a dynamic process emphasizing the belief that meaning—in any context—can be constructed in collaboration with others.

DESIGN OF THE BOOK

In order to help students make meaning of a work and ultimately to write effectively about it, this book is organized to focus on two broad areas of activity:

Exploring Works Actively and Collaboratively (Part I):   In order to write comfortably about a literary work, readers need to become familiar with the work and to develop ideas about which they can feel confident. Chapter 1 introduces readers to the practice of exploring literature collaboratively. Chapters 2–5 examine the various activities involved in that exploration (active reading, writing in a double-entry journal, discussing in groups, and conducting informal research), and include examples taken from actual student responses, as well as exercises that provide students with practice in exploring literature collaboratively. Chapter 6 includes the four selections used throughout the book, as well as examples of student responses to the works (including annotations, journal entries, transcripts of group discussions, and comments on informal research).

Communicating Views and Conclusions Formally (Part II): When readers move from exploring ideas informally to presenting them formally, their concerns shift from finding good ideas to presenting those ideas for the approval of others. This section provides students with strategies for sharing ideas generated through the exploratory process and for helping other people to recognize the value of these ideas. Chapters 7 and 8 explore the process that most writers go through as they seek to formalize their responses to literature (generating topics, drafting and revising, responding to works in progress). Chapter 9 introduces students to some forms of literary analysis, including types of formal presentations (explications, analyses, and evaluations). Chapter 10 explains the conventions agreed upon by literary scholars (quoting, paraphrasing, and summarizing sources, and documenting sources used in a presentation). These chapters include extensive examples from actual student work. Chapter 11 invites students to respond to literature creatively, either by composing their own creative work or by adding to the works they've read. This chapter includes both examples and exercises to guide students through the creative process.

Chapter 12 includes eight additional literary works divided into two groups. In order to encourage students to make their own meaning of the works, there is no apparatus in these sections. Students are invited to come to their own conclusions regarding the meanings of these selections, both individually and as parts of a thematic unit. The Appendices cover collaborative projects and essay assignments, and the brief glossary provides students with definitions of some of the terms they might encounter in an introduction to literature course.

ACKNOWLEDGMENTS

We wish to thank the four students who agreed to work through the collaborative process on the selections covered in the Case Study and to allow us to make a record of their activity. Debbie Carlisle, Eric Labbe, Kelly Leighton, and Cinde Veinot put into this project the same time and energy that they put into their coursework—their insights and observations allowed us to reinforce theory with clear, accessible examples. Our thanks go as well to the other students whose work is used here: Michael Damphousse, Sheila Dodson, Angela Fusco, Heather Hussey, Mary Massa, Lynn Michaud, Kathy Royal, and Babette Duncan Wilson. And of course we thank the students in our literature classes for their affirmation of the value of collaborative learning.

This text is itself a product of the collaborative process: Beyond the collaboration among the authors and their students, *Exploring Literature* has benefited from the contributions of reviewers and editors. We wish to thank the following individuals who read drafts of the manuscript and provided many useful suggestions and criticisms: Chris Anson, University of Minnesota; Patricia Bizzell, College of the Holy Cross; Betsy Bowen, Fairfield University; H. Eric Branscomb, Stonehill College; Elizabeth Chiseri-Strater, University of Chicago; Rex Easley, University of Cincinnati; Lisa Ede, Oregon State University; Cheryl Glenn, Oregon State University; Muriel Harris, Purdue University; C. Jeriel Howard, Northeastern Illinois University; Thomas E. Martinez, Villanova University; Joan Rothstein-Vandergriff, University of Missouri—Kansas City; Eugene Smith, University of Washington; and Louise Z. Smith, University of Massachusetts, Boston.

Without the advice and support of the editorial staff at Allyn and Bacon, *Exploring Literature* might still be an idea in search of a practical format. Amy Capute and Brenda Conaway facilitated communication between authors, editors, and reviewers. Susan McIntyre expertly oversaw production of the text, and Kathy Smith braved a hurricane to ensure that production was kept on schedule. Finally, Joe Opiela deserves special thanks for his keen vision—Joe's understanding of what makes a text work kept us on course throughout the process of transforming a proposal into a pedagogically sound textbook.

Special thanks go to our families: Jim and Shannon Cain; Donna, Abigail, and Aaron DeCiccio; and Joan, Martha, and Rebecca Rossi. Their support and encouragement—not to mention their putting up with irritable would-be authors—was invaluable throughout the process of producing this text.

1 "Whether They Work Together Or Apart"

An Introduction to Working Collaboratively

Writing about literature begins with reading or experiencing literature, thinking about it, and gaining familiarity with sharing your responses and thoughts with other people. Sharing reactions, feelings, experiences, perceptions, and ideas—that's what makes socializing with friends, attending sporting events, arguing about politics, or participating in countless other activities enjoyable. That's also what should make reading and responding to literature enjoyable. This book invites you to approach literature as an occasion for the mutual sharing with others of reactions, feelings, experiences, perceptions, and ideas concerning literary works.

In other words, you are invited to approach literature as a social activity: to read literature and to respond to it not merely as an isolated individual but in community with others as a participant in an active give-and-take process. Besides finding this interaction enjoyable in itself, you'll see that it leads to a more complete and satisfying experience of the literary works discussed. You'll also find that it leads you, as the natural outgrowth of your activity, to a desire to communicate in writing about literature. You'll find that writing about literature is not an isolated activity, detached from the rest of experience, but simply another, more formal way of sharing with others.

If approaching literature as a social activity is new to you, then you may be surprised to discover that literature has always had a strong social dimension. Historically, literature was more commonly intended to be experienced in community—stimulating conversation, thought, and reaction—rather than privately experienced in solitude. This social dimension has always made, and continues to make, literature a powerful means to delight, entertain, and instruct.

The social dimension of literature also suggests one reason why simply reading a literary work may not be enough to make everything about it clear right away. To be food for discussion, and a stimulus to thinking and conversation, literature ought to offer people something to talk about. It might present ideas or views to react against; it might puzzle and raise questions; or it might focus attention inward on aspects of its artistic craft or outward to aspects of its social and political context. Those literary works that have been termed classics, or Literature with a capital "L," are often simply works that seem continually to offer us new avenues for discussion.

When you first start working with literature, you may find that it helps to view literary works in terms of everyday questions. Literature is similar to open-ended questions instead of closed questions. Closed questions really ask, *Can you come up with 'X'?* (everything else would be the wrong answer). Open-ended questions ask, *What can you come up with?* (a variety of answers is expected, and each answer competes for the recognition of our peers as, in some way, being better than other answers). For example, the question, "Should alcohol be banned at campus events?" is a closed question, while "How would you respond to the alcohol problem on campus?" is an open-ended question. The open-ended question is "better" because it prompts further discussion, offers new ideas, stimulates thinking, or pulls together pieces of earlier discussion as parts of a coherent picture. Of course, open-ended questions do expect people to stay within reasonable boundaries in order to provide relevant answers. Take, for example, the boundaries given in this open-ended question from a survey: "Recently, a student group stated that alcohol abuse is becoming a serious problem on college campuses. What are your reactions to that statement?" The idea of alcohol use on college campuses sets the boundary for a wide range of relevant responses, but out-of-bounds would be comments about such matters as sexism in chemistry exams, alcohol use in industry, or even other drugs on campus.

Literary works are similar to open-ended questions in that they also offer boundaries for relevant discussion. At times, some of these boundaries may be obvious because writers often have some notions about where they would like discussion to lead. In fact, writers frequently offer signposts to their readers. For example, Shakespeare's *Romeo and Juliet* opens with a prologue labeling the lovers "star cross'd" and condemning the anger and bloodshed that mark their families' feud, inviting with these signposts a discussion of the place of fate (versus free will) in human affairs on one hand, and the relative power of hatred versus love on the other hand. That play's broader boundaries are established by all it presents to readers for response (just as the sample survey question set its boundaries by presenting the topic of alcohol abuse on campus for response). Outside the boundaries would be whatever has little or nothing to do with what the play presents. Often, discussion of literary works focuses on what signposts and boundaries their authors have actually provided.

People sometimes find the open-endedness of literature troubling because they feel more secure with *answers* than with *questions*. They would rather agree with a "right" answer than take the risk of thinking for themselves and discussing, or even negotiating about, their ideas with others.

That attitude is unproductive at best, dangerous at worst. Think about it for a moment: With that attitude in science, people would still "know" that the earth is flat and the sun moves around the earth. So, if you find literature puzzling, if it raises questions for you, if it makes you react strongly in disagreement with something depicted in it, if it makes you think about how a piece works artistically, or even if it makes you think about your similar experiences, you are thinking for yourself. You may be ready to join in a give-and-take because you have something to say, a desire to know, a reaction to get off your mind, or something to share—and an openness to consider what other people wish to share with you. You may be ready to approach literature and to get the most out of doing so.

People sometimes seek a "right" answer in order to avoid the discomfort of feeling confused. But confusion is not necessarily a bad thing. In fact, in the study of literature—as in life itself—confusion is often the first step toward understanding. Since it's usually counterproductive to work through confusion alone, most people almost instinctively seek out another person when they don't know what to do. When you approach someone else, however, you don't do so simply to get the right answer. Instead, you do so to begin a discussion, to begin the process of making sense of things—to begin to make meaning.

GETTING BY WITH A LITTLE HELP FROM YOUR FRIENDS

Imagine the following scene in a college writing center: Jason walks in, frustrated about a paper assignment in his Introduction to Literature class. He complains to Kim, a tutor, that he can't figure out what the symbols in a story mean. After a little hesitation, he blurts out, "Come on, you're an English major—tell me what it means!" Instead, Kim encourages Jason to compare notes with other members of his class, asking each other questions, trying out ideas, and arguing different responses. Kim assures Jason that this process is exactly what she and other majors do when they're trying to come to terms with a literary work.

In this scene, Jason does what comes naturally to all of us in looking for someone to talk to. But he tries to take a shortcut by asking to be given an answer instead of asking for help in talking through his confusion. If Jason had been genuinely lost and Kim had simply told him what the story "means" (even though hers would probably be just one of many legitimate interpretations), he would still be at a loss to explain in his paper how or why that meaning fits the story. Worse yet, the next time he found himself faced with a difficult literary work, he'd have to head right back to the writing center for the "answer" instead of having some idea of how to go about making meaning of literature himself. Kim helps Jason toward independence when she shows him, instead of the "answer," a process that has worked for her in making meaning of confusing material.

What happens if Jason follows Kim's advice? As he tries to talk about the story with others, he'll become more certain about what's happening in it, he'll begin to figure out what he thinks of the story, and he'll start to articulate his ideas. The story will begin to make more sense through the discussion among students. As Jason continues talking to others in his class, he'll probably hear ideas different from his. That will force both him and his fellow students to reexamine their ideas, to try to justify them, and to entertain the possibility that there may be more than one way to come to terms with the story. As some interpretations are discarded, others will be strengthened, and still others will be altered to accommodate different views. Ultimately, the group engaged in the discussion will have a better understanding of the story, and Jason will have rehearsed informally what he needs to do formally in his paper in order to present his ideas and to show how or why they are valid for this story.

As a student who explores literature collaboratively, you are obviously at an advantage: You come to an understanding of a work not through listening to an "expert," but through the normal give-and-take of conversation. You gain confidence in your interpretation because you have already put it to the test. When faced with another difficult work, you feel much more comfortable about trying to understand it on your own. And you also discover something far more valuable than any given interpretation: You begin to understand that meaning doesn't exist somewhere "out there," waiting for you to find it. Literary critics present their interpretations of particular works only after thinking and writing about their own ideas, sharing those ideas with others, listening to others' ideas, reworking their own ideas, and engaging in research. When you work collaboratively, you are applying, in a more immediate way, the same kind of give-and-take that critics practice in making meaning of a text.

In order for the method to succeed, however, you have to recognize that there's no such thing as one "correct" interpretation of a work. If there were, most critics would be out of business, there would be no profit in writing or reading essays about literature, and there would be very little enjoyment to be had from reading literature. The true excitement of reading literature comes from the social activity it engenders—the conversation between the author and reader, as well as between readers. It is only through that conversation that a literary work comes to have meaning, and it is only through that conversation that a literary work can achieve its ultimate goal, which is to delight and entertain as well as to instruct.

One of the cornerstones of this book is the view that learning is shared. We believe that before you can become confident about putting in writing your individual response to literature, you need to become confident in your ability to share what you think you know with others. We believe that cooperation among individuals builds community and that community, in time, supports individuals. According to this view, the literature classroom—like all classrooms—should be abuzz with talk: debate, propositions, and instruction. In this way, you will learn that making meaning is a collaborative effort, not an exercise in how to uncover the teacher's clues for understanding his or her meaning for a poem, a play, a story, or an essay. In the end, we believe that you will learn the process critics, teachers, and writers themselves have internalized in understanding literature: read actively, write honestly, discuss with others, reassess, and so on.

COLLABORATION IN ACTION

If you're wondering just how the collaborative process can lead to a finished work, think for a moment about what you're reading now. We'd like to share the story of how we began the last portion of this chapter: a formal introduction to making meaning of a poem collaboratively.

For one of us, the idea for a book like this goes back to an experience similar to Jason's in the vignette. Having come across Robert Frost's poem "A Tuft of Flowers," he was at first puzzled. But having read a good deal about ways of making meaning, and having discussed such issues with colleagues, he began to look at the poem as something more than an account of a pastoral scene. When he showed the poem to the other two authors, a conversation began. Through writing and talking about "The Tuft of Flowers," we three concluded that, regardless of Frost's original intent in writing the poem, he had certainly communicated to us a message about collaborative learning. We discovered that Frost's poem illustrated our notions of collaborative learning and of how to make meaning of a work of literature. *We had made our own meaning of the poem.* Following the poem are transcriptions of some of the conversations that led to our conclusions, and finally the written portion of this chapter that grew out of our conversations.

THE TUFT OF FLOWERS

Robert Frost

I went to turn the grass once after one
Who mowed it in the dew before the sun.

The dew was gone that made his blade so keen
Before I came to view the leveled scene.

I looked for him behind an isle of trees;   5
I listened for his whetstone on the breeze.

But he had gone his way, the grass all mown,
And I must be, as he had been—alone,

"As all must be," I said within my heart,
"Whether they work together or apart."   10

But as I said it, swift there passed me by
On noiseless wing a bewildered butterfly,

Seeking with memories grown dim o'er night
Some resting flower of yesterday's delight.

And once I marked his flight go round and round,   15
As where some flower lay withering on the ground.

And then he flew as far as eye could see,
And then on tremulous wing came back to me.

I thought of questions that have no reply,
And would have turned to toss the grass to dry;   20

But he turned first, and led my eye to look
At a tall tuft of flowers beside a brook,

A leaping tongue of bloom the scythe had spared
Beside a reedy brook the scythe had bared.

The mower in the dew had loved them thus,   25
By leaving them to flourish, not for us,

Nor yet to draw one thought of ours to him,
But from sheer morning gladness at the brim.

The butterfly and I had lit upon,
Nevertheless, a message from the dawn,   30

That made me hear the wakening birds around,
And hear his long scythe whispering to the ground,

And feel a spirit kindred to my own;
So that henceforth I worked no more alone;

But glad with him, I worked as with his aid,   35
And weary, sought at noon with him the shade;

And dreaming, as it were, held brotherly speech
With one whose thought I had not hoped to reach.

"Men work together," I told him from the heart,
"Whether they work together or apart."   40

In the first segment of our conversation, we discussed why we thought the poem was relevant:

> AD: Using the poem . . . isn't a new idea for me. It's a poem that's been mentioned by others who've talked about collaborative approaches. I think it ties into what we're saying because we normally think that the meaning to a poem is something that an individual alone has to find. That's what's happening in "Tuft" too. Frost leads the person in the poem to understand that everybody is connected—so the final lines are poignant for me because there's a change, a reversal, an understanding when the speaker says, "Men work together whether they work together or apart." I feel that ties into everything we've been trying to say so far, . . . especially with the idea that works of literature are conversations that we're invited to partake in [and] that writers of literature speak to their readers.

> MR: In part what we're doing here is investing this poem with an additional meaning by saying, "Now let this poem represent something that Frost probably was unaware of when he wrote it, although his general idea is probably similar to what we're thinking about." When we envision the poem as a symbol for collaboration, it's a symbol that *we've* created out of what was already there. We're really . . . investing the poem with another meaning, and interestingly enough it's a meaning that doesn't conflict with what was there in the beginning.

In this segment, we found ourselves talking about two things at once: first, the poem itself regardless of our ideas about collaborative learning, and second, how the poem fit in with those ideas. What we found interesting was that we couldn't separate the two strands of thought. We kept coming back to what the poem meant *to us*:

> KSC: One of the tougher parts of the poem is why this tuft of flowers was left in the first place. Maybe it's so basic it's unanswerable for someone who's never attempted to leave a tuft while mowing the lawn.

> MR: Have you ever left a tuft of flowers while mowing the lawn? It's pretty . . . hard to do these days with riding mowers.

> AD: Next to fences, around the sheds—and they're never flowers, always weeds.

MR: I know; that's a good question, though. He [the speaker or the turner] speculates and says . . . he knows the mower must have loved the flowers but left "them to flourish, not for us, nor yet to draw one thought of ours to him, but from sheer morning gladness at the brim." The message that he and the butterfly light upon is a message from the dawn. The connectedness goes beyond just them so that the whole is greater than the sum of its parts—which is ultimately what we're saying when we talk about collaboration.

AD: It sounds very romantic to me. The guy [the mower] who left the tuft was the person who feels things more strongly than other people and then the weeder or the mower [turner] who comes across the tuft has understood this and is part of that circle. It seems to me a whole lot like what happens in class with collaboration. It all has to do with the dawn . . . where all images and symbols reside.

MR: I'm afraid my literal mind simply says, "What better time to cut the grass than dawn. Start our day early, and mow the grass so that it can dry in the sun."

KSC: But that's what a lot of pastoral poetry is about. That very ordinary practical and reasonable nature stuff is evocative. So the dawn, even though you're talking about sensible mowing times, also says something about oneness with nature and beauty and truth and all that.

AD: But the interesting thing here is that Frost doesn't press oneness with nature so much as oneness with other people. It's sort of a *social* connectedness. Nature is only the *intermediary*, the world in which it happens.

KSC: And that connectedness is what we're talking about in collaborative learning—the classroom is our "field."

AD: . . . I like the idea of the connection that this poem brings to mind between collaborative learning and the reader's response, because our reading is not perhaps the traditional reading of the poem. I think that the idea of the reader's response has something to do with students' journals and with coming together in class and then giving a report to the class afterwards.

KSC: Yes. I was just thinking the other day about the poem, and I decided that he [the turner] knows from the beginning that people work together. He has to—this is an assembly-line type of operation: one person mows, another turns the grass to dry its other side, and later someone comes to fork it onto a wagon. This is a process, not a series of unrelated activities. But in the end he knows it from the heart. . . . It strikes me as a good parallel to the collaborative group work where people go through it by rote and only after awhile come to realize that it really works. Those

journals seem isolated, but they're like the mower's work; they're connected to what comes later. . . .

Now that you've listened in on parts of that conversation, we'd like to
show you how it translated into a more formal introduction to making
meaning collaboratively.

By the way, the tapes of our conversation revealed quite a bit of digres-
sion—talk about families, school politics, current baseball standings, and so
on. And the conversations excerpted here led to other conversations as we
looked at notes and drafts, decided against producing a sample essay about
literature generated by our conversation, and chose to use our conversation
to help explain what collaborative learning is. We think that both our
interpretation itself and the method we use to relate the poem to our ideas
illustrate the premise of this book. See if you agree.

MAKING MEANING OF "THE TUFT OF FLOWERS"

The closing lines of Robert Frost's "Tuft of Flowers" are memorable, and
they would make a good motto for this text: "Men work together . . .
Whether they work together or apart" (39–40). But how can people work
together if they work *apart*? Is Frost just playing with words? What does he
mean?

Readers often start to think about a literary work when something seems
puzzling or questions come to mind. When they begin to wonder, the work
begins to challenge them. It invites them to add the thrill of the hunt for
knowledge to the pleasure of sharing whatever experience the work presents. Thus, the same puzzlement and questions which inexperienced readers of literature so often dread are what experienced readers of literature
welcome as invitations full of promise. They search for questions when the
questions don't come on their own.

The puzzling point, or the questions that start each person thinking, are
often different, however. What each reader notices, recognizes, or understands will differ because each person is the unique product of his or her
individual history, personality, experiences, and education. A point that is
puzzling to one person may seem obvious to another person, and the other
person may be puzzled by what seems obvious to the first. This is one reason
that sharing through discussion with others is helpful. Each person has
something valuable to share, and each person has something to learn from
others. How far one question or another can lead differs too. So sharing
through discussion with others often helps to identify the more promising
questions for further thought and discussion.

Sometimes, when you first begin working with literature, it's easy to find questions but hard to find a way to get started answering them. If you find yourself or your discussion group becoming stuck as you try to answer your questions, you can get things moving by talking about what you know or what seems obvious to you. Just talking over the facts often leads to further discussion. To arrive at what you don't know, talk through what you do know. (This strategy also works when members of your group think that they have no questions or that they have nothing to say.) Remember, what is obvious to one person may not be obvious to another. In many areas of life, people argue about the "facts" as hotly as they argue about what the facts mean. If you discover that everyone in your group doesn't agree on the facts, your group may have far more to discuss than you originally expected. This strategy of reviewing what you know—what seems obvious to you—can be especially helpful when discussing poetry, since the way language is used in poetry often leaves readers a little uncertain about the facts. Consider how more than one idea is packed into "once after one" (1), "an isle of trees" (5) or even "on noiseless wing" (12). What exactly do these phrases mean?

Let's try it. What do you know about Frost's poem? You know the speaker has come to a field to complete a task: turning over the newly mown grass. Someone else (he does not know who) mowed the field early in the morning and left after completing the job. Before the speaker can start his work, however, a butterfly appears and seems confused to find all the grass and flowers gone. Eventually, the butterfly finds a tuft of flowers left uncut near a brook. The speaker notices this and decides that the mower must have left the tuft on purpose.

In addition to these bare facts, some additional information can be noted. The speaker tells us what he is thinking. He also attributes thoughts to the butterfly and the mower that actually tell us more about his own thinking (since he can't really know what the butterfly or the mower was thinking). Moreover, the poem chronicles a change in the speaker's view of life: he changes from believing that all work "alone" (8) to all work "together" (39) when he repeats the line, "Whether they work together or apart" (10; 40).

You might also notice that the butterfly and the tuft play key roles in bringing about this change, and because they have key roles both probably have some symbolic value. But the butterfly and the tuft are actually helpful rather than merely mysterious. The butterfly appears at the moment the speaker expresses the view that everyone exists in isolation. When he is just about to cease watching the butterfly and begin his solitary work (20), the butterfly leads the speaker to the tuft of flowers which, in his thoughts, provides a link between him and the mower. The link produces a sense of kinship which fosters a sense of community for the speaker in place of his earlier isolation.

Much of the information about the poem in the preceding description would probably be found on a second or third reading of the poem or early in discussions with other readers. (Of course, coming to agreement on the facts and putting the description together in writing, as it is done here, would take more time and effort.) Notice that the description cannot really confine itself to facts. It begins to slip into interpretations of fact and finally to suggest ideas about theme when the ending is discussed in terms of upholding community over isolation. Reviewing the known has gotten things moving here. It is even beginning to direct attention back toward that question of how individuals working apart can actually be working together. Alternatively, reviewing the known can lead to new questions to explore. What is important is to begin thinking and discussing.

You might find that instead of reviewing facts, you can comfortably begin directly with a key question such as, "How can people work *together* if they work *apart*?" Or you might be intrigued by other possibilities: You might find that you want to know more about haying as a process, especially about the importance of the speaker's role of turning the cut grass and the value of harvesting grass in the first place. You might recall and wish to examine a similar experience in your own past. You might want to know more about Frost's life and to consider identifying the speaker to a greater extent with Frost himself rather than considering him a fictional person. Or you might want to think about relating the poem to one of Frost's major interests, poetry. Each of these possibilities could serve equally well to get things moving.

Take, for example, the following possibility: Because we are interested in collaborative learning, we might choose to read the poem's commentary on community in terms of the collaborative approach to literature. We might wish to understand the entire meadow as a literary text and the tuft as that part of the text that calls the reader's attention to others involved in the conversation between writer and readers. Everyone approaches the meadow differently: the mower from one perspective, the speaker from another, the butterfly from still another. The tuft might be the point at which all observers recognize their connectedness. If so, does the meadow mean something different to each of them, whereas the tuft holds much the same meaning for all? Can the butterfly be a catalyst, a participant in the community of readers who makes a key contribution without being fully aware of its importance? Or maybe the butterfly is aware—a *facilitator* who, more receptive to the whole message than the speaker, recognizes the unity of the three participants and points it out to the speaker. But is the mower aware of the community of readers?

Would any of these possible interpretations really work? Maybe not. But exploring them through discussions with others would undoubtedly produce valuable insights about the poem. Notice that interpretations often end with yet another question, opening new avenues to explore. We're not going to develop any particular interpretation here because our purpose is not to have you accept a particular interpretation of Frost's "Tuft of Flowers." Instead, our purpose is to introduce you to the method—the method of exploring literature and coming to agreement on an interpretation in community with others. In the following chapters, you will practice the method outlined here, making your own meaning of the literary works you read. As you do so, you will discover that making meaning from literature is an ongoing process involving reading, asking questions, formulating hypotheses, rereading, asking more questions, reformulating hypotheses. . . . Now that we have begun the conversation, we ask you to carry on with it.

2 Active Reading
Preliminary Reading and Annotating Texts

The following scenario is probably familiar to most students in literature classes:

> Immediately after an instructor or a student offers an observation on a literary work, one member of the class blurts out: "I just can't understand it! How can you *come up* with that stuff? I read the same story and I didn't get *anything* out of it!"

This student's frustration results from a relatively common misperception about understanding literature—that some people can read a story once and can go on for an hour discussing its significance. Would that it were so easy! In fact, instructors and experienced students of literature are able to come up with observations not because of some genetic literary superiority but because of the way they read a literary work. What critics and professors—and experienced students of literature—do is called **active** reading. Most of us do a good deal of **passive** reading every day: we scan newspaper or magazine articles; we read letters and notes. But there's a big difference between this type of reading and the type necessary to appreciate fully a work of literature. Perhaps an analogy to listening would help explain the difference: Although people are surrounded by music much of the time, they don't always *listen* to it. When the radio is on in the background—in the cafeteria, in the car, at home—people rarely really pay attention to the music. They know it's there, but they don't appreciate it fully. Even when people are dancing, they don't hear much more than the beat. But when a person has just bought her favorite artist's new CD, or when a person is settling in to listen to a live concert, they pay attention. They hear the melodies; they listen to the lyrics; they distinguish between various instruments in the production. It's at these times that people truly appreciate the music. The same holds true for reading: there's a time to treat reading as a chore, or as a type of background music, and there's a time to truly pay attention to it. In order to appreciate what literature can reveal about humanity, its history, and its prospects, it is necessary to take the time to explore or analyze works of literature.

"Easy for you to say," you may be thinking. Actually, it is easy for experienced readers of literature to say—after all, they have developed an aptitude for analysis. But this appreciation is not something reserved for the literary scholar. Active reading can be learned, and it can benefit even the most skeptical reader.

READING ACTIVELY

What happens when you read actively? Put simply, you become engaged in a conversation with the author. This is the beginning of the larger conversation that this book is all about. The conversation starts privately, between the reader and the writer. Since you, the reader, are just feeling your way around the material, you can't expect to make much meaning from it at first. You and the author don't know each other yet. You might consider the analogy of a couple's first meeting on a blind date, or of college roommates meeting for the first time. You converse, and you understand each other's words, but you don't yet know that your roommate is a very reticent, low-key person whose "It's all right" is the equivalent of your "Wow, this is terrific!" You only get to know those things after paying close attention to the other person's way of speaking, to his or her "style." You do much the same thing with the literature you read. Some writers are like the roommate—their prose is clipped, sparse, and seemingly not very demonstrative. Others, however, write with an abundant, complex, and rich style. You can't know this when you first encounter an author. And even if you've already read something by an author, you can't know his or her characters or the situation in a new book until you've lived with them for awhile. That roommate whom you were sure you'd never understand may well become your best friend by the end of the semester; the blind dates who seemed completely inscrutable to each other may end up spending the rest of their lives together. In both cases, continuing the conversation makes it possible for the parties to understand each other better. So the moral of this story is this: Look upon the mystery of a literary work as a challenge, an adventure of sorts. Getting to know a story or a play can be enjoyable in much the same way that getting to know another person is—if you take the time and put in the effort.

The first thing to do when you're setting out to read a literary work actively is to leave yourself enough time to get into it. Consider Susan Glaspell's *Trifles* (p. 68), for example. This brief play wouldn't take more than about twenty minutes to read passively. But such a reading would at best clue you in on the basic plot of the story. If you're to get a sense of the flavor of Glaspell's language, the significance of her imagery, or the motivations of her characters, you have to slow down. This chapter and the next (on the double-entry journal) will discuss ways in which you can enter the conversation that leads to making meaning of literature. Since that conversation begins with the reader and the writer, this chapter will focus on you and the literary text (the author's side of the conversation) by introducing you to two stages involved in active reading: **preliminary reading** and **annotating the text.** The following outline provides a glimpse of what will be covered in the remainder of the chapter:

Preliminary Reading
    Reviewing Prior Knowledge
    Asking Questions
Annotating the Text
    Commenting on Language
    Making Note of Familiar Passages
    Commenting on Characterizations
    Making Note of Difficult Passages

PRELIMINARY READING

Even before you begin reading, you can prepare yourself to get the most out of a work of literature. The first steps to take in active reading might be more accurately called **preliminary reading: reviewing prior knowledge** and **asking questions.**

Reviewing Prior Knowledge

What's prior knowledge? Quite simply, it's what you may already know that's relevant to the literary work you're studying. Perhaps you've read something before by this author, or heard the author's name in another class. Perhaps you're familiar with the *genre* (the type of literature: play, poem, short story, novel, essay) or with the setting of the work. In addition to considering what you already know, you may also want to begin thinking about any relevance a literary work may have to your own experience. When asked to make a few observations after reading the opening stage directions for *Trifles*, Eric Labbe jotted down the following notes:

Eric Labbe's Preliminary Reading Observations for *Trifles*
- Plays—have to look closely at dialogue, not much description
- Men & women seem completely different creatures—rigid sex roles in early part of century (Amer. History class)
- Dismal, unkempt kitchen—my kitchen a happy, secure place—food, family, treats

- Rural life can be isolating—we lived out in the "sticks" when I was a kid—no other kids to play with

The point is, no matter how irrelevant prior knowledge may seem at first, it can come in handy in making the material familiar to you. Eric's observation on plays, for example, prepared him to read this work differently from the way he read novels or short stories. And his knowledge of turn-of-the-century sex roles made it easier for him to understand the men's disdain for the women's "trifles." The kitchen as described in the opening stage directions, in contrast to Eric's childhood experience, seemed positively ominous. That contrast provided him with some early insight into the nature of the play: perhaps this house is not a happy one, since the warmth usually associated with kitchens is missing. Finally, Eric knew first-hand how isolated rural life can be, thus providing himself with an appreciation for the loneliness of the lives he would encounter in the play. Eric's prereading observations on this play should assure you that regardless of the extent of your general knowledge or the nature of your personal experience, drawing on prior knowledge offers a unique perspective from which to consider a literary work.

ASKING QUESTIONS

Most students have been afraid, at one time or another, that their questions might sound stupid to others—especially to an instructor. Granted, it's sometimes difficult to ask a question in front of an entire class, but when you're in the privacy of your own reading space, who cares how stupid the question may seem to be? Nobody's there to hear it but you, and most "stupid" questions aren't stupid at all. In fact, you should be asking questions throughout your reading process, and beyond it in your discussions of the literary work. However, the initial questions you ask can help you make sense of what you're reading. One of the first and most common questions readers have about literary works is, "Why this title?" In fact, each of the students cited in these chapters asked precisely that question about the title of Glaspell's play. In doing so, they prepared themselves to look out for anything in the play that might be characterized as a trifle. And, in fact, only a few pages into the action the sheriff comments disdainfully on Mrs. Wright's concern over her preserves:

SHERIFF. Well, can you beat the women! Held for murder and worryin' about her preserves.

Later in the play the men continue to disparage the work of the women, and it isn't long before the irony of the men's behavior becomes apparent to both the women and the reader. Thus just one question at the beginning of your reading can lead you to a clearer understanding of an apparently significant theme in the play.

More "academic questions" may lead you to do a little research even before reading a literary work. We treat research in this book as an activity that occurs well after reading, writing journal entries, and discussing in groups—it is an expansion of your initial conversations. Occasionally, however, you may find yourself interested enough to do a little preliminary research. For example, you may want to learn something about the author before reading the work. While it's not necessary to have biographical information before reading a text, it's sometimes interesting to get an idea of the mind behind the material. The first communication in exploring literature collaboratively is the conversation between writer and reader. Often two parties engaged in conversation try to find out something about one another; in this case, if you, the reader, want to "check up" on the author, there are a couple of avenues you can pursue. Perhaps somewhere in the book there's a brief biographical sketch, or perhaps you have access to the *Dictionary of Literary Biography*, or a more specific biographical index of authors from a particular country or time period. Biographical information won't unlock any mysteries found in a literary work. However, in much the same way that people discussing any subject sometimes like to know a little about their partners in conversation, readers sometimes feel more comfortable if they know a little about the author before they begin to read.

When Debbie Carlisle first approached *Trifles*, she asked not only the title question discussed previously, but a couple of other questions as well:

Debbie Carlisle's Initial Questions about *Trifles*
- How can such a short play have anything to say to readers?
- Why is the whole play set in a small farmhouse kitchen?
- Who is Glaspell, and what else did she write?

Note that Debbie's first two questions express some skepticism about the value of this play. That's a valid response—the author has a responsibility to convince the reader that this literary work is worthwhile. Debbie also asks about the author. Regardless of the nature of your preliminary questions, they provide you with a perspective from which to begin your reading.

EXERCISE 1

Take a look at the opening stage directions in Glaspell's *Trifles*:

SCENE:
The kitchen in the now abandoned farmhouse of JOHN WRIGHT, a gloomy kitchen, and left without having been put in order—unwashed pans under the sink, a loaf of bread

outside the breadbox, a dish towel on the table—other signs of incompleted work. At the rear the outer door opens, and the SHERIFF comes in, followed by the COUNTY ATTORNEY and HALE. The SHERIFF and HALE are men in middle life, the COUNTY ATTORNEY is a young man; all are much bundled up and go at once to the stove. They are followed by the two women—the SHERIFF'S WIFE first; she is a light wiry woman, a thin nervous face. MRS. HALE is larger and would ordinarily be called more comfortable looking, but she is disturbed now and looks fearfully about as she enters. The women have come in slowly and stand close together near the door.

Write down anything you already know (either from personal experience, from other classes, or from your reading) that might help you begin to understand the play. Make note also of any questions that come to mind. Then look up Susan Glaspell's name in the *Dictionary of Literary Biography* or a similar reference work, and take a few notes on biographical information that you think might be relevant. Compare your preliminary notes to those of Debbie Carlisle and Eric Labbe. What are the similarities? Differences?

ANNOTATING THE TEXT

Whether you've made extensive prereading notes or simply jotted down a few questions, the next steps in active reading will truly be active, engaging you in that conversation with the author we've been promising you throughout this chapter. As you begin to read more closely, you will begin **annotating** the text, underlining significant words, phrases, and passages, as well as writing observations and questions in the margins. Sometimes you'll find yourself underlining passages (brief ones) that simply "grab" you. That's fine. If a passage is compelling, then it's worth remembering, and it may help you understand the story better. You may also find your pen drawn to sections that make you think, perhaps a segment in which the author seems to spend an inordinate amount of time on something that seems irrelevant. For example, in *Trifles* Glaspell seems to focus our attention on the preserve jars in the cupboard. While we eventually realize the importance of things like the canary and sewing, the preserves don't seem related to the story as clearly. You can underline that passage and make a note in the margin—perhaps by simply writing, "What's with the preserves?" Later, when you've finished your close reading of the story, you may be able to put that note together with others to get a sense of how they fit together.

As you read you will find other reasons for underlining passages or making marginal notes. Perhaps a description reminds you of a religious image, for example, or a name sounds like it comes from a famous Greek myth. Perhaps a certain phrase recurs several times in a poem or other literary work, or a character has a distinctive way of speaking. Or perhaps you come across a passage that intrigues or baffles you—you're not quite sure of what it means or what to make of it. When you come across such references or uses of language, it's worth making note of them. At first you may be uncertain about what to annotate, but rest assured, the more you engage in active reading, the more comfortable you'll be with how and when to annotate the text. (As you discuss your annotations with fellow students, you'll also discover that each reader responds differently to a text.)

A word of caution: Underlining significant passages is fine as long as you don't overdo it. When you begin to talk about the literary work, and especially when you begin to write about it, you don't want to look at pages and pages filled top to bottom with underlined passages. If you underline too much, you defeat the purpose of the exercise. Remember, underlining should be reserved for *selected* important passages.

Now that you're familiar with the "how-to," what are some of the things you'll look for when you annotate a selection? Again, what you choose to annotate depends on your experience, your familiarity with the author or the genre, and your personal response to the literature. What follows is a discussion of some common types of annotation that you may find helpful as you become accustomed to reading actively. The following outline lists the areas that will be covered.

Commenting on Language
    Images
    Descriptions
    Repetition
    Similes and metaphors
Making Note of Familiar Passages
    Cross-references
    Reminders of your own experience
    References to myths, religion, or classical figures
Commenting on Characterizations
    Personalities of characters
    Dialogue
Making Note of Difficult Passages
    Intriguing Sections

In the following discussion you'll encounter examples from a number of different literary works not found in this text. Don't be concerned if you're not familiar with many of them; it's not necessary to understand the entire work in order to appreciate, for example, an author's use of language. In fact, it's only through careful attention to language, dialogue, and references *as you read* that you can come to a fuller understanding of a literary work. (At the end of the chapter we'll provide a few samples from student annotations of *Trifles* for you to compare with your own annotations.)

COMMENTING ON LANGUAGE

Frequently, when readers are engrossed in a story, they pay little conscious attention to the language used by the author. But in fact, it's precisely that language that makes the story so engrossing. Think for a moment: Don't you know people who always tell a great story, or others who can bore and confuse you with even the most exciting material? Anyone who has heard the same story from two different sources understands how important language is. Naturally, then, one of the first things you will find yourself looking at as you annotate a text is how the author presents the material. The following examples illustrate various uses of language and should give you an idea of what to look for as you make note of significant passages.

Images

You may be familiar with F. Scott Fitzgerald's *The Great Gatsby*. The last line of that book creates a very powerful image: "And so we beat on, boats against the current, borne back ceaselessly into the past." Some of you may also be familiar with William Butler Yeats' poem "The Second Coming," which ends with the question:

> And what rough beast, its hour come round at last,
> Slouches toward Bethlehem to be born?

Each of these passages focuses on an *image*, a picture created by the writer to help the reader understand what he is saying. Some readers find that Fitzgerald's image suggests frustration. Even without having read the book, someone who thinks about these lines can feel the drag of the current (the past) on the boats (people trying to move beyond the past). Similarly, reading Yeats' last lines creates a picture in some readers' minds: A "rough beast" is surely something to fear, especially since the poet tells us that its time (to rule?) has come "at last." It is through an understanding of images like these—an understanding that arises not from the intellect but from the emotions—that readers begin to make sense of the larger work.

Descriptions

One of the most powerful tools a writer has at her or his disposal is *description*; the mark of a skilled writer is the ability to convey a sense of place so that the reader can truly experience it. In *Incidents in the Life of a Slave Girl*,

Harriet Jacobs describes the tiny attic space in which she hid from her master for almost seven years:

> The garret was only nine feet long and seven wide. The highest part was three feet high, and sloped down abruptly to the loose board floor. There was no admission for either light or air. . . . To this hole I was conveyed as soon as I entered the house. The air was stifling; the darkness total. A bed had been spread on the floor. I could sleep quite comfortably on one side; but the slope was so sudden that I could not turn on the other without hitting the roof. The rats and mice ran over my bed; but I was weary, and I slept such sleep as the wretched may, when a tempest has passed over them.

Note that there is no "flowery" language used in this description; the garret is described in the simplest and most ordinary terms. But that's precisely what makes the scene so compelling—to think that this "hole," as Jacobs calls it, was her home for almost seven years! No amount of inflated prose extracted from the pages of a thesaurus could come close to this matter-of-fact, photographic account of Jacobs' prison.

Sometimes, however, it's appropriate to use more lavish language to describe a scene. Consider Elizabeth Barrett Browning's apocalyptic vision in "The Cry of the Human":

> The plague runs festering through the town,
> And never a bell is tolling,
> And corpses, jostled 'neath the moon,
> Nod to the dead-cart's rolling;
> The young child calleth for the cup,
> The strong man brings it weeping,
> The mother from her babe looks up,
> And shrieks away its sleeping.
> Be pitiful, O God!

The language here is certainly less ordinary than that of Jacobs. Each writer is describing a fearsome place, but the approach is quite different in Browning's work. The fact that she chooses to use language that cries out with emotion tells the reader that her purpose is different from Jacobs'. There has to be a *reason* why Jacobs doesn't choose to use the kind of language Browning uses; as readers continue to annotate, write about, and discuss the literature, these reasons will become clear. But the first step is simply making note of the fact that the writer has used a particular kind of description—an underlined passage, with the marginal note "vivid language," is enough to remind the reader that the language is worth remembering.

Repetition

The importance of repetition in verse is indisputable: from the song-games children play to the music adults listen to, the refrain plays an important role in conveying meaning. In speeches, repetition is particularly effective, even when the speeches are only read rather than heard. Many of you are probably familiar with one of the most famous phrases in modern American history, the "I have a dream" refrain from Martin Luther King, Jr.'s speech at the 1963 March on Washington.

Even in fiction, repetition can take on the role of a refrain. Consider, for example, the opening section of Leslie Marmon Silko's short story "Yellow Woman." At the opening of the story the narrator, having awakened on a riverbank before her lover, mounts a horse, observing that the animal "felt warm underneath me." Then as she talks to her mysterious lover she remembers the previous night and "his warmth around me." Later, as they embrace, she says, "All I could know was the way he felt, warm, damp, his body beside me." At the end of the section, when he finally brings her to his house, he says, "Yellow Woman, come inside where it's warm." If you read this section of the short story closely, you can't help but make a mental note of the repetition of the word "warm." Clearly, that sensation is important to the narrator. Simply making note of this refrain, either by underlining the repeated words or by writing a marginal note, will help you come to terms with the remainder of the story.

Similes and Metaphors

Perhaps the most powerful tools of language that the writer can use are similes and metaphors. Sometimes referred to collectively as "figurative language," similes and metaphors allow the writer to use a familiar image to help explain something that may not be so familiar to the reader, or to convey a particular impression. In Nadine Gordimer's *A Sport of Nature*, for example, the following simile appears: "He talked about 'his book' as a companion and a leg-iron by which he had been shackled a long time, dragging it around the world with him." The comparison of a book that one is writing to a companion is something most of us might understand. But comparing it to a leg-iron is something else again: some readers will sense that the task of writing can sometimes imprison the author.

Metaphors, unlike similes, actually present an equation without using the words "like" or "as." The main character in James Joyce's "The Dead" uses a metaphor to convey the feeling he gets while listening to a song: "To follow the voice, without looking at the singer's face, was to feel and share the excitement of swift and secure flight." Clearly the song in this instance has a profound effect upon Gabriel; he feels himself take wing as he listens.

Both metaphors and similes help readers understand what writers and their characters want to convey. As readers make note of these figures of speech, they can begin to put the figures together with other elements of the literary work to make its meaning clearer.

EXERCISE 2

When Kelly Leighton annotated *Trifles*, she noted the repetition of words having to do with communication: *telephone, talk, ask, tell, conversation*, and the like. Cinde Veinot focused on figures of speech: the metaphors of knotting and quilting. As you begin your active reading of *Trifles*, annotate the text for Glaspell's use of *language*, looking for images, descriptions, and metaphors/similes as well as repetition. (You probably won't find examples of everything mentioned in the section, but try to note as many different uses of language as you can.) Find other references to language in the sample annotations on pp. 29–34, and compare them to your responses. What are the similarities? Differences?

MAKING NOTE OF FAMILIAR PASSAGES

One of the reasons why literature provides pleasure for so many readers is the sense of familiarity it offers. As readers enter the world created by the author, they become familiar with settings, characters and action. Sometimes they find material that relates to their own lives, and sometimes they discover references to other works they've read, particularly classics, myths, or religion. This familiarity not only provides pleasure, but it also helps readers make meaning of literary works.

Cross-References

Dictionaries, encyclopedias, and other reference books make frequent use of **cross-references**, references in one part of the book to related material in another part. For example, in an encyclopedia entry on "World Series" you might find the cross-reference "See also 'Baseball.'" In a literary work, the author frequently makes reference to other parts of the work. The reference might be in the form of dialogue, with different characters saying almost the same thing at different times. Or an author might use similar terms or images to describe different settings or characters. It's up to the reader to make note of those cross-references. As you read a literary work, you will become aware gradually of references to other parts of the selection. In August Wilson's *Joe Turner's Come and Gone*, for example, characters continually make reference to travel and roads: In the first scene a character talks of men "working on the road gang with the sweat glistening on them." Later in that same scene a newcomer tells where he's come from: "Come from all over. Whicheverway the road take us that's the way we go." Toward the end of the scene a woman tells of her lost love, who "was born in Alabama then ...come to West Texas and find me and we come here. ... [Then] he started walking down the road and ain't never come back." This story is followed closely by a young man's asking her to be his companion: "You wanna go along the road a little ways with me?" When considered together, these and numerous other references to roads, wandering, and travel lead some readers to discover a *theme* of instability and searching in the play. A reader who has underlined such references and made marginal notes of pages where references appear will be able to recognize the pattern that emerges.

Reminders of Your Own Experience

Often readers find themselves drawn to works that reflect their own experience. Literature is an exploration of the human condition; therefore it's only natural that readers find characters, settings, or concepts that remind them of their own experience. For example, someone reading Donne's "The Good Morrow" might recall that feeling brought on by first deep love:

> I wonder, by my troth, what thou and I
> Did till we loved?
> . . .
> If ever any beauty I did see,
> Which I desired, and got, 'twas but a dream of thee.

Most people reading this poem will have experienced deep love at least once, and many will sympathize with Donne's wondering what he and his lover did all their lives until they met, as well as with his belief that all other beauty is "but a dream" of the only true beauty, his love.

References to Myths, Religion, or Classical Figures

At times readers recognize references to myths, religion, or classical figures. Since most writers are themselves avid readers, such references abound in all kinds of literature. Consider, for example, Thomas Pynchon's *The Crying of Lot 49*. Pynchon's main character, Mrs. Oedipa Maas, must solve the "riddle" of the estate left by real estate mogul Pierce Inverarity. (Note, by the way, that the names in the novel call attention to themselves; would any reader know real people by those names? This is a fairly clear indication that the names are significant.) Many readers will recognize that "Oedipa" is the feminine form of "Oedipus." The fact that she must solve a riddle of sorts recalls the ancient Greek play by Sophocles in which Oedipus must solve the riddle of the sphinx. A reader familiar with the Oedipus myth will be able to make use of the reference in coming to terms with the novel.

References to religion also abound in literature. Regardless of the author's affiliation, he or she can draw on religious images familiar in the culture. In "I dreaded that first Robin," for example, Emily Dickinson calls the bird "The Queen of Calvary." Many readers will recognize the reference to the hill on which Jesus of Nazareth was executed. That reference underscores the "dread" the speaker feels in the first line, calling up a vivid image of pain, suffering, and death.

In Robert Bolt's *A Man for All Seasons* a particular reference to a classical figure is found. The "man for all seasons" is Thomas More, the great humanist and Chancellor of England under King Henry VIII. When Henry insists that More sign an oath declaring the King to be the head of the Church in England, More cannot—even though his refusal means certain death. When told that he has been dubbed "the English Socrates," More replies, "Socrates! I've no taste for hemlock, Your Excellency, if that's what you require." This scene calls to mind quite specifically the ancient Greek philosopher's suicide after being condemned for his teachings. The reference not only emphasizes Thomas More's intense desire to avoid martyrdom, but it also reinforces the greatness of his character. After all, few people in history are as widely known and respected as Socrates.

Of course, you may not be familiar with all of the references cited here. They assume a familiarity with the concept of romantic love, with classical mythology, with the New Testament of the Bible, and with ancient Greek philosophers. Every reader encounters unfamiliar references on occasion: sometimes a literary work is grounded in a culture unfamiliar to you, or sometimes you find reference to "classic" works of your own culture that you haven't yet encountered. Most literary works, however, can be understood without a thorough knowledge of all references; furthermore, many college texts provide footnotes to acquaint readers with unfamiliar references. And as you continue your education, you'll become better acquainted with your own and other cultures. Regardless, you'll still find many references to familiar material in your reading, and paying close attention to those references can enhance your appreciation of the work.

EXERCISE 3

In his annotations of *Trifles*, Eric Labbe makes note of his own rural experience, as well as noting cross-references to cold and warmth throughout the play. Go back to *Trifles* and annotate the text for *familiar passages*. (While you may not find many examples of mythic, religious, or classical references, you should have no problem finding cross-references and references to your own experience.) Find other references to familiar passages in the sample annotations on pp. 29–34, and compare them to your responses. What are the similarities? Differences?

COMMENTING ON CHARACTERIZATIONS

Personalities of Characters

Readers come to know characters in literary works in much the same way that they come to know others in "real life." The character's own words and actions are are often revealing, as is what others (in literature, narrators and/or authors) say about the character. In Margaret Atwood's *Cat's Eye*, for example, the young girl narrating the story describes her only friend at school, Carol. The passage reads like half of a conversation in which one person is describing to another her initial impressions of a third person:

> She tells me her hair is honey-blond, that her haircut is called a pageboy, that she has to go to the hairdresser's every two months to get it done. . . . Carol and her younger sister have matching outfits for Sundays: fitted brown tweed coats with velvet collars, round brown velvet hats with an elastic under the chin to hold them on. They have brown gloves and little brown purses. She tells me all this.

This description reveals to readers a little girl caught up in appearance, probably well-to-do, and perhaps a bit of a snob. (Of course, the narrator also reveals something about herself as she describes Carol: There's more than a touch of envy in the lines.) A reader might underline or bracket this passage and make a marginal note referring to both Carol's character and the narrator's envy.

Dialogue

Often a character is best understood through his or her own words. In real life, of course, initial impressions are often formed to a great extent through conversation. It's possible to tell where a person comes from, her social class, education, likes and dislikes simply by listening to her in conversation. Characters in literature provide readers with the same opportunity. In drama readers expect to become acquainted with characters through their words, since plays are almost exclusively dialogue. But fiction writers also use dialogue to allow their characters' personalities to emerge. Eudora Welty does precisely this in her story "Petrified Man." In the following conversation, the beautician Leota and her customer Mrs. Fletcher are discussing how they met their husbands. Mrs. Fletcher says, "I met Mr. Fletcher, or rather he met me, in a rental library." Leota responds with, "Honey, me an' Fred, we met in a rumble seat eight months ago and we was practically on what you might call the way to the altar inside of half an hour." Mrs. Fletcher's reference to her husband as "Mr. Fletcher," her self-correction (it's not ladylike for a woman to introduce herself to a man), and her reference to the "rental library" reveal a woman who prides herself on propriety. Leota, on the other hand, calls Mrs. Fletcher "honey," calls her husband "Fred," uses nonstandard English ("me an' Fred," "we was"), and jokingly intimates that their physical relationship preceded their marriage vows. Leota is clearly not one to pay much attention to proper behavior; in fact she seems to revel in her earthiness. Each of these women is characterized without the author's ever having commented on her; the women themselves reveal their personalities. Noting these personality characteristics in the margins of the text allows readers to recall how they made judgments about the two women.

EXERCISE 4

In her annotations of *Trifles* (pp. 33–34), Debbie Carlisle notes passages which characterize the County Attorney. Go back to *Trifles* and annotate the text for *characterization*. (Make sure to pay attention to stage directions as well as to dialogue.) Compare Debbie's annotations to your responses. What are the similarities? Differences?

MAKING NOTE OF DIFFICULT PASSAGES

At one time or another every reader encounters confusing or intriguing passages in a literary work. Sometimes it's only after several readings and a good deal of conversation that the passages begin to have meaning. Simply making note of them by underlining and perhaps putting a question mark in the margin is all you need to do as you annotate. Often you will come to a clearer understanding of the passage as you continue to read. If not, you can address the issue as you write in your journal and discuss your responses (see Chapters 3 and 4).

Intriguing Sections

Often poetry presents readers with intriguing sections. Because of the need to say so much in so little space, and the need to pay close attention to rhythms as well as to meaning, poetry can be difficult to understand on first reading. But it is precisely that difficulty that makes reading poetry so rewarding—in poetry, more so than in any other genre, the reader is aware of the interaction, the conversation, between writer and audience. A case in point is Gerard Manley Hopkins' "I wake and feel the fell of dark." The last two stanzas of this poem read as follows:

I am gall, I am heartburn. God's most deep decree
Bitter would have me taste: my taste was me;
Bones built in me, flesh filled, blood brimmed the curse.

Selfyeast of spirit a dull dough sours. I see
The lost are like this, and their scourge to be
As I am mine, their sweating selves; but worse.

Why would the speaker describe himself as "gall" and "heartburn"? Is he tasting something or is he talking about what he tastes like? What is "selfyeast" and why does the "dull dough" sour? And what does sweating have to do with anything? All of these questions seem unanswerable, but in fact, if you were reading this poem and began addressing them, you'd begin to make meaning of the poem. Simply making note of the lines as you annotate will call your attention to them later as you write in your journal and discuss your responses.

EXERCISE 5

In her annotations of *Trifles* (pp. 33–34), Debbie Carlisle poses a couple of questions. Go back to *Trifles* and annotate the text for *difficult or intriguing passages*. While the play appears to be simple and straightforward and thus easy to understand, you may be intrigued by the playwright's treatment of seemingly insignificant matters. Find other references to difficult or intriguing passages in the sample annotations on pp. 29–34, and compare them to your responses. What are the similarities? Differences?

SAMPLE ANNOTATED PASSAGES FROM *TRIFLES*

The following are several annotated sections from *Trifles*. Not all of the types of annotations mentioned previously are represented here; that would be impossible for almost any single work of literature. In fact, as you annotate literary works, you'll often find yourself focusing on one or two general types of annotation—metaphors and classical references, for example. This selectivity is dictated in part by the author: Some authors are known for metaphors and classical references. But it's also dictated in part by the reader's experience and tastes: Some readers are more attuned to metaphors and classical references. Note in the following selections that different students focused on different types of annotation, even when reading the same passages.

HALE. Harry and I had started to town with a load of potatoes. We came along the road from my place; and as I got
here, I said, "I'm going to see if I can't get John Wright
to go in with me on a party telephone." I spoke to Wright
about it once before, and he put me off, saying folks
talked too much anyway, and all he asked was peace and
quiet—I guess you know about how much he talked
himself; but I thought maybe if I went to the house and
talked about it before his wife, though I said to Harry
that I didn't know as what his wife wanted made much
difference to John—

phone p. 69

talk!

COUNTY ATTORNEY. Let's talk about that later, Mr. Hale. I
do want to talk about that, but tell now just what happened when you got to the house.

talk/
communica-
tion

HALE. I didn't hear or see anything; I knocked at the door,
and still it was all quiet inside. I knew they must be up,
it was past eight o'clock. So I knocked again, and I
thought I heard somebody say, "Come in." I wasn't sure,
I'm not sure yet, but I opened the door—this door [indi-
cating the door by which the two women are still standing],
and there in that rocker—[pointing to it] sat Mrs. Wright.
[They all look at the rocker.]

communica-
tion

COUNTY ATTORNEY. What—was she doing?

HALE. She was rockin' back and forth. She had her apron in
her hand and was kind of—pleating it.

COUNTY ATTORNEY. And how did she—look?

HALE. Well, she looked queer.

communica-
tion

COUNTY ATTORNEY. How do you mean—queer?

HALE. Well, as if she didn't know what she was going to do
next. And kind of done up.

COUNTY ATTORNEY. How did she seem to feel about your
coming?

HALE. Why, I don't think she minded—one way or other.
She didn't pay much attention. I said, "How do, Mrs.
Wright, it's cold, ain't it?" And she said, "Is it?"—and
went on kind of pleating at her apron. Well, I was surprised; she didn't ask me to come up to the stove, or to
set down, but just sat there, not even looking at me, so I
said, "I want to see John." And then she—laughed. I

guess you would call it a laugh. I thought of Harry and the team outside, so I said a little sharp: "Can't I see John?"

"No," she says, kind o' dull like. "Ain't he home?" says I. "Yes," says she, "he's home." "Then why can't I see him?" I asked her, out of patience. "'Cause he's dead," says she. "Dead?" says I. She just nodded her head, not getting a bit excited, but rockin' back and forth. "Why— where is he?" says I, not knowing what to say. She just pointed upstairs—like that [himself pointing to the room above]. I got up, with the idea of going up there. I walked from there to here—then I says, "Why, what did he die of?" "He died of a rope around his neck," says she, and just went on pleatin' at her apron. Well, I went out and called Harry. I thought I might—need help. We went upstairs, and there he was lyin'—

silent communication

COUNTY ATTORNEY. I think I'd rather have you go into that upstairs, where you can point it all out. Just go on now with the rest of the story.

talk

HALE. Well, my first thought was to get that rope off. I looked . . . [Stops, his face twitches.] . . . but Harry, he went up to him, and he said, "No, he's dead all right, and we'd better not touch anything." So we went back downstairs. She was still sitting that same way. "Has anybody been notified?" I asked. "No," says she, unconcerned. "Who did this, Mrs. Wright?" said Harry. He said it businesslike—and she stopped pleatin' of her apron. "I don't know," she says. "You don't know?" says Harry. "No," says she. "Weren't you sleeping' in the bed with him?" says Harry. "Yes," says she, "but I was on the inside." "Somebody slipped a rope round his neck and strangled him, and you didn't wake up?" says Harry. "I didn't wake up," she said after him. We must 'a looked as if we didn't see how that could be, for after minute she said, "I sleep sound." Harry was going to ask her more questions, but I said maybe we ought to let her tell her story first to the coroner, or the sheriff, so Harry went fast as he could to Rivers' place, where there's a telephone.

questions/ communica- tion

phone p. 68

COUNTY ATTORNEY. And what did Mrs. Wright do when she knew that you had gone for the coroner?

HALE. She moved from that chair to this over here . . . [Pointing to a small chair in the corner.] . . . and just sat there with her hands held together and looking down. I got a feeling that I ought to make some conversation, so I said I had come in to see if John wanted to put in a telephone, and at that she started to laugh, and then she stopped and looked at me—scared. [*The* COUNTY ATTORNEY, *who has had his notebook out, makes a note.*] I dunno, maybe it wasn't scared. I wouldn't like to say it was. Soon Harry got back, and then Dr. Lloyd came, and you, Mr. Peters, and so I guess that's all I know that you don't.

"conversa-tion"!

phone p. 68

Notice that Kelly focuses on Glaspell's use of **language**, particularly the **images** of talk, conversation, and communication. She also uses **cross-references** to help remind herself of connections between passages in the play.

Cinde Veinot

COUNTY ATTORNEY [*as one turning from serious things to little pleasantries*]. Well, ladies, have you decided whether she was going to quilt or *knot it?*

"trifles"

MRS. PETERS. We think she was going to—*knot it.*

COUNTY ATTORNEY. Well, that's interesting, I'm sure. [*Seeing the birdcage.*] Has the bird flown?

**"knot"—
a noose**

bird: Mrs. W.

MRS. HALE [*putting more quilt pieces over the box*]. We think the—cat got it.

**quilt =
investigation?**

COUNTY ATTORNEY [*preoccupied*]. Is there a cat?

[MRS. HALE *glances in a quick covert way at* MRS. PETERS.]

cat: Mr. W.

MRS. PETERS. Well, not now. They're superstitious, you know. They leave.

COUNTY ATTORNEY [*to* SHERIFF PETERS, *continuing an interrupted conversation*]. No sign at all of anyone having come from the outside. Their own rope. Now let's go up again and go over it piece by piece. [*They start upstairs.*] It would have to have been someone who knew just the—

**quilt =
investigation?**

[MRS. PETERS *sits down. The two women sit there not looking at one another, but as if peering into something and at the same time holding back. When they talk now, it is in the manner of feeling their way over strange ground, as if afraid of what they are saying, but as if they cannot help saying it.*]

simile

Notice that Cinde, like Kelly, focuses on **language**, but on **metaphor and simile** rather than on images. Notice too that she picks up on the mention of a "trifle," recalling the title of the play.

Eric Lobbe

Scene: The kitchen in the now abandoned farmhouse of JOHN WRIGHT, *a gloomy kitchen, and left without having been put in order—unwashed pans under the sink, a loaf of bread outside the breadbox, a dish towel on the table—other signs of incompleted work. At the rear the outer door opens, and the* SHERIFF *comes in, followed by the* COUNTY ATTORNEY *and* HALE. *The* SHERIFF *and* HALE *are men in middle life, the* COUNTY ATTORNEY *is a young man; all are much bundled up and go at once to the stove. They are followed by the two women—the* SHERIFF'S WIFE *first; she is a light wiry woman, a thin nervous face.* MRS. HALE *is larger and would ordinarily be called more comfortable looking, but she is disturbed now and looks fearfully about as she enters. The women have come in slowly and stand close together near the door.*

COUNTY ATTORNEY [*rubbing his hands*]. This feels good. Come up to the fire, ladies.

MRS. PETERS [*after taking a step forward*]. I'm not—cold.

SHERIFF [*unbuttoning his overcoat and stepping away from the stove as if to mark the beginning of official business*]. Now, Mr. Hale, before we move things about, you explain to Mr. Henderson just what you saw when you came here yesterday morning.

COUNTY ATTORNEY. By the way, has anything been moved? Are things just as you left them yesterday?

SHERIFF [*looking about*]. It's just the same. When it dropped *below* zero last night, I thought I'd better send Frank out this morning to make a fire for us—no use getting pneumonia with a big case on; but I told him not to touch anything except the stove—and you know Frank.

> gloomy, not like my memory of farmhouse

> cold/stove

> fire/cold/stove (our stove so warm!)

> fire/cold/stove

Eric's **images** focus on sensations—cold and warmth, and he seems particularly interested in the stove. His attention to the stove may well result from his noting a **familiar passage**, namely the stage directions that cause him to recall his own childhood experiences in a farmhouse.

Debbie Carlisle

Scene: The kitchen in the now abandoned farmhouse of JOHN
WRIGHT, *a gloomy kitchen, and left without having been put in
order—unwashed pans under the sink, a loaf of bread outside
the breadbox, a dish towel on the table—other signs of incompleted work. At the rear the outer door opens, and the*
SHERIFF *comes in, followed by the* COUNTY ATTORNEY *and*
HALE. *The* SHERIFF *and* HALE *are men in middle life, the*
COUNTY ATTORNEY *is a young man; all are much bundled up
and go at once to the stove. They are followed by the two
women—the* SHERIFF'S WIFE *first; she is a light wiry woman, a
thin nervous face.* MRS. HALE *is larger and would ordinarily be
called more comfortable looking, but she is disturbed now and
looks fearfully about as she enters. The women have come in
slowly and stand close together near the door.*

men, women
act different
women fear-
ful?

COUNTY ATTORNEY [*rubbing his hands*]. This feels good.
Come up to the fire, ladies.

MRS. PETERS [*after taking a step forward*]. I'm not—cold.

woman—hesi-
tant

man—assert-
ive

SHERIFF [*unbuttoning his overcoat and stepping away from the
stove as if to mark the beginning of official business*]. Now,
Mr. Hale, before we move things about, you explain to
Mr. Henderson just what you saw when you came here
yesterday morning.

COUNTY ATTORNEY. By the way, has anything been moved?
Are things just as you left them yesterday?

SHERIFF [*looking about*]. It's just the same. When it dropped
below zero last night, I thought I'd better send Frank out
this morning to make a fire for us—no use getting pneumonia with a big case on; but I told him not to touch
anything except the stove—and you know Frank.
    . . . .

Why the de-
tail?

HALE. Harry and I had started to town with a load of potatoes. We came along the road from my place; and as I got
here, I said, "I'm going to see if I can't get John Wright
to go in with me on a party telephone." I spoke to Wright
about it once before, and he put me off, saying folks
talked too much anyway, and all he asked was peace and
quiet—I guess you know about how much he talked
himself; but I thought maybe if I went to the house and
talked about it before his wife, though I said to Harry

Why the de-
tail?

that I didn't know as what his wife wanted made much difference to John—

men/women

COUNTY ATTORNEY. Let's talk about that later, Mr. Hale. I do want to talk about that, but tell now just what happened when you got to the house.

HALE. I didn't hear or see anything; I knocked at the door, and still it was all quiet inside. I knew they must be up, it was past eight o'clock. So I knocked again, and I thought I heard somebody say, "Come in." I wasn't sure, I'm not sure yet, but I opened the door—this door [*indicating the door by which the two women are still standing*], and there in that rocker—[*pointing to it*] sat Mrs. Wright. [*They all look at the rocker.*]

. . . .

What's the big deal?

COUNTY ATTORNEY [*as one turning from serious things to little pleasantries*]. Well, ladies, have you decided whether she was going to quilt or knot it?

arrogant man!

MRS. PETERS. We think she was going to—knot it.

COUNTY ATTORNEY. Well, that's interesting, I'm sure. [*Seeing the birdcage.*] Has the bird flown?

Condescending

MRS. HALE [*putting more quilt pieces over the box*]. We think the—cat got it.

COUNTY ATTORNEY [*preoccupied*]. Is there a cat?

[MRS. HALE *glances in a quick covert way at* MRS. PETERS.]

MRS. PETERS. Well, not now. They're superstitious, you know. They leave.

Ignores women/ listens to men on p. 68

COUNTY ATTORNEY [*to* SHERIFF PETERS, *continuing an interrupted conversation*]. No sign at all of anyone having come from the outside. Their own rope. Now let's go up again and go over it piece by piece. [*They start upstairs.*] It would have to have been someone who knew just the—

ignores women

These are the same passages that Kelly, Cinde, and Eric annotated, but notice that Debbie does not pay attention to the same issues that the other students do. Neither does she focus on one issue. Instead, Debbie pays attention to **characterization**, particularly of Mr. Wright's and the County Attorney's attitudes toward women. She also notices different **images** of men and women. Finally, she seems perplexed by the detail, annotating several **intriguing passages**.

CONCLUSIONS

When you begin doing prereading activities and reading actively, perhaps all you'll do is follow the steps outlined earlier. That's all right; frequently it's only later, after reflection, that you begin to put some of these annotations together to make sense. (That reflection is most productive when it takes place in a journal—covered in Chapter 3.) You'll also develop your own "style" of making notes and annotating, using symbols and code words that have evolved as you feel more and more comfortable reading literature. In fact, once you become accustomed to reading actively, you may find yourself unable to pick up a literary work without a pen in your hand. You may also find yourself willingly—sometimes eagerly—rereading lines, passages, and sometimes even whole sections of a work. When that happens, you'll know that you've taken your place in the initial conversation that leads to making meaning of a text.

3 Interactive Reading

Exploring Actively with a Double-Entry Journal

In Chapter 2 you began the collaborative process by engaging in a "conversation" with the author of a literary work. In this chapter, you'll extend this conversation—you'll record what you believe to be significant about a work—by formalizing your active reading notes. You'll write your reactions about what you've read, and then you'll write notes about those reactions. The **journal writing** presented in this chapter will help you to add your voice to the ongoing conversation about literature.

The following dialogue—about what to do with his writing—takes place in the head of Peter Elbow, a professional writer and professor of English at the University of Massachusetts:

"Give it."

"No."

"You have to give it if you want to write."

"I don't want to give it. I'll loan it or disguise it or sell it even. I'll give it to certain people if they promise to like it—or if they promise to suffer. But I won't just give it away."

In the **double-entry journal** described in this chapter you'll be doing much the same thing, only you'll be debating with yourself about the feelings and ideas suggested by the literary work you've read. The give-and-take in your own head may seem odd or forced, at first—as does Elbow's entry. However, you'll soon recognize it is precisely such active give-and-take (with your classmates, your instructor, and the literary critics you'll be asked to read) that will later give rise to insightful, persuasive responses (both oral and written) that you'll make about literature. You'll also find that practice with the double-entry journal will produce topics for you to develop in formal presentations. A natural outgrowth of the double-entry journal activity

---

This chapter draws heavily on Ann Berthoff's "A Curious Triangle and the Double-Entry Notebook; or How Theory Can Help Us Teach Reading and Writing," in *The Making of Meaning* (41–47). See also Peter Elbow's "Methodological Doubting and Believing" in *Embracing Contraries* (151–53).

should be a wish to communicate—in Elbow's words, to **give**—in writing your experiences with literature.

THE IDEA BEHIND ACADEMIC JOURNALS

Journals (logs, diaries, sketchbooks) have a long tradition. Columbus recorded what he observed when he came to the so-called New World 500 years ago. Some of his observations are noticeable in the following excerpt:

> And I certify to Your Highnesses that nowhere under the sun do I think that there can be found lands superior in fertility, in moderation of cold and heat, in abundance of good and healthy water, and the rivers are not like those of Guinea, which are all pestilential.

Donald Murray, a former professor of English at the University of New Hampshire and a current writer for the *Boston Globe,* has an extensive collection of bound journals—what he calls *daybooks.* The following entry formed the basis for a later *Globe* article Murray wrote, entitled "Scenes Frozen in Memory":

> "Why I'm not going to Tullahoma."
>
> When we were driving through Tennessee, I saw the road to Tullahoma where I was trained as a paratrooper 45 years before.
>
> For a moment I decided to turn west to Tullahoma but I kept on the highway south to Birmingham. Over sixty, I knew Tullahoma would not be there, not my Tullahoma.
>
> It was easy to kill and easy to die.
>
> How many Tullahomas do I have? Places that are no longer what they were. And were never what they were. The good old days weren't. The experience and in the immediate recovery of that experience, it is changed. We distort experience into our own meanings. These are necessary lies.
>
> Unrelatived
>
> Ian and his war stories
>
> He tells the same story different ways
>
> I want to go back to specifics:
>
> | | |
> |---|---|
> | Tullahoma | NH woods |
> | Maine Beach | Boston |
> | UNH student | UNH teacher |

In the years between these two extracts, there have been countless others who have kept some type of journal. At some point in your life you've probably kept a journal—or diary, at least—yourself. Why a journal? People have long known that the memory is deceptive. A journal is a good way to file away ideas, questions, insights, and the like for future reference. The specific journal discussed here works on a similar principle: It allows you to generate information about works of literature that you may later develop into oral and written responses.

To prepare yourself for practicing a **double-entry journal**, try first a journal entry in the spirit of those written by Columbus and Murray. Specifically, read the following passage from "The Story of an Hour" by Kate Chopin, and record for future reference any ideas, questions, or perceptions that the passage elicits.

From "The Story of an Hour"

There would be no one to live for during those coming years; she would live for herself. There would be no powerful will bending hers in that blind persistence with which men and women believe they have a right to impose a private will upon a fellow-creature. A kind intention or a cruel intention made the act seem no less a crime as she looked upon it in that brief moment of illumination. And yet she had loved him—sometimes. Often she had not. What did it matter! What could love, the unsolved mystery, count for in face of this possession of self-assertion which she suddenly recognized as the strongest impulse of her being!

IDEA BEHIND THE DOUBLE-ENTRY JOURNAL

The double-entry journal reinforces the close connection between reading and writing, a connection sometimes forgotten in the struggle to "get through" a course. The main activity of each is to make meaning. Yet in the end, words do not **transmit** a writer's meaning into a reader's head; they simply provide **guidelines** for making meaning. When writers and readers keep this in mind, they sustain a process—an ongoing conversation, if you will—that frequently leads the reader pretty close to what the writer intended.

In this respect, you may find it worthwhile to consider the line in boldface from Cinde Veinot's double-entry journal entry, which is reprinted in full on p. 41, for Kate Chopin's "The Story of an Hour": "Is the title important? **The one hour of freedom for Louise!**" Note the exclamation mark. It may indicate that Cinde has determined for herself what one of the author's guidelines (the title) has contributed to her own understanding of "The Story of an Hour." It may also be construed as an early cue Cinde is providing herself that exploring the idea of freedom in the short story may lead to an informative response when it comes time for her to write about Chopin's work.

KEEPING A DOUBLE-ENTRY JOURNAL

So what makes a double-entry journal so important? According to legend, the mythological god Janus was two-headed, able to look ahead and behind. And, as the legend goes, this is the reason for January in our Roman calendar—the first month of the new year, reminding us of the preceding year and leading us to anticipate the upcoming year. In the process of making meaning, Janusian thinking refers to what comes about as a result of the puzzlement concerning objects, like literary texts, which people want to understand.

The double-entry journal was originally devised by Ann Berthoff in her book *The Making of Meaning*. Berthoff writes:

> I ask my students (all of them: freshmen, upperclassmen, teachers in graduate seminars) to furnish themselves with a notebook, spiral bound at the side, small enough to be easily carried around but not so small that writing is cramped. . . . What makes this notebook different from most, perhaps, is the notion of the double-entry: on the right side readings notes, direct quotations, observational notes, fragments, lists, images— verbal and visual—are recorded; on the other (facing) side, *notes about those notes*, summaries, formulations, aphorisms, editorial suggestions, revisions, comments on comments are written. The reason for the double-entry format is that it provides a way for the student to conduct that "continuing audit of meaning" that is at the heart of learning to read . . . critically. The facing pages are in dialogue with each other.

Sounds simple, doesn't it? And it really is that easy. To start, all you need is a notebook and a pen or pencil. Then, either fold each page in half, or draw a line down each page from top to bottom. The idea here is to enable yourself to make two sets of observations so that the entries will be in dialogue with one another.

Continuous practice with a double-entry journal should demonstrate how the dialogue forces you to read more actively and insightfully—to apply Berthoff's "continuing audit of meaning." In the end, practicing such a journal should help you to draw meaning from a text about which you were originally confused. In challenging your own reactions in the double-entry journal, you'll be prepared for the responses your classmates and your instructor may offer as you develop the meaning you have made. No longer will you feel completely lost when asked to respond to a work of literature; rather, through the process of writing a double-entry journal, you'll grow in confidence as you seek to make your reactions about literature available to others.

EXERCISE 2

Read "The Story of an Hour" (p. 81). As you read, **on the right side of your journal notebook,** pause to write down words, details, images, questions, or thoughts that strike you. **(This is not note-taking, so don't get anxious about having to summarize everything.)** Encourage yourself to make notes of words and ideas and reactions that catch your attention. If you find you have not written anything down after awhile, stop and ask yourself what you noticed or how you were feeling; then simply write down your answers. At the end of your reading make a few more notations to capture quickly what's in your head as you complete the work.

The double-entry journal lets you be Janus for awhile—using two heads instead of one, the whole idea behind a collaborative approach to literature. Thus your second entry is significant. Recall, for a moment, what Berthoff says: "The reason for the double-entry format is that it provides a way for the student to conduct that 'continuing audit of meaning' that is at the heart of learning to read . . . critically. The facing pages are in dialogue with each other." Also bear in mind that you'll be asked later on to share your journal notes with others. In so doing, you'll be learning from others how they go about making meaning of texts, just as they'll be learning from you. As you get used to such collaboration, you'll begin to master a process that will lead you from initial confusion, through interesting reactions, and to more fully developed responses about what you've read. You'll notice that the more collaboration involved in attempting to construct meaning, the clearer the complex process involved in understanding difficult material will become.

EXERCISE 3

Reread "The Story of an Hour." Now, read slowly the entry you came up with for Exercise 2. While you do this, **on the left side of your notebook,** jot down what comes to mind about the short story as you read the right side. Try to respond to each right-side observation, but skip over those that may not demand further response. Try not to worry about the difference between the two sides of your journal. What's really important about this whole process is to get your thoughts about the text to be in a dialogue with each other.

Reprinted below are several complete double-entry journal entries students wrote for Chopin's "The Story of an Hour." As you read through the entries, note each student's internal give-and-take and the topics each student generates. Try to sense also how strongly the students indicate a desire to discuss Chopin's story more fully. Don't be concerned that, after reading these students' entries, you may not have added anything more significant about the story. Recall that Chapter 2 helped you to come up with your own questions, key images, and so forth; you've therefore already prepared yourself for adding your own voice to the conversation about Chopin's work. You'll notice, too, that Debbie's interpretation is very personal and rather different from either Cinde's or Eric's. And you'll see that Eric certainly pursues a different path than the one Cinde travels. All the responses to Chopin's work have not been exhausted—probably never will be exhausted. Consider the exercises you've completed in this way: The conversation about "The Story of an Hour" was merely begun by the three students we've quoted; you've taken advantage of the opportunity to make it more stimulating.

Cinde Veinot

I think she set you up so that you expect something to happen. Many clues!

Does Chopin clue us in with the first line?

The one hour of freedom for Louise!

Is the title important?

Obviously, each character has a different view of Mrs. Mallard. Like the sister, they think Louise can't handle much.

Why does the sister think she's making herself ill?

I think this quotation symbolizes both Louise's freedom and Brently's return.

Does "distant song" indicate anything?

Richards seems suspicious to me.

Is Richards significant?

Debbie Carlisle

I read this on Valentine's Day so that may color my impressions. I like the story. It's very powerful and sad. I can imagine this wife's pain mingled with exultation at the thought that her husband has died as I suppose only someone who has felt trapped in a pain-filled marriage can, but it still shocked me a little.

Her power of observation seems heightened by her grief.
Foreshadowing? ¶2 & 3 Why did the lines in her face "bespeak repression"?

Years that would belong to her alone—wouldn't *she* grow to be lonely?

The idea of freedom and "no powerful will" bending hers intrigues me.

"A kind intention or a cruel intention made the act seem no less a crime"—moment of illumination; CONTROL ISSUES

She prayed that "life might be long when only yesterday she had thought with a shudder that life might be long."

Can love ever be justified when it's controlling?

Image of wife as goddess of Victory is powerful. I like this. She died of "heart disease—of joy that kills."

Love vs. possession or self-assertion = "the strongest impulse of her being." Is it? A very feminist story.

How terrible this story strikes me as being. Was death the only escape from marriage back then? Couldn't she just leave him?

Eric Labbe

Despite the red herring, the story works because it shows a woman's (Mrs. Louise Mallard's) struggle with repression, her joy in liberation, the possibility of a new life, and her shocking death.

Mr. Mallard "killed"—a red herring?

Chopin sets us up nicely for Louise's heart attack through the details that show us her anxiousness. Mrs. Mallard goes through stages: from instant pain and grief, then recognizing something coming to her [her freedom? or her heart attack?], beating it back and trying to reject it, then embracing it and exulting in it.

All the heightened description of Mrs. Mallard's embracing her supposed freedom reminds us of her heart condition.

It only takes Louise an hour to truly get over Brently's death. She seems to have been thinking about it for quite awhile. His being "killed" gave her a chance to realize her full potential by getting out of a marriage in which her attributes were muted.

"Repression," this seems the key. How can the ending be seen as anything but silly?

Maybe if we read the ending as an allegory of a kind, then it can be said to be symbolic of certain oppressive forces in society (Chopin's and even our own).

As you can see, Cinde, Debbie, and Eric debate with themselves their individual reactions to Chopin's work. Debbie follows up on a *personal* experience that the story prompts: "I can imagine this wife's pain mingled with exultation at the thought that her husband has died *as I suppose only someone who has felt trapped in a pain-filled marriage can.*" Cinde and Eric try to make sense of the work by recalling *formal critical strategies* they have learned: Cinde writes, "Does 'distant song' indicate anything? I think this quotation *symbolizes* both Louise's freedom and Brently's return." Eric writes, "Maybe if we read the ending as an *allegory* of a kind, then it can be said to be *symbolic* of certain oppressive forces in society (Chopin's and even our own)." All three raise topics that might be developed more fully later on: *repression, self-assertion, freedom, rebirth, death, foreshadowing,* and so forth. All indicate a desire to talk with others about what they've discovered: When Debbie writes, "Can love ever be justified when it's controlling?" she has raised a question that she probably wants to answer—for herself and for her listeners or readers. The same may be said of the following notes written by Eric: "'*Repression*'—*this seems the key*. It only takes Louise an hour to truly get over Brently's death. She seems to have been thinking about it for quite awhile. His being 'killed' gave her a chance to realize her full potential by getting out of a marriage in which her attributes were muted." Cinde certainly seems to have hit upon something when she writes: "*Why does the sister think she's making herself ill?* Obviously, each character has a different view of Mrs. Mallard. Like the sister, they think Louise can't handle much."

Taken together, Exercises 2 and 3 helped you to complete an important process in making meaning of a literary work. As those exercises demonstrate—indeed, as the preceding entries demonstrate—such a process (give-and-take, generating topics, and desiring further discussion) is integral to extending that ongoing human conversation about literature, specifically "The Story of an Hour." While you read the rest of this chapter and practice the double-entry journal, try to keep this process in mind. And when you write your own entries, read particular works with the idea of learning from them and reflecting on them.

EXERCISE 4

Compare your completed entry on "The Story of an Hour" with those by Cinde, Debbie, and Eric. Make a list of similarities and differences. Jot down what you've contributed to the ongoing conversation about Chopin's work. Then, using your entry, make another list—of key issues, perceptions, and questions you think you'd like to explore later.

A DOUBLE-ENTRY JOURNAL CHECKLIST

Just as there's no single meaning for a literary work such as Chopin's, there's no single correct way to do the double-entry journal. You do want to make sure, however, that your comments are in dialogue with one another. The following is a checklist of suggestions and questions that might make your journal activity more profitable. (An added benefit of the checklist, you'll certainly notice, is that it provides a useful process to follow for generating topics. And these may be topics that you'll want to explore more fully later with your classmates and your instructor):

> **Summary.** *Look for what keeps coming up in your entries, for what seems to be most important. What connections can you make between and among your observations? Can you draw any conclusions? What now seems important or unimportant?*

Notice how often Cinde, Debbie, and Eric referred to the *title*, to *repression*, and to *freedom*. Notice how they made connections—between their lives and the work, between and among characters within the work, and between ideas they generated the first time through the work, on the right-hand side of their journals.

Reflections. *What second thoughts do your entries prompt?*

Notice how Cinde became inquisitive about characters (*Richards* and *Louise's sister*). Note that Eric reconsidered his opinion about the ending being silly when he applied a little *prior knowledge* (what he knew about *allegory*) to it. Debbie, you may have observed, became as disturbed by Louise's need to control as she was upset with Louise's being part of an oppressive domestic situation.

Associations. *How do your observations about the work of literature relate to other parts of your life—to your deepest concerns or interests?*

Personalizing is perfectly all right here. It's worth looking at that part of Debbie's entry which shows why: "I read this on Valentine's Day so that may color my impressions. I like the story. It's very powerful and sad. I can imagine this wife's pain mingled with exultation at the thought that her husband has died as I suppose only someone who has felt trapped in a pain-filled marriage can, but it still shocked me a little."

Reactions to your reactions. *What do your entries tell you about what you're interested in, how your mind works?*

It may be worth recalling how Eric challenged his original notion of the ending being silly: "*How can the ending be seen as anything but silly?* Maybe if we read the ending as an allegory of a kind, then it can be said to be symbolic of certain oppressive forces in society (Chopin's and even our own)."

Dialogue with the author. *What do you have to say to the author? How would he or she reply?*

Note the questions Debbie asked, presumably, of the author: "How terrible this story strikes me as being. Was death the only escape from marriage back then? Couldn't she just leave him?"

Going public. *Who do you want to talk to about your observations? What would you explain or ask?*

In the end of his journal, Eric certainly indicated his desire to want to go public: "It only takes Louise an hour to truly get over Brently's death. She seems to have been thinking about it for quite awhile. His being 'killed' gave her a chance to realize her full potential by getting out of a marriage in which her attributes were muted."

Practice the double-entry journal on one of the other selections from the Case Study. But this time, after completing the journal, use the suggestions in the preceding checklist as you write in your journal. Discuss in a paragraph or two the difference between writing this entry with the checklist and writing one for "The Story of an Hour" without it.

OTHER TYPES OF JOURNAL WRITING

In this chapter, you've been given a glimpse of other types of journal writing—the logs of Columbus and Murray. Before concluding this chapter, we'd like to discuss two specific forms of journal writing a little more fully.

Academic Journal Writing

The kind of talking to themselves that members of the academy (teachers, writers, critics) conduct is termed **academic** journal writing. Frequently, academicians will write to themselves about the writing they are preparing for publication, sometimes without consciously knowing they are doing so. Consider the following entries:

> Harry Stephen told his old stories, wrinkled his nose, & alluded several times to his great age. He is 58. An undoubted failure; but that has a refreshing effect upon people; they are more irresponsible than the successes; but yet one can't call Harry exactly irresponsible either. He is modest; humorous; all his pride for his father & ancestors. He still *takes out an enormous pocket knife, & slowly half opens the blade, & shuts it.* [our italics]
>
> —Virginia Woolf

> Again (working on doubting/believing). Had experience of feeling an objection to my argument. Bothered me: kept tickling my mind. Didn't know how to answer it. I kept trying to put it aside, not think about it—and sort of hope that readers wouldn't notice. Then I remembered the idea (my own idea) that it's better to write these things down. (But reluctant to do so. I'm in a hurry; trying to finish this version; don't want to fiddle with it—don't want to deal with these objections.) Took out a separate sheet and wrote out the objection. Immediately it led to an answer to the objection that I'd not been able to think of before. The answer is short and will be useful for this draft—didn't waste a lot of time.
>
> —Peter Elbow

These excerpts demonstrate what we mean by academic journal writing, for both Virginia Woolf and Peter Elbow talk to themselves (one more consciously than the other) about the work they're readying for publication. What's remarkable about this kind of journal writing is that sometimes the writer will end up recording, almost verbatim, something he or she will later reproduce in a published work. In the preceding Virginia Woolf entry, for example, the italicized line about Harry Stephen turns up as follows in Woolf's novel *Mrs. Dalloway* during a section involving her character Peter Walsh: "Putting his hand into his pocket he took out a large pocket-knife and half opened the blade." Elbow's entry is more a commentary on the way he worked out a problem he encountered in writing his very famous piece on the doubting and believing game that writers and readers play. However, the point here is that talking to yourself while you are trying to overcome a sticky situation, such as making meaning of literature, can be at worst therapeutic and at best surprisingly fruitful.

Focused Freewriting

When students are asked to compose—in a short period of time, say, 5–10 minutes—what's in their minds about a particular topic, they are conducting what is termed **focused freewriting.** Unlike freewriting, which is fast, nonstop, spontaneous writing on anything that comes to mind, focused freewriting must deal squarely with the assigned topic. Consider the following examples of focused freewriting:

> Although some of Wells's biological talk was hard to understand, I do understand what Dr. Moreau was doing—vivisection. I don't believe it was right. Dr. Moreau seemed willing to disturb other lives for his own sake. I felt compassion for the beasts: their lives were disrupted and someone interested in playing God was trying to make them something they were not. I don't know why our narrator—Prendick—didn't try to escape earlier.
>
> —Kathy Royal

> While reading Dr. Moreau's explanations of his experiments to Prendick, I couldn't help but feel totally disgusted. This man was playing around with the natural order of things and creating monsters and yet he could talk about it so rationally—amazing! The entire story was quite disturbing and I found myself feeling sorry for the animals. They suffered extreme pain, were transformed into something totally different, and expected to deny their natural instincts. I must say, when Moreau was killed, I thought he got exactly what he deserved.
>
> —Lynn Michaud

Kathy and Lynn fulfilled the task of focused freewriting when they were asked to write down their feelings upon completing H. G. Wells's *The Island of Dr. Moreau,* an 1895 novel about scientific experimentation on animals and its effect on the evolutionary theory. Often, as these entries show, strong assertions are made that may later be developed insightfully. However, because the goal of focused freewriting is simply to get some feelings down for further discussion about the work, the kinds of connections and internal debate prompted by the double-entry journal may not always emerge.

These and other forms of journal writing all serve the purpose of getting you to record ideas, questions, and insights you may find useful to explore in a more formal way. However, the double-entry journal illustrates why making meaning of literature is a social or collaborative activity. While all journal writing is valuable, the double-entry form, even more than any other form of journal, can make you conscious of the process (give-and-take, generating topics, and desiring further discussion) involved in making meaning of a literary work.

EXERCISE 6

Focused freewriting: Write nonstop for, say, 5–10 minutes about your feelings or reactions to the following excerpt from Chopin's story. Then, in a paragraph or two, describe the difference between what you generated by doing this focused freewriting and what you generated by writing a double-entry journal entry for the Chopin story. For example, did the double-entry journal provide you with any issues or topics that the focused freewriting didn't?

From "The Story of an Hour"

It was her sister Josephine who told her, in broken sentences; veiled hints that revealed in half concealing. Her husband's friend Richards was there, too, near her. It was he who had been in the newspaper office when intelligence of the railroad disaster was received, with Brently Mallard's name leading the list of "killed." He had only taken the time to assure himself of its truth by a second telegram, and had hastened to forestall any less careful, less tender friend in bearing the sad message.

She did not hear the story as many women have heard the same, with a paralyzed inability to accept its significance. She wept at once, with sudden, wild abandonment, in her sister's arms. When the storm of grief had spent itself she went away to her room alone. She would have no one follow her.

CONCLUSIONS

Cinde Veinot, Debbie Carlisle, and Eric Labbe demonstrated Janusian thinking in their double-entry journal entries. Yours probably did as well. The notes on the right-hand side showed their attempts to *look ahead*, past the confusion, toward the text's meaning; those on the left-hand side showed us reflections, *looking backward* at initial confusion, concerns, and questions in an attempt to make some meaning out of the original puzzlement. These entries and your practice with the double-entry journal should help you to see it as a fruitful activity.

The goal of this chapter has been to get you used to a process that will allow you to respond significantly to a work of literature. By practicing a double-entry journal (a personal reflection that lets you talk to, or to be in dialogue with, yourself before you have to do the same with others), you'll learn to pay more attention to the *way* you read—*the reading process*. You'll soon see an added benefit: This practice will get you to pay more attention to the *way* you write—*the writing process*. Both reading and writing are similar in demanding debate and change before meaning is either offered or apprehended.

So to begin reading more constructively, especially when something is as puzzling as a new work of literature, it helps to be aware of the process by which readers build meanings out of other people's words. A double-entry journal can help you to do this. It can help in your determination of what happens when you're engaged in making meaning of a text. *How do you feel about the subject matter? strong? indifferent? bored? Likewise, how do you feel about the writer? What connections can you make with other things you know or with other things in your life as you're reading? Do you make pictures as you read or as you relate what you're reading to other things you've read? Do you concentrate on ideas or the style of writing? What are the things you overlook?* As these questions suggest, we do not know the **rules** for making meaning—no one really does. But all readers can pay more attention to the way they themselves make meaning of new and puzzling texts. And you can learn to be more active and more sensitive as you read. When you become more active, you may be able to detect holes in the interpretation you're trying to construct. When you become more sensitive, you can even learn something about how and why you construct the meanings you construct. Engaging yourself this way in a work of literature is certainly more rewarding than throwing down the book in exasperation.

4 Sharing and Responding

Exploring Together in Groups

So far in this book, through active reading and double-entry journal writing, you have prepared yourself for sharing and responding—for exploring works of literature together with your classmates and teacher. In this chapter, you'll learn about the benefits of collaboratively exploring works of literature. When you explore the meaning of such works collaboratively, you'll be seizing the opportunity to voice your own concerns about them. Moreover, sharing and responding to literature as part of a group provides a practical aid to your learning how to interpret texts, because the kinds of issues you'll need to explore formally later on can be sorted out by you and your peer group. The real purpose of this chapter is to show you that it isn't a bad thing to work with others, especially when you are engaged in the complex process of making meaning of literature.

THE ROLE OF THE TEACHER CHANGES IN A COLLABORATIVE CLASSROOM

Traditionally, literature teachers provided their own insights to students who were too confused by a difficult poem, play, short story, or novel to worry about making meaning on their own. Such teachers were clearly in charge in their classrooms. In the collaborative classroom, the situation is more equal; the teacher is less conspicuous about being the authority. The teacher in such a classroom is more a guide, leading students through the difficult process of making meaning—a process that he or she has learned through many years of study and practice. The teacher in such a classroom is also like a referee, standing in the way of chaos, directing confusion toward productive conversation rather than destructive anarchy. The teacher in such a classroom arranges for conversation, sustaining the dialogue so that it really does become ongoing. In a collaborative classroom, both teacher and student come to view learning as a process, a strategy for coming to know something (what a text means, for instance) as opposed to reciting information (how many sonnets Shakespeare wrote, for instance).

THE ROLE OF A STUDENT CHANGES IN
A COLLABORATIVE CLASSROOM

John Trimbur, a professor of English at Worcester Polytechnic Institute, wrote a letter that Kenneth Bruffee, a professor of English at Brooklyn College, included in his textbook about collaborative learning, *A Short Course in Writing*. Trimbur's letter illustrates what is meant by saying that learning is, by and large, the result of changes in the kinds of relationships that occur among the people involved; in other words, learning is social or collaborative. The letter described how in a collaborative classroom the students are responsible and responsive to one another. Trimbur explained that, whether writing by themselves in their journals, or debating issues face-to-face in their groups, students in a collaborative classroom were always engaged with someone as they worked their way through the assigned task. Trimbur's letter was the proof Bruffee needed to verify that line in Frost's "Tuft of Flowers" we have cited in opening this book: "Men [and women] work together whether they work together or apart."

It is important to note here that, as students in a collaborative classroom, you are not competing to outdo one another. Instead, you'll be working to celebrate one another's success in learning the difficult process of making sense of literature. Learning collaboratively is indeed liberating and democratic: you always have a stake in the outcome and you have to be skillful at negotiation and compromise. Learning to share and respond to literature collaboratively exemplifies what it means to say that meaning is *constructed*, not *uncovered*: many voices (yours included), at first—and perhaps often—discordant, chime in rather harmoniously in the end.

THE ENVIRONMENT CHANGES IN A
COLLABORATIVE CLASSROOM

In most classrooms, as you've probably noticed, the format calls for the teacher to lecture from the front of the room, delivering the lesson to neat rows of students making up the rest of the room. The teacher's voice, perhaps occasional student voices posing questions or offering observations—this is as much as you'll hear in such classrooms. The collaborative classroom is designed for noise because the social nature of the learning that takes place within it demands conversation—lots of it. You've probably already noticed that the desks are not in neatly arranged rows, nor is the teacher poised in the traditional place at the front of the room. Instead, desks are often arranged in circles—several circles at first, then one large circle when the class as a whole convenes to construct meaning of a text. You may have already come to see the idea of the circle as both symbolic and sustaining. It is symbolic because everyone gets to look at and to talk with everyone else in a conversation that is literally continuous, mirroring the larger ongoing conversation called literature. It is sustaining because voices like yours that might be soft or usually silent become audible, supported by the unending circle of co-laborers engaged in the difficult process of making meaning.

BEING PREPARED TO SHARE AND RESPOND

There are times when some students really appreciate traditional, teacher-led classrooms—even, perhaps especially, literature classrooms. Usually, these times occur when such students haven't adequately prepared for a particular lesson, perhaps because they haven't been urged to engage consistently in the process of making meaning of the subject. During these times, some students find it comforting to learn that they can just sit erect, pen poised, and take notes on what the teacher has prepared on the subject. While most literature instructors certainly have a great deal to offer their students, the danger in such a practice is that it may prevent students from ever really learning the subject on their own. If you were to adopt this attitude, you might come to view meaning in literary texts as existing in some absolute form, rather than as something that can be made. While you might take in a wealth of information, such passive learning could make it difficult for you to participate enthusiastically in any larger, ongoing conversations regarding literature—or any other subject for that matter.

Such scenarios are impossible in the collaborative classroom. From the start of this book, you've been alerted to the fact that you're responsible for becoming involved in making meaning of literature. From reading a text actively to notetaking to writing in the double-entry journal, you've been preparing yourself for the more formal tasks of sharing your views with others—students, teachers, and other readers. In fact, right now, you possess a wealth of material that will enable you to engage in productive conversation. In this chapter, you'll discover how that material can be debated and focused for more formal written and oral projects.

EXERCISE 1

Find several like-minded peers who have worked on the same text for Exercise 5 in Chapter 3. Form a group and, outside of class, share your responses for about an hour. (Refer to you annotations, notes, and journals for responses.) Be sure you have chosen someone to record notes on your conversation. Be prepared to compare the results of your group work with those cited in the remaining pages of this chapter.

AGREEING TO SHARE: THE FIRST STEP

In the remaining sections of this chapter, we have reproduced parts of the transcript that four students (Debbie Carlisle, Eric Labbe, Kelly Leighton, and Cinde Veinot) developed when they discussed the essay "Polygamy" (p. 88). Having annotated their texts and written in their journals, the students engaged in conversation about the literary works they had read. As you read through the transcript, notice the tug of war among the students—the way they speak out, debate, negotiate, and then complete their conversation.

> *Cinde:* Do you believe this man of ninety claiming he was seventy? The poor daughter-in-law has no idea what she's getting herself into. What do you think? He puts her on the spot.
>
> *Kelly:* I thought he was creepy. . . .
>
> *Debbie:* . . . these women are subjected to this man.
>
> *Eric:* But it doesn't bother them.
>
> *Debbie:* It should.

In this initial section, notice how readily each person takes up the conversation; that's what active preparation will enable you to do. The transcript shows the informal, rather emotional responses the students had toward the subject matter of the essay. As friends are likely to do, the four offer candid remarks. But notice, too, how quickly each student follows up an initial foray into conversation. Even in their early conversations these students can conceive of a subject that has to do with "the man" in the essay "Polygamy," a topic that might prove fruitful for further discussion or formal presentation. Still, should you find yourself a little unsure about collaborating in this way, don't worry. You can move past such a common reaction rather easily once you're focused on the goal of making meaning of a text.

EXERCISE 2

In the conversation you have begun with your peers to complete Exercise 1, analyze your initial responses to the chosen text. Are they also informal, personal, candid? Compare them to the responses highlighted previously.

INVITING RESPONSE: LEARNING TO FOCUS COLLABORATIVELY

One of the advantages of collaborative learning is that it helps those involved to solve a problem faster and better than they could possibly do on their own. In the case of responding formally to literature, either in writing or orally, collaborating can help you to determine if your informal responses merit further investigation. Notice that in the following two excerpts, a student advances an informal response, and it is taken very seriously by the student's peers.

Kelly: I thought about the concept of temporary marriage. I said [in my journal] it was something we should look into.

Eric: For whom?

Kelly: What do you mean? For us, for everyone.

Eric: Do you really think Americans should consider . . . temporary marriage?

Kelly: Well I mean if the partners both agree they want to be married for a year and then that's it. . . .

[Conversation then shifts to another topic.]

Cinde: I really didn't buy the story at all. I bought the narrator. She was pretty believable. . . . The funny thing about the narrator is that I thought she had already made a judgment by the first paragraph on the second page. It just seemed like her whole tone was completely negative. She just said, "Well I'm not really close to it but I don't know how I feel." I don't buy that. I really think that she had already made up her mind just by the way she said, "What do you think of this?" I think that maybe more than the TV the more threatening thing is her because you can tell by her reaction that she's very Westernized. It took a lot for him to say, "What do you think?"

Debbie: I thought it was interesting that he was selective about the customs he chose to protect or to keep. The thing about the chairs I thought was just stubborn. But the television. I think that would be the most threatening object or idea threatening to his culture.

Kelly: I find it sort of a joke.

Eric: I just read this recently . . . and it seems like a diary. It doesn't seem like she's making any kind of a decision either way. There's a decision right there. That's a decision in itself. She decided to be tolerant. I thought it was kind of interesting how the medium bridges cultures and how that works and what the dynamic is there.

In the first excerpt, Kelly wants to get some response to her focusing on "temporary marriage." Eric responds, but the conversation quickly trails off, perhaps indicating to Kelly that such a topic might not justify the amount of time she may have to invest in it. In the second excerpt, however, Cinde's decision to focus on the narrator and on cultural notions elicits interesting responses from the others. Cinde can assume from this exchange that either area might deserve further attention.

EXERCISE 3

In the conversation you have begun with your peers to complete Exercise 2, analyze your responses that are followed up by your peers. How does the follow-up conversation indicate to you whether or not the focus of your topic merits further time and energy? Compare what you come up with to the responses highlighted previously.

MAKING MEANING OF INITIAL RESPONSES: ISOLATING TOPICS

In exploring literature collaboratively, you can be assured that all you have thought about regarding a particular text will be tested, through thoughtful and often heated debate, by those with whom you work. In the end those ideas that receive the most treatment will probably be those topics you'll want to explore formally—in either a written or an oral report. In the lengthy transcript that follows, notice how intensely Eric and Debbie argue for their different points of view regarding polygamy, marriage, women, and culture. Kelly and Cinde chime in from time to time, but we can assume that, if they wanted, it would be up to the two principal speakers to develop more formal pieces centered on these topics, knowing full well what kinds of arguments will trigger further response (friendly or not) from their readers or listeners.

> *Eric:* It doesn't seem that the polygamy is all that bad for these people. It seems like culture. These two women are happy. They seem happy and there aren't a lot of cultural customs and overtones. If you're from Arabia and you're from a Nomadic culture that sort of thing is going to happen. You've got to have some sort of a legal attitude towards marriage; otherwise it just doesn't work. There have to be certain rules and laws to keep things together so I can see how we would complain in the West that this isn't a romantic, sharing, co-dependent relationship. . . .
>
> *Cinde:* . . . But that's us telling them what they should be bothered about.
>
> *Eric:* What I mean is that you have this woman from the West with Western values going to an Eastern place and there's a clash there.
>
> *Debbie:* So you think Eastern women don't value equality and respect as individuals.
>
> *Kelly:* I'm sure they do.

Eric: No they don't. I don't think they know about it.

Cinde: They may now.

Debbie: Don't you think there is something wrong with that?

Eric: To us but not to them because that's all they know.

Kelly: But isn't there something wrong with that?

Eric: No. To you or to us but to a Buddhist? For us to say this is wrong and attempting to change, that's forcing our cultural values on them. We don't agree with it. I don't happen to agree with the Australian Aborigines carving the cheeks of their young when they're in the adolescent rites. We would call that scarification and that's bad, but it serves a purpose. Yes, we don't agree with polygamy.

Cinde: Do you think they should object more to it? Are you saying they are not believable enough?

Debbie: No. I'm just saying that he brought up that this is the culture and that this is Western culture and you should accept the culture for what it is. I'm saying no, dammit. Subjection is subjection—and very objectionable.

Eric: I think everybody should object to that. But this is different.

Kelly: Are these women dehumanized?

Eric: Is this a human rights issue? But for these women I don't know because with these women this is the way they see it and they've gone into it. You can't educate the whole world.

Cinde: No, you can't. It's nowhere near the same thing. You're talking about a set of cultural values that are based on Western tradition in the 50s.

Debbie: So you're justifying this? You don't think there is anything wrong with these women serving this man?

Eric: I don't think . . . there is any way we can change that. I don't think there is any way we can pass judgment on it.

Debbie: There is nothing wrong with it!

Eric: I don't agree with polygamy but I don't think that therefore we have to pass judgment on another culture.

Kelly: You don't necessarily have to agree with it.

Cinde: This is a very provocative piece of writing.

Eric: They're not objecting to it so it's not up to us to. It's fine that we don't agree with it.

Debbie: We feel sympathy for them.

Eric: I don't think any of us are arguing for polygamy here. For them it works.

Debbie: I don't like it at all.

EXERCISE 4

In the conversation you have begun with your peers to complete Exercise 3, analyze those responses to the chosen text that are contested. How does the debate indicate to you whether or not the topic(s) should be formalized in writing or in an oral report? Compare what you come up with to the responses highlighted previously.

COMING TOGETHER: JOINING THE LARGER COMMUNITY

Once you've shared your responses about a text with members of your collaborative group, your teacher will probably want to convene the entire classroom for further discussion. He or she will want reports from each of the classroom's groups so that all students will benefit by a thorough discussion of a work like the essay "Polygamy."

If you consider what the four students discussed concerning "Polygamy," you can well imagine the scenario that would result from bringing up at least their ideas for debate in front of the entire class. You can probably bank on a lively response to the issue of polygamy that Eric and Debbie debated. Perhaps it would be more intense than that generated by the issue Cinde brought up about the narrator's perspective in the piece. Yet, even that issue, along with the others (temporary marriage, the "man" in society), would prompt response.

In a typical class of twenty-five students, you could then expect four additional reports like this one, with up to four more topics per report. Ideally, you could get from such a set-up approximately twenty separate topics! If it is approached earnestly, a collaborative approach to making meaning of literature can make a profound difference in the sheer number of ideas generated in a given class session. Rather than being left on your own to make sense of your confusion about a work of literature, in a collaborative classroom, you would be allowed to turn to others—a support group, if you will—who will enable you to direct that negative energy into something positive, a process for approaching the work that can reveal a number of profitable topics for more formal investigation.

What transpires in your group will likely follow in the classroom: debate, consensus, more topics for consideration, etc. In the end, without having one person tell you all he or she could remember or research about a text, you'll be the recipient of many ideas about how to approach your text in a formal way (a paper or oral presentation). You'll hear the arguments in favor and against such ideas. Thus you'll be prepared to investigate the text more thoroughly and insightfully than you might have thought possible when you first read it.

EXERCISE 5

For the conversations you have had with your peers to complete Exercises 1–4, choose a recorder to be responsible for relating to the class as a whole the debate that took place in your group, the consensus you reached, as well as the areas of disagreement that remain. Be prepared to help out your recorder should he or she be called upon to present your responses.

CONCLUSIONS

Two heads are certainly better than one when it comes time to solving academic problems. You know this from your experience in studying for exams you've taken before you came to this course. You probably sought the assistance and support of your friends when you had a test in an area about which you just weren't sure—the same principle applies to collaboratively learning how to make meaning of literature. Even the best literary critics will not deny that literature is confusing. Thus, they will readily admit that individual interpretations can be challenged, debated, changed. That's what happens in a collaborative classroom—except that it occurs **before** a formal individual response is presented. The advantage of such intense conversations as those represented in this chapter, as well as those you engaged in with your peers, is that there will be many suggestions about a literary text in the course of small and large group discussions. So when the time comes for formal conversation (a paper, a presentation), your voice won't be concealed.

5 Adding Research and Following Up

Consulting Experts and Renewing Discussion

We said in the Preface that exploring literature can be considered an ever-widening conversation, first between the author and the reader, then between readers in group discussions, and then between readers in written observations. One of the more intriguing features of this latter conversation is its breadth and scope—readers wishing to discover more about a literary work can consult literary critics to see how others have interpreted the work, biographers to see how the work relates to the author's life, literary and art historians to discover the artistic environment in which the author worked, historians to understand the social and political climate in which the author lived, philosophers to explore the thinking and values that permeated the author's culture—and the list goes on. Children are often fascinated to discover that the author of one of their favorite books is a real person; they delight in seeing the author in a context other than that of the book. Sometimes that sense of wonder is lost as students move on through the academic process. The collaborative classroom can rekindle the desire to find out more about an author, his or her life, and his or her world.

In Chapter 2 we mentioned that you may want to do a little preliminary biographical or social research before reading a selection. This chapter discusses more substantive (but still informal) research, namely research conducted in order to clarify issues and answer questions that arise in the course of group discussions. There are any number of reasons why you may wish to extend your conversation to those who have written about an author and his or her times—you may want to find more biographical information, to read more of the author's work, to find out how literary critics have interpreted a particularly intriguing passage, to explore the social/political/cultural context in which the author wrote, or to discover more about a central topic in the literary work. Any of these reasons are valid for pursuing informal research, and your informal research may lead you to a topic worthy of more formal exploration in a research paper. Because research involves a special kind of conversation, a silent one involving reader and writer rather than two speakers, this chapter may sound similar to research chapters in college handbooks. This chapter is not intended to be a complete guide to conducting formal research; rather, we are introducing you to sources that can extend the conversation begun when you first encountered a literary work.

AREAS OF RESEARCH

As you discuss literary works, your natural curiosity can lead to informal research in four general areas: biography; commentary/criticism; social/cultural/political context; topic/theme.

Biography

As you discuss a literary work with other students, you will often come up with questions that the work itself cannot answer. Sometimes those questions are objective, such as, "Was Lady Mary Chudleigh married or not?" Others are more open-ended, such as, "Was she influenced by any great thinkers of her age?" Regardless of the simplicity or complexity of your question, research can provide you with or lead you to a response. In the discussions of "To the Ladies" (p. 94) for example, Kelly Leighton makes the following observation:

> The first thing I thought of when I read this was, like, did this woman have a really awful marriage? Was she abused by her husband? Who is she, anyway? I've never read anything else by her. . . .

Kelly's questions are a natural lead-in to research. In the reference room of the college library she was able to find sources providing some information on Lady Mary Chudleigh's life, information which helped the group gain a new perspective on the poem. For instance, Kelly discovered that Chudleigh was unhappy in her marriage, and that she was heavily influenced by the contemporary feminist Mary Astell. Kelly brought back to the group the following observations:

> I couldn't find out anything about her marriage except some reference to her unhappiness—at least that confirms our suspicions that the poem is in some ways autobiographical. What's really interesting, though, is the relationships she had with women. She was really into feminism—I couldn't believe it; in the eighteenth century! These women were writing all sorts of stuff to defend women's rights. What a crowd! I'd always thought the eighteenth century had only Pope and Jonson and those guys, but there was really a lot going on then that doesn't get into the major literature.

Look up the entry on Lady Mary Chudleigh in two of the sources listed here. In your journal, take down any information you consider relevant to the poem. Before meeting with your group, compare the biographical sketches: Does one source give more space than others to Chudleigh? What does each source emphasize? Why do you think the sources emphasize what they do? When your group meets, compare responses: Do some students emphasize certain aspects of her life more than others? Discuss any differences in your interpretations of her life and its influence on her poem.

Dictionaries of biography provide readers with brief life-histories of noted people, and usually include bibliographies (lists of the authors major works, lists of critical works, full-length biographies). If you wish to find out more about an individual author, consult an appropriate reference from the following list:

Contemporary Authors

Everyman's Dictionary of Literary Biography: English and American. Rev. Ed.

A Dictionary of British and American Women Writers 1660–1800.

Dictionary of Literary Biography. 38 volumes plus supplements.

Dictionary of National Biography. 21 volumes.

Commentary/Criticism

Occasionally in your exploration of literature, you come across passages that remain intriguing, perhaps even difficult to interpret, despite extensive group discussion. And on occasion members of the group will disagree on the value of a particular work. Consider, for example, Eric Labbe's evaluation of Chudleigh's poem:

> Here's proof that injustice doesn't always lead to great poetry. It's an interesting description of the way things were back then, even the way the hierarchical patriarchal system works today. I bet a lot of women looked at it and silently agreed with her. I can't really say much about it. It's pretty straightforward. The woman had guts to speak out that way back then, to let her voice be heard. But I wish she had written a better poem.

In the past, when Eric wished to pursue further the question of excellence regarding other writers, he consulted critical works. He found bibliographies in anthologies in which a work appeared (anthologies frequently include bibliographies for major writers); he also used reference works devoted entirely to listing critical works. This time Eric sought information on

Chudleigh in a couple of poetry anthologies, to no avail. He then consulted the *MLA Bibliography,* and found one reference to Chudleigh in an index. Alas, when he checked the full reference for the article, he discovered that it was written in German! Eric even consulted the English Department's Eighteenth Century Literature specialist—to no avail. What Eric encountered in his frustrating search is something you should be prepared for: Occasionally you will encounter a writer about whom little has been written. In Eric's case, the search proved all but fruitless. He found general reference to Chudleigh's reception in the dictionaries of biography, but found little else to support (or challenge) his assessment of her poetry. In the case of critical response to Chudleigh's poem, then, the conversation could not be extended to include those who had written about her work. Eric's experience, however, did lead him to draw some conclusions, which he reported to the group:

> Even though I didn't think the poem was that great, I expected to be able to find *something* about her in the critics—especially after seeing what she'd written and the people she hung around with. It makes me wonder about why some writers are obscure and some are considered "masters." I've read poets who don't seem any better than Chudleigh and they've got all sorts of books and articles written about them. Why? Is it really because they're better poets? Could her obscurity have something to do with her sex or the subjects she wrote about? Seems to me that except for Aphra Behn, there's just no women in the eighteenth-century anthologies. And most of the stuff written on her has been done in the last ten years or so.

EXERCISE 2

Look up Chudleigh in one of the bibliographies listed here (other than the MLA). Can you find any reference to Chudleigh? Then look up Aphra Behn in one of the bibliographies (including the MLA), and report to the group how many references to her you find. Finally, discuss Eric's conclusions about women writers—how do you respond to his suggestion that Chudleigh's sex or subject matter may be responsible for her obscurity? If you can think of any other obscure writers who may have been ignored for reasons other than the value of their work, discuss what those reasons might be.

Bibliographies are invaluable resources for critical analyses of literature. Many are specialized, focusing on a particular period of literary history, on a particular group of writers, or sometimes on a particular writer. As you do your own research, consult bibliographies from the following list:

Arts & Humanities Citation Index
Essay and General Literature Index

Literary Criticism Index

MLA International Bibliography of Books and Articles on the Modern Languages and Literature

Library of Literary Criticism of English and American Authors. 8 volumes plus extension.

Social/Cultural/Political Context

As you may have noticed in reading the journal entries and transcripts of group discussions in Chapters 3 and 4, conversation about literary works often involves discussion of social issues. Perhaps the primary reason for this phenomenon is that literature (as we've said several times before in this book) is not written in a vacuum. The author is a living, breathing human being who is a member of a particular society. No author can avoid being influenced to some extent by outside forces. While some writers are more conscious than others of making a social statement (Arthur Miller, for example, wrote *The Crucible* as a condemnation of McCarthyism), virtually all writers reflect in some way the society in which they live. It can be fascinating to discover what kind of world a writer lived in—and it can be informative as well. When discussing "To the Ladies," for example, Kelly Leighton made the following observation:

> . . . I thought first it was surprising to hear a feminist view more than three centuries ago be brought out because the views on marriage are amazingly contemporary. I was curious about the reaction of her audience and what kind of reception she got. I'm surprised they didn't burn her at the stake. . . .

In trying to pursue these thoughts, Kelly had quite a task before her. It's relatively easy to look up information on a particular author's biography, and criticism is easy to find as well. But where should she begin looking for information on the views of women in the eighteenth century? Actually, Kelly's task was simpler than it appeared at first. Because the poem is so clearly political in its content, the chances of the topic's being mentioned in biographical material were high. Thus a look in the dictionary of biography that Kelly had consulted earlier provided a little information on the reception Chudleigh's work received. Desiring more information, however, Kelly consulted a history of English literature, where she found information on the stir caused by early feminists and a discussion of a group of literary women that Chudleigh associated with. This is what she reported to the group:

> Apparently eighteenth-century feminists were causing enough of a stir that prominent men found it necessary to address the issue. Chudleigh

went to this wedding in 1700 ... where the minister preached a sermon about how morally weak women were and that was why they had to obey their husbands in everything. Chudleigh got so mad she went home and wrote her most famous poem in response. It was called *The Ladies Defence: or, The Bride-Woman's Counsellor Answer'd*. Her reputation really took off after it was published. She also belonged to a group of feminist writers led by Mary Astell, who published a couple of books on women's rights. Astell's work was well-known enough to be referred to by Defoe and Steele. I guess there was more going on in that area [women's rights] than we realized.

EXERCISE 3

From the biographical sources used for Exercise 1, choose an interesting area of Chudleigh's life and times—perhaps someone who influenced her, or an issue she was involved in. Find information about your choice in an appropriate source from the following list. In your journal, take notes on the information you find. Share your notes with the group, comparing the different kinds of information members find in different sources.

Depending on the nature of the information you're looking for, you will find yourself consulting different sources. Some literary works will send you off to consult philosophers or theologians, others to historians or political scientists, still others to psychologists or sociologists. Sometimes too you will find yourself curious about how a writer's contemporaries treated similar subject matter, as well as what contemporary visual artists or musicians were doing. As you follow your curiosity in such matters, you can consult sources from the following list:

Literary Histories

Cambridge History of American Literature. 3 volumes.

Cambridge History of English Literature. 15 volumes.

Literary History of the United States. 2 volumes. 4th ed. rev.

The Oxford Companion to American Literature. 5th ed.

The Oxford Companion to Classical Literature.

The Oxford Companion to English Literature. 5th ed.

Philosophy/Religion

The Encyclopedia of Philosophy. 4 volumes.

An Encyclopedia of Religion.

History

New Cambridge Modern History. 14 volumes.

An Encyclopedia of World History.

Harvard Guide to American History. Rev. ed. 2 volumes.

Social Sciences

Encyclopedia of Psychology. 2nd ed.

International Encyclopedia of the Social Sciences. 8 volumes plus supplement.

Art/Music

Encyclopedia of World Art. 15 volumes.

International Cyclopedia of Music and Musicians. 11th ed.

General Encyclopedias/Almanacs

Encyclopedia Americana. 30 volumes. Updated with yearbooks.

The New Encyclopaedia Britannica. 32 volumes. Updated with yearbooks.

World Almanac and Book of Facts.

Topic/Theme

At times your response to a literary work focuses more on the topic itself than on other matters. For example, in discussing Chudleigh, Debbie Carlisle found herself asking questions about the progress—or lack thereof—of women's rights over the past two centuries. When Cinde mentioned how contemporary Chudleigh's views seemed, Kelly offered the following comments:

> This is also frightening because if they'd been around this long, they predate the 20th Century. Will it take three hundred more years for people to wake up? So I guess what I'm frightened of is just how little attitudes towards women have changed, and how today people relate, and how many men still see wives as their servants or their subordinates and I think that's kind of sad too.

These questions led Debbie to investigate the history of women's rights, especially with regard to marriage. Her research was not directly related to the poem, of course, but it certainly was relevant to the conversation begun by Lady Mary Chudleigh. Such an issue is frequently covered in the popular press, so Debbie was able to look up the topic in a periodical and a newspaper index, as well as to consult a book she found through a computerized database. She reported this information to the group:

> Even though there were a lot of women writing about the stuff Chudleigh wrote about in the early eighteenth century, Mary Wollstonecraft's *A Vindication of the Rights of Women* didn't come out until almost a hundred years after Chudleigh wrote, and it took almost another hundred years before British wives were finally granted the right to own their own property. They didn't even get the right to vote until 1928! . . . seems to me her gripes are understated if anything—now I understand why she cautions women to avoid marriage if they're wise.

EXERCISE 4

Look up the subject of womens rights in marriage in one of the sources listed here. Read one source cited in the reference work. (If you're consulting books, read the preface or introduction, and look through the table of contents to get an idea of what the book is about.) Take notes on the source in your journal, and compare your findings in group discussion. How does the information you've found affect your reading of the poem?

Indexes and databases will provide you with the names of articles and books on a given subject. If you need help in determining the appropriate heading to look under, consult the *Library of Congress Subject Headings*, a multivolume reference that lists all of the subject headings used by the Library of Congress in cataloging books. This resource can be found in the reference room of the library.

General Periodicals Index (InfoTrac). (computer index)

Magazine Index Plus (InfoTrac). (computer index)

National Newspaper Index (InfoTrac). (computer index)

New York Times Index.

Readers Guide to Periodical Literature.

Your library's computerized database or card catalogue.

CONCLUSIONS

This chapter has been brief—its intent was simply to acquaint you with some of the general sources you may consult when you want to know a bit more about a writer and his or her work. Although this information can help you understand the work better by providing you with different perspectives from which to approach it, you shouldn't think that it's always necessary to consult "experts" in order to make meaning of a literary work. As we've said throughout the book so far, meaning is made as readers enter into a dialogue with writers and other readers. The research mentioned in this chapter extends the conversation beyond the classroom, allowing other voices to contribute. In fact, none of the students in the group changed their minds significantly about the poem after consulting other sources. What the students gained from their research was confidence in consulting others when seeking to make meaning of a literary work, familiarity with general reference works, and experience in dealing with the occasional fruitless search for information.

As you prepare to present your ideas formally, you will find yourself consulting sources beyond those mentioned in this chapter. The references listed here can provide you with invaluable assistance in beginning your formal research, however. Many of the reference works listed include bibliographies; some are devoted entirely to bibliography. Using these sources as a starting point, you will be able to focus your research according to the needs of your project, bringing into your presentation a collection of voices. But this chapter should have convinced you that research isn't something relegated to a major project; it can make for interesting informal discussion as well.

6 Case Study

An Overview of the Exploration Process

In this section you have a chance to observe how other students completed the work you've been assigned in the preceding chapters. The four students (Debbie Carlisle, Eric Labbe, Kelly Leighton, and Cinde Veinot) worked with four texts representing four genres (short story, poem, essay, and drama) that focus on similar themes (communication, a woman's or wife's role, men and women). The sample annotations, journal entries, conversations, and comments on research reflect different students' responses to the same material.

Perhaps the most important feature of the Case Study is the students' conversation about the work. Each reflects the genuine talk that the students engaged in after having annotated the texts and after having written in their double-entry journals. As you read the conversations, note the similarities and differences that arise, as well as the many topics and issues the students generate. For these students, the conversations marked a critical point in their exploration of the literature: They brought their private observations to the group, and came away with different perspectives that allowed them to explore the literature further. In Chapters 8 and 9 we provide two sample papers generated from the students' exploration of this literature—if you review the Case Study after reading those papers, you should be able to see quite clearly how the formal presentation results from the initial exploration.

The format for the works (*Trifles*, "The Story of an Hour," "Polygamy," and "To the Ladies,") is as follows:

- The Selection
- Annotations
- Double-Entry Journal Entries
- Group Discussion
- Comments on Informal Research

Annotations and journal entries are presented exactly as the students produced them; conversations are edited to make reading easier. We also chose not to point out anything particular in the student responses, preferring to allow you to compare Debbie's, Eric's, Kelly's, and Cinde's responses to your own.

TRIFLES

Susan Glaspell

SCENE:

The kitchen in the now abandoned farmhouse of JOHN WRIGHT, *a gloomy kitchen, and left without having been put in order—unwashed pans under the sink, a loaf of bread outside the breadbox, a dish towel on the table—other signs of incompleted work. At the rear the outer door opens, and the* SHERIFF *comes in, followed by the* COUNTY ATTORNEY *and* HALE. *The* SHERIFF *and* HALE *are men in middle life, the* COUNTY ATTORNEY *is a young man; all are much bundled up and go at once to the stove. They are followed by the two women—the* SHERIFF'S WIFE *first; she is a slight wiry woman, a thin nervous face.* MRS. HALE *is larger and would ordinarily be called more comfortable looking, but she is disturbed now and looks fearfully about as she enters. The women have come in slowly and stand close together near the door.*

COUNTY ATTORNEY [*rubbing his hands*]. This feels good. Come up to the fire, ladies.

MRS. PETERS [*after taking a step forward*]. I'm not—cold.

SHERIFF [*unbuttoning his overcoat and stepping away from the stove as if to mark the beginning of official business*]. Now, Mr. Hale, before we move things about, you explain to Mr. Henderson just what you saw when you came here yesterday morning.

COUNTY ATTORNEY. By the way, has anything been moved? Are things just as you left them yesterday?

SHERIFF [*looking about*]. It's just the same. When it dropped below zero last night, I thought I'd better send Frank out this morning to make a fire for us—no use getting pneumonia with a big case on; but I told him not to touch anything except the stove—and you know Frank.

COUNTY ATTORNEY. Somebody should have been left here yesterday.

SHERIFF. Oh—yesterday. When I had to send Frank to Morris Center for that man who went crazy—I want you to know I had my hands full yesterday. I knew you could get back from Omaha by today, and as long as I went over everything here myself—

COUNTY ATTORNEY. Well, Mr. Hale, tell just what happened when you came here yesterday morning.

HALE. Harry and I had started to town with a load of potatoes. We came along the road from my place; and as I got here, I said, "I'm going to see if I can't get John Wright to go in with me on a party telephone." I spoke to Wright about it once before, and he put me off, saying folks talked too much anyway, and all he asked was peace and quiet—I guess you know about how much he talked himself; but I thought maybe if I went to the house and talked about it before his wife, though I said to Harry that I didn't know as what his wife wanted made much difference to John—

COUNTY ATTORNEY. Let's talk about that later, Mr. Hale. I do want to talk about that, but tell now just what happened when you got to the house.

HALE. I didn't hear or see anything; I knocked at the door, and still it was all quiet inside. I knew they must be up, it was past eight o'clock. So I knocked again, and I thought I heard somebody say, "Come in." I wasn't sure, I'm not sure yet, but I opened the door—this door [*indicating the door by which the two women are still standing*], and there in that rocker—[*pointing to it*] sat Mrs. Wright. [*They all looked at the rocker*].

COUNTY ATTORNEY. What—was she doing?

HALE. She was rockin' back and forth. She had her apron in her hand and was kind of—pleating it.

COUNTY ATTORNEY. And how did she—look?

HALE. Well, she looked queer.

COUNTY ATTORNEY. How do you mean—queer?

HALE. Well, as if she didn't know what she was going to do next. And kind of done up.

COUNTY ATTORNEY. How did she seem to feel about your coming?

HALE. Why, I don't think she minded—one way or other. She didn't pay much attention. I said, "How do, Mrs. Wright, it's cold, ain't it?" And she said, "Is it?"—and went on kind of pleating at her apron. Well, I was surprised; she didn't ask me to come up to the stove, or set down, but just sat there, not even looking at me, so I said, "I want to see John." And then she—laughed. I guess you would call it a laugh. I thought of Harry and the team outside, so I said a little sharp: "Can't I see John?" "No," she says, kind o' dull like. "Ain't he home?" says I. "Yes," says she, "he's home." "Then why can't I see him?" I asked her, out of patience. "'Cause he's dead," says she. "*Dead?*" says I. She just nodded her head, not getting a bit excited, but rockin' back and forth. "Why— where is he?" says I, not knowing what to say. She just pointed upstairs—like that [*himself pointing to the room above*]. I got up, with the idea of going up there. I walked from there to here—then I says, "Why, what did he die of?" "He died of a rope around his neck," says she, and just went on pleatin' at her apron. Well, I went out and called Harry. I thought I might—need help. We went upstairs, and there he was lyin'—

COUNTY ATTORNEY. I think I'd rather have you go into that upstairs, where you can point it all out. Just go on now with the rest of the story.

HALE. Well, my first thought was to get that rope off. I looked . . . [*Stops, his face twitches.*] . . . but Harry, he went up to him, and he said, "No, he's dead all right, and we'd better not touch anything." So we went back downstairs. She was still sitting that same way. "Has anybody been notified?" I asked. "No," she says, unconcerned. "Who did this, Mrs. Wright?" said Harry. He said it business-like—and she stopped pleatin' of her apron. "I don't know," she says. "You don't *know?*" says Harry. "No," says she. "Weren't you sleepin' in the bed with him?" says Harry. "Yes," says she, "but I was on the inside." "Somebody slipped a rope round his neck and strangled him, and you didn't wake up?" says Harry. "I didn't wake up," she said after him. We must 'a looked as if we didn't see how that could be, for after a minute she said, "I sleep sound." Harry was going to ask her more questions, but I said maybe we ought to let her tell her story first to the coroner, or the sheriff, so Harry went fast as he could to Rivers' place, where there's a telephone.

COUNTY ATTORNEY. And what did Mrs. Wright do when she knew that you had gone for the coroner?

HALE. She moved from that chair to this over here . . . [*Pointing to a small chair in the corner.*] . . . and just sat there with her hands held together and looking down. I got a feeling that I ought to make some conversation, so I said I had come in to see if John wanted to put in a telephone, and at that she started to laugh, and then she stopped and looked at me—scared. [*The* COUNTY ATTORNEY, *who had his notebook out, makes a note.*] I dunno, maybe it wasn't scared. I wouldn't like to say it was. Soon Harry got back, and then Dr. Lloyd came, and you, Mr. Peters, and so I guess that's all I know that you don't.

COUNTY ATTORNEY. [*looking around*]. I guess we'll go upstairs first—and then out to the barn and around there. [*To the* SHERIFF]. You're convinced that there was nothing important here—nothing that would point to any motive?

SHERIFF. Nothing here but kitchen things.

[*The* COUNTY ATTORNEY, *after again looking around the kitchen, opens the door of a cupboard closet. He gets up on a chair and looks on a shelf. Pulls his hand away, sticky.*]

COUNTY ATTORNEY. Here's a nice mess.

[*The women draw nearer.*]

MRS. PETERS [*to the other woman*]. Oh, her fruit; it did freeze. [*To the* LAWYER.] She worried about that when it turned so cold. She said the fire'd go out and her jars would break.

SHERIFF. Well, can you beat the women! Held for murder and worryin' about her preserves.

COUNTY ATTORNEY. I guess before we're through she may have something more serious than preserves to worry about.

HALE. Well, women are used to worrying over trifles.

[*The two women move a little closer together.*]

COUNTY ATTORNEY [*with the gallantry of a young politician*]. And yet, for all their worries, what would we do without the ladies? [*The women do not unbend. He goes to the sink, takes a dipperful of water from the pail and, pouring it into a basin, washes his hands. Starts to wipe them on the roller towel, turns it for a cleaner place.*] Dirty towels! [*Kicks his foot against the pans under the sink.*] Not much of a housekeeper, would you say, ladies?

MRS. HALE [*stiffly*]. There's a great deal of work to be done on a farm.

COUNTY ATTORNEY. To be sure, and yet . . . [*With a little bow to her.*] . . . I know there are some Dickson county farmhouses which do not have such roller towels. [*He gives it a pull to expose its full length again.*]

MRS. HALE. Those towels get dirty awful quick. Men's hands aren't always as clean as they might be.

COUNTY ATTORNEY. Ah, loyal to your sex, I see. But you and Mrs. Wright were neighbors. I suppose you were friends, too.

MRS. HALE. [shaking her head]. I've not seen much of her of late years. I've not been in this house—it's more than a year.

COUNTY ATTORNEY. And why was that? You didn't like her?

MRS. HALE. I liked her all well enough. Farmers' wives have their hands full, Mr. Henderson. And then—

COUNTY ATTORNEY. Yes—?

MRS. HALE [looking about]. It never seemed a very cheerful place.

COUNTY ATTORNEY. No—it's not cheerful. I shouldn't say she had the homemaking instinct.

MRS. HALE. Well, I don't know as Wright had, either.

COUNTY ATTORNEY. You mean that they didn't get on very well?

MRS. HALE. No, I don't mean anything. But I don't think a place'd be any cheerfuler for John Wright's being in it.

COUNTY ATTORNEY. I'd like to talk more of that a little later. I want to get the lay of things upstairs now. [He goes to the left, where three steps lead to a stair door.]

SHERIFF. I suppose anything Mrs. Peters does'll be all right. She was to take in some clothes for her, you know, and a few little things. We left in such a hurry yesterday.

COUNTY ATTORNEY. Yes, but I would like to see what you take, Mrs. Peters, and keep an eye out for anything that might be of use to us.

MRS. PETERS. Yes, Mr. Henderson.

[The women listen to the men's steps on the stairs, then look about the kitchen.]

MRS. HALE. I'd hate to have men coming into my kitchen, snooping around and criticizing. [She arranges the pans under the sink which the LAWYER had shoved out of place.]

MRS. PETERS. Of course it's no more than their duty.

MRS. HALE. Duty's all right, but I guess that deputy sheriff that came out to make the fire might have got a little of this on. [Gives the roller towel a pull.] Wish I'd thought of that sooner. Seems mean to talk about her for not having things slicked up when she had to come away in such a hurry.

MRS. PETERS [Who has gone to a small table in the left rear corner of the room, and lifted one end of a towel that covers a pan]. She had bread set. [Stands still.]

MRS. HALE. [eyes fixed on a loaf of bread beside the breadbox, which is on a low shelf at the other side of the room. Moves slowly toward it.] She was going to put this in there. [Picks up loaf, then abruptly drops it. In a manner of returning to familiar things.] It's a shame about her fruit. I wonder if it's all gone. [Gets up on the chair and looks.] I think there's some here that's all right, Mrs. Peters. Yes—here; [Holding it toward the window.] this is cherries, too. [Looking again.] I declare I believe that's the only one. [Gets down, bottle in her hand. Goes to the sink and wipes it off on the outside.] She'll feel awful bad after all her hard work in the hot weather. I remember the afternoon I put up my cherries last summer. [She puts the bottle on the big kitchen table, center of the room, front table. With a sigh, is about to sit down in the rocking chair. Before she is seated realizes what chair it is;

with a slow look at it, steps back. The chair, which she has touched, rocks back and forth.]

MRS. PETERS. Well, I must get those things from the front-room closet. [*She goes to the door at the right, but after looking into the other room steps back.*] You coming with me, Mrs. Hale? You could help me carry them.

[*They go into the other room; reappear,* MRS. PETERS *carrying a dress and skirt,* MRS. HALE *following with a pair of shoes.*]

MRS. PETERS. My, it's cold in there. [*She puts the cloth on the big table, and hurries to the stove.*]

MRS. HALE [*examining the skirt*]. Wright was close. I think maybe that's why she kept so much to herself. She didn't even belong to the Ladies' Aid. I suppose she felt she couldn't do her part, and then you don't enjoy things when you feel shabby. She used to wear pretty clothes and be lively, when she was Minnie Foster, one of the town girls singing in the choir. But that—oh, that was thirty years ago. This all you was to take in?

MRS. PETERS. She said she wanted an apron. Funny thing to want, for there isn't much to get you dirty in jail, goodness knows. But I suppose just to make her feel more natural. She said they was in the top drawer in this cupboard. Yes, here. And then her little shawl that always hung behind the door. [*Opens stair door and looks.*] Yes, here it is. [*Quickly shuts door leading upstairs.*]

MRS. HALE [*abruptly moving toward her*]. Mrs. Peters?

MRS. PETERS. Yes, Mrs. Hale?

MRS. HALE. Do you think she did it?

MRS. PETERS [*in a frightened voice*]. Oh, I don't know.

MRS. HALE. Well, I don't think she did. Asking for an apron and her little shawl. Worrying about her fruit.

MRS. PETERS [*starts to speak, glances up, where footsteps are heard in the room above. In a low voice*]. Mr. Peters says it looks bad for her. Mr. Henderson is awful sarcastic in a speech, and he'll make fun of her sayin' she didn't wake up.

MRS. HALE. Well, I guess John Wright didn't wake up when they was slipping that rope under his neck.

MRS. PETERS. No, it's strange. It must have been done awful crafty and still. They say it was such a—funny way to kill a man, rigging it all up like that.

MRS. HALE. That's just what Mr. Hale said. There was a gun in the house. He says that's what he can't understand.

MRS. PETERS. Mr. Henderson said coming out that what was needed for the case was a motive, something to show anger, or—sudden feeling.

MRS. HALE [*who is standing by the table*]. Well, I don't see any signs of anger around here. [*She puts her hand on the dish towel which lies on the table, stands looking down at the table, one half of which is clean, the other half messy.*] It's wiped here. [*Makes a move as if to finish work, then turns and looks at loaf of bread outside the breadbox. Drops towel. In that voice of coming back to familiar things.*] Wonder how they are finding things upstairs? I hope she had it a little more red-up there. You know, it seems kind of *sneaking.* Locking her up in town and then coming out here and trying to get her own house to turn against her!

MRS. PETERS. But, Mrs. Hale, the law is the law.

MRS. HALE. I s'pose 'tis. [*Unbuttoning her coat.*] Better loosen up your things, Mrs. Peters. You won't feel them when you go out.

[MRS. PETERS *takes off her fur tippet, goes to hang it on hook at back of room, stands looking at the under part of the small corner table.*]

MRS. PETERS. She was piecing a quilt. [*She brings the large sewing basket, and they look at the bright pieces.*]

MRS. HALE. It's log cabin pattern. Pretty, isn't it? I wonder if she was goin' to quilt or just knot it?

[*Footsteps have been heard coming down the stairs. The* SHERIFF *enters, followed by* HALE *and the* COUNTY ATTORNEY.]

SHERIFF. They wonder if she was going to quilt it or just knot it. [*The men laugh, the women look abashed.*]

COUNTY ATTORNEY [*rubbing his hands over the stove*]. Frank's fire didn't do much up there, did it? Well, let's go out to the barn and get that cleared up.

[*The men go outside.*]

MRS. HALE [*resentfully*]. I don't know as there's anything so strange, our takin' up our time with little things while we're waiting for them to get the evidence. [*She sits down at the big table, smoothing out a block with decision.*] I don't see as it's anything to laugh about.

MRS. PETERS. [*apologetically*]. Of course they've got awful important things on their minds. [*Pulls up a chair and joins* MRS. HALE *at the table.*]

MRS. HALE [*examining another block*]. Mrs. Peters, look at this one. Here, this is the one she was working on, and look at the sewing! All the rest of it has been so nice and even. And look at this! It's all over the place! Why, it looks as if she didn't know what she was about! [*After she has said this, they look at each other, then start to glance back at the door. After an instant* MRS. HALE *has pulled at a knot and ripped the sewing.*]

MRS. PETERS. Oh, what are you doing, Mrs. Hale?

MRS. HALE [*mildly*]. Just pulling out a stitch or two that's not sewed very good. [*Threading a needle.*] Bad sewing always made me fidgety.

MRS. PETERS [*nervously*]. I don't think we ought to touch things.

MRS. HALE. I'll just finish up this end. [*Suddenly stopping and leaning forward.*] Mrs. Peters?

MRS. PETERS. Yes, Mrs. Hale?

MRS. HALE. What do you suppose she was so nervous about?

MRS. PETERS. Oh—I don't know. I don't know as she was nervous. I sometimes sew awful queer when I'm just tired. [MRS. HALE *starts to say something, looks at* MRS. PETERS, *then goes on sewing.*] Well, I must get these things wrapped up. They may be through sooner than we think. [*Putting apron and other things together.*] I wonder where I can find a piece of paper, and string.

MRS. HALE. In that cupboard, maybe.

MRS. PETERS. [*looking in cupboard*]. Why, here's a birdcage. [*Holds it up.*] Did she have a bird, Mrs. Hale?

MRS. HALE. Why, I don't know whether she did or not—I've not been here for so long. There was a man around last year selling canaries cheap, but I don't know as she took one; maybe she did. She used to sing real pretty herself.

MRS. PETERS [glancing around]. Seems funny to think of a bird here. But she must have had one or why should she have a cage? I wonder what happened to it?

MRS. HALE. I s'pose maybe the cat got it.

MRS. PETERS. No, she didn't have a cat. She's got that feeling some people have about cats—being afraid of them. My cat got in her room, and she was real upset and asked me to take it out.

MRS. HALE. My sister Bessie was like that. Queer, ain't it?

MRS. PETERS [examining the cage]. Why, look at this door. It's broke. One hinge is pulled apart.

MRS. HALE [looking, too]. Looks as if someone must have been rough with it.

MRS. PETERS. Why, yes. [She brings the cage forward and puts it on the table.]

MRS. HALE. I wish if they're going to find any evidence they'd be about it. I don't like this place.

MRS. PETERS. But I'm glad you came with me, Mrs. Hale. It would be lonesome for me sitting here alone.

MRS. HALE. It would, wouldn't it? [Dropping her sewing.] But I tell you what I do wish, Mrs. Peters. I wish I had come over sometimes when she was here. I— [Looking around the room.] —wish I had.

MRS. PETERS. But of course you were awful busy, Mrs. Hale—your house and children.

MRS. HALE. I could've come. I stayed away because it weren't cheerful—and that's why I ought to have come. I—I've never liked this place. Maybe because it's down in a hollow, and you don't see the road. I dunno what it is, but it's a lonesome place and always was. I wish I had come over to see Minnie Foster sometimes. I can see now—[Shakes her head.]

MRS. PETERS. Well, you mustn't reproach yourself, Mrs. Hale. Somehow we just don't see how it is with other folks until—something comes up.

MRS. HALE. Not having children makes less work—but it makes a quiet house, and Wright out to work all day, and no company when he did come in. Did you know John Wright, Mrs. Peters?

MRS. PETERS. Not to know him; I've seen him in town. They say he was a good man.

MRS. HALE. Yes—good; he didn't drink, and kept his word as well as most, I guess, and paid his debts. But he was a hard man, Mrs. Peters. Just to pass the time of day with him. [Shivers.] Like a raw wind that gets to the bone. [Pauses, her eye falling on the cage.] I should think she would 'a wanted a bird. But what do you suppose went with it?

MRS. PETERS. I don't know, unless it got sick and died. [She reaches over and swings the broken door, swings it again; both women watch it.]

MRS. HALE. You weren't raised round here, were you? [MRS. PETERS shakes her head.] You didn't know—her?

MRS. PETERS. Not till they brought her yesterday.

MRS. HALE. She—come to think of it, she was kind of like a bird herself—real sweet and pretty, but kind of timid and—fluttery. How—she—did—change. [*Silence; then as if struck by a happy thought and relieved to get back to everyday things.*] Tell you what, Mrs. Peters, why don't you take the quilt in with you? It might take up her mind.

MRS. PETERS. Why, I think that's a real nice idea, Mrs. Hale. There couldn't possibly be any objection to it, could there? Now, just what would I take? I wonder if her patches are in here—and her things. [*They look in the sewing basket.*]

MRS. HALE. Here's some red. I expect this has got sewing things in it. [*Brings out a fancy box.*] What a pretty box. Looks like something somebody would give you. Maybe her scissors are in here. [*Opens box. Suddenly puts her hand to her nose.*] Why— [MRS. PETERS *bends nearer, then turns her face away.*] There's something wrapped up in this piece of silk.

MRS. PETERS. Why, this isn't her scissors.

MRS. HALE [*lifting the silk*]. Oh, Mrs. Peters—it's— [MRS. PETERS *bends closer.*]

MRS. PETERS. It's the bird.

MRS. HALE [*jumping up*]. But Mrs. Peters—look at it. Its neck! Look at its neck! It's all—other side *too*.

MRS. PETERS. Somebody—wrung—its neck.

[*Their eyes meet. A look of growing comprehension of horror. Steps are heard outside.* MRS. HALE *slips box under quilt pieces, and sinks into her chair. Enter* SHERIFF *and* COUNTY ATTORNEY. MRS. PETERS *rises.*]

COUNTY ATTORNEY [*as one turning from serious things to little pleasantries*]. Well ladies, have you decided whether she was going to quilt it or knot it?

MRS. PETERS. We think she was going to—knot it.

COUNTY ATTORNEY. Well, that's interesting, I'm sure. [*Seeing the birdcage.*] Has the bird flown?

MRS. HALE [*putting more quilt pieces over the box*]. We think the—cat got it.

COUNTY ATTORNEY [*preoccupied*]. Is there a cat?

[MRS. HALE *glances in a quick covert way at* MRS. PETERS.]

MRS. PETERS. Well, not now. They're superstitious, you know. They leave.

COUNTY ATTORNEY [*to* SHERIFF PETERS, *continuing an interrupted conversation*]. No sign at all of anyone having come from the outside. Their own rope. Now let's go up again and go over it piece by piece. [*They start upstairs.*] It would have to have been someone who knew just the—

[MRS. PETERS *sits down. The two women sit there not looking at one another, but as if peering into something and at the same time holding back. When they talk now, it is in the manner of feeling their way over strange ground, as if afraid of what they are saying, but as if they cannot help saying it.*]

MRS. HALE. She liked the bird. She was going to bury it in that pretty box.

MRS. PETERS [*in a whisper*]. When I was a girl—my kitten—there was a boy took a hatchet, and before my eyes—and before I could get there— [*Covers her face an instant.*] If they hadn't held me back, I would have— [*Catches herself, looks upstairs where steps are heard, falters weakly.*] —hurt him.

MRS. HALE [*with a slow look around her*]. I wonder how it would seem never to have had any children around. [*Pause.*] No, Wright wouldn't like the bird—a thing that sang. She used to sing. He killed that, too.

MRS. PETERS [*moving uneasily*]. We don't know who killed the bird.

MRS. HALE. I knew John Wright.

MRS. PETERS. It was an awful thing was done in this house that night, Mrs. Hale. Killing a man while he slept, slipping a rope around his neck that choked the life out of him.

MRS. HALE. His neck. Choked the life out of him.

MRS. PETERS [*with rising voice*]. We don't know who killed him. We don't *know.*

MRS. HALE [*her own feeling not interrupted*]. If there'd been years and years of nothing, then a bird to sing to you, it would be awful—still, after the bird was still.

MRS. PETERS [*something within her speaking*]. I know what stillness is. When we homesteaded in Dakota, and my first baby died—after he was two years old, and me with no other then—

MRS. HALE [*moving*]. How soon do you suppose they'll be through, looking for evidence?

MRS. PETERS. I know what stillness is. [*Pulling herself back.*] The law has got to punish crime, Mrs. Hale.

MRS. HALE [*not as if answering that*]. I wish you'd seen Minnie Foster when she wore a white dress with blue ribbons and stood up there in the choir and sang. [*a look around the room.*] Oh, I *wish* I'd come over here once in a while! That was a crime! That was a crime! Who's going to punish that?

MRS. PETERS [*looking upstairs*]. We mustn't—take on.

MRS. HALE. I might have known she needed help! I know how things can be—for women. I tell you, it's queer, Mrs. Peters. We live close together, and we live far apart. We all go through the same things—it's all just a different kind of the same thing. [*Brushes her eyes, noticing the bottle of fruit, reaches out for it.*] If I was you, I wouldn't tell her her fruit was gone. Tell her it *ain't.* Tell her it's all right. Take this in to prove it to her. She—she may never know whether it was broke or not.

MRS. PETERS [*takes the bottle, looks about for something to wrap it in; takes petticoat from the clothes brought from the other room, very nervously begins winding this around the bottle. In a false voice.*] My, it's a good thing the men couldn't hear us. Wouldn't they just laugh! Getting all stirred up over a little thing like a—dead canary. As if that could have anything to do with—with—wouldn't they *laugh!*

[*The men are heard coming downstairs.*]

MRS. HALE [*under her breath*]. Maybe they would—maybe they wouldn't.

COUNTY ATTORNEY. No, Peters, it's all perfectly clear except a reason for doing it. But you know juries when it comes to women. If there was some definite thing. Something to show—something to make a story about—a thing that would connect up with this strange way of doing it.

[*The women's eyes meet for an instant. Enter* HALE *from outer door.*]

HALE. Well, I've got the team around. Pretty cold out there.

COUNTY ATTORNEY. I'm going to stay here awhile by myself. [*To the* SHERIFF.] You can send Frank out for me, can't you? I want to go over everything. I'm not satisfied that we can't do better.

SHERIFF. Do you want to see what Mrs. Peters is going to take in?

[*The* LAWYER *goes to the table, picks up the apron, laughs.*]

COUNTY ATTORNEY. Oh, I guess they're not very dangerous things the ladies have picked up. [*Moves a few things about, disturbing the quilt pieces which cover the box. Steps back.*] No, Mrs. Peters doesn't need supervising. For that matter, a sheriff's wife is married to the law. Ever think of it that way, Mrs. Peters?

MRS. PETERS. Not—just that way.

SHERIFF [*chuckling*]. Married to the law. [*Moves toward the other room.*] I just want you to come in here a minute, George. We ought to take a look at these windows.

COUNTY ATTORNEY [*scoffingly*]. Oh, windows!

SHERIFF. We'll be right out, Mr. Hale.

[HALE *goes outside. The* SHERIFF *follows the* COUNTY ATTORNEY *into the other room. Then* MRS. HALE *rises, hands tight together, looking intensely at* MRS. PETERS, *whose eyes take a slow turn, finally meeting* MRS. HALE's. *A moment* MRS. HALE *holds her, then her own eyes point the way to where the box is concealed. Suddenly* MRS. PETERS *throws back quilt pieces and tries to put the box in the bag she is wearing. It is too big. She opens box, starts to take bird out, cannot touch it, goes to pieces, stands there helpless. Sound of a knob turning in the other room.* MRS. HALE *snatches the box and puts it in the pocket of her big coat. Enter* COUNTY ATTORNEY *and* SHERIFF.]

COUNTY ATTORNEY [*facetiously*]. Well, Henry, at least we found out that she was not going to quilt it. She was going to—what is it you call it, ladies?

MRS. HALE [*her hand against her pocket*]. We call it—knot it, Mr. Henderson.

CURTAIN

Cinde Veinot (Annotations)

COUNTY ATTORNEY [*as one turning from serious things to <u>little pleasantries</u>*]. Well, ladies, have you decided whether she was going to quilt or <u>knot it</u>?	"trifles" "knot"—a noose
MRS. PETERS. We think she was going to—<u>knot it.</u>	
COUNTY ATTORNEY. Well, that's interesting, I'm sure. [*Seeing the birdcage.*] <u>Has the bird flown?</u>	bird: Mrs. W.
MRS. HALE [*putting more <u>quilt pieces</u> <u>over the box</u>*]. We think the—cat got it.	quilt = investigation?
COUNTY ATTORNEY [*preoccupied*]. <u>Is there a cat?</u>	
[MRS. HALE *glances in a quick covert way at* MRS. PETERS.]	cat: Mr. W.

MRS. PETERS. Well, <u>not now.</u> They're superstitious, you know. They leave.

COUNTY ATTORNEY [*to* SHERIFF PETERS, *continuing an interrupted conversation*]. No sign at all of anyone having come from the outside. Their own rope. Now let's go up again and go over it <u>piece by piece.</u> [*They start upstairs.*] It would have to have been someone who knew just the—

quilt = investigation?

[MRS. PETERS *sits down. The two women sit there not looking at one another, but as if peering into something and at the same time holding back. When they talk now, it is in the manner of feeling their way over <u>strange ground,</u> as if afraid of what they are saying, but as if they cannot help saying it.*]

simile

Eric Labbe (Double-Entry Journal)

I think the most important theme here is of the way people's roles blind them to looking outside of the roles. The Attorney and the Sheriff feel that there could be nothing of importance in the kitchen, where "women are use to worryin' over trifles," so they look everywhere but the important places. What are they doing looking in the barn? Isn't that where a <u>man</u> would look for clues?

Good theme—result of tension and characterization

It's the women, with their careful attention to trifles, and their knowledge of a woman's psychology, who are able to figure things out: the queer stitching, the separation, no kids, frigid husband, killed canary. They are able to put all these ideas together while the men are looking in the barn. You can also see this because the women were concerned about Mrs. Wright as a person. They are able to discover things about her: by trying to bring her the quilt, they discover the bird. It's these "trifles" that help solve the murder.

"Women are used to worryin' over trifles" some thing going on about women's and men's roles.

Bird cage? Dead bird = husband

But they don't give her away! In some sense, they feel that what happened was just. Even Mrs. Peters— "Who's married to the law?"—tries to cover up the evidence. But she's not married to the law—"Just that way." Mrs. Hale is the real representative here for women's rights: "We live close together, and we live far apart." She knows that the years of loneliness did Mr. Wright in.

Eventually, women think she did it.

Debbie Carlisle (Double-Entry Journal)

I loved this play. It's wonderful—especially the women being upset by the men criticizing the housekeeping.

I was especially interested in the contrast of gender specific views.

The women see clearly what has gone on. They remember the young, cheerful woman who sang vs. the married woman who didn't.

What strikes the women as human strikes the men as criminal. Different values, different empathies.

The bird was Mrs. Wright's child substitute. To the women it seems like justifiable homicide, not murder. Women protect their friend from male justice.

Tragic situation. Murder over what some see as trifles!

"Women are used to worryin' over trifles." Are feelings trifles? Is women's work trifling to men? Yes. A person can be pushed too far—at least Mrs. Peters thinks so. She's not only <u>not</u> married to the law; she helps hide the evidence to protect Mrs. Wright.

Are feelings ever trifles? Whose feelings count? Can a person be pushed too far?

Group Discussion

Kelly: I think the most important theme here is the way people's roles, not dinner rolls—regular roles, blind them to looking outside of those roles. They are kind of set in their ways. The attorney and the sheriff feel there could be nothing of importance in the kitchen where women are used to worrying over trifles but they look everywhere but the important places to solve this case. What are they doing looking in the barn? It's kind of stupid looking in the barn but isn't that where a man would look for clues? The women with their careful attention to trifles and their knowledge of a woman's psychology were able to figure things out—the queer stitching, the separation, no kids, the frigid husband and the dead canary. They can put all these little tiny things together while the men are out looking in the barn. You can also see that because the women were concerned about Mrs. Wright as a person, they were able to discover things about her. By trying to bring her the quilt, they discover the bird. It's those trifles that solve the murder. But they don't give her away. They don't turn her in. In some way they feel that what happened was just. Even Mrs. Peters, who's married to the law, tries to cover up the evidence. But she's not married to the law in just that way. Mrs. Hale is the real representative here for women's rights. She says, "We live close together and we live far apart." She knows that it's the years of loneliness that did Mr. Wright in, that Mrs. Wright couldn't handle it any more. The men here are stereotypical men though. Any self-respecting detective who suspected the wife for murder and knew she was found sitting in the kitchen would search the kitchen. It just stands to reason. He still might not put two and two together because he would never catch the stitching which was an important clue for the women, but any detective who's trained would look in the kitchen. It just makes sense.

Cinde: Maybe I read this quickly or something but is everybody sure that she did it?

Kelly: The women are.

Cinde: I mean you guys.

Debbie: Oh yes. Definitely she did it.

Eric: Well there were descriptions where they said she was very frail and thin.

Cinde: I thought it was really strange and I felt it was a little rough on the men. It really set her up as being stupid and mean. I understand that he broke the canary's neck but is that reason to choke somebody? I understood that maybe she was . . . oh, I don't know.

Kelly: I don't know what you mean.

Eric: Well wasn't that supposedly the reason she killed him?

Debbie: That was the straw that broke the camel's back.

Kelly: That was the breaking point. He broke the canary's neck and she killed him—and then really covered it up. He couldn't find a motive so obviously she would probably get off. First of all could she kill her husband and second of all could these women approve of it and sort of cover it up?

Cinde: I just thought it was really hard on men.

Eric: Actually I thought it was hard on the men but I went along with the women. It seemed like this woman had gone through an awful lot. Thirty some odd years or however many years of sitting around all by herself.

Cinde: I understand that but, then again, did anyone really comprehend that?

Kelly: The women do.

Eric: The women know.

Cinde: It seems they're sympathizing with her because she's a woman. It's sort of like a sisterhood and that's enough reason to cover up for her. She did kill him. She murdered him.

Kelly: I really like this. I especially like the part where the women talk about what they saw going on and remembered her as a young cheerful girl who sang and thought of the bird as her child because she didn't have children. She loved the bird. It was all the joy she had and he killed it.

Debbie: She just sort of lost it after years and years and years of trying to maintain it.

Cinde: I think the author is trying to get us to agree with the two women that it was just the men's fault; she makes them out to be so bad and so stupid. They wouldn't be that stupid.

Eric: This is not high quality drama.

Kelly: Well I think this also is a political statement of the time it is written—the late 1800's.

Cinde: I don't think there was enough of a reason to kill.

Debbie: There wasn't enough of a motive?

Cinde: The covering up I didn't agree with. Maybe the motive is there but I didn't buy it. I didn't go along with the author. I wasn't taken in.

Debbie: But as far as what's going on in this play, we all agree with what's going on.

Kelly: Well, um. . . .

Eric: Yeah.

Eric Labbe (Comments on Informal Research)

I was curious about how Glaspell is viewed in terms of other playwrights. One critic considers her the only other member of the Provincetown Players, aside from Eugene O'Neill, who can be considered a major talent. This guy even says Glaspell is better than O'Neill in some ways—she's more controlled, and she doesn't go on and on like he does. The only O'Neill play I've ever read is *A Long Day's Journey Into Night,* and at least with that play, I can see what he [the critic Bigsby] means. O'Neill has these long speeches, and seems to want to spell everything out, while Glaspell only gives you little snippets of conversation. He also made me notice something I hadn't paid attention to before—just like the women figure everything out by looking at trifles, Glaspell makes up the whole play out of trifles, little gestures or images. He talks about how the broken hinge on the cage makes us think about the broken necks of the bird and Mr. Wright, and the broken spirit of Mrs. Wright. I really saw the play differently after I read this guy.

THE STORY OF AN HOUR

Kate Chopin

Knowing that Mrs. Mallard was afflicted with a heart trouble, great care was taken to break to her as gently as possible the news of her husband's death.

It was her sister Josephine who told her, in broken sentences; veiled hints that revealed in half concealing. Her husband's friend Richards was there, too, near her. It was he who had been in the newspaper office when intelligence of the railroad disaster was received, with Brently Mallard's name leading the list of "killed." He had only taken the time to assure himself of its truth by a second telegram, and had hastened to forestall any less careful, less tender friend in bearing the sad message.

She did not hear the story as many women have heard the same, with a paralyzed inability to accept its significance. She wept at once, with sudden, wild abandonment, in her sister's arms. When the storm of grief had spent itself she went away to her room alone. She would have no one follow her.

There stood, facing the open window, a comfortable, roomy armchair. Into this she sank, pressed down by a physical exhaustion that haunted her body and seemed to reach into her soul.

She could see in the open square before her house the tops of trees that were   5 all aquiver with the new spring of life. The delicious breath of rain was in the air. In the street below a peddler was crying his wares. The notes of a distant song which some one was singing reached her faintly, and countless sparrows were twittering in the eaves.

There were patches of blue sky showing here and there through the clouds that had met and piled one above the other in the west facing her window.

She sat with her head thrown back upon the cushion of the chair, quite motionless, except when a sob came up into her throat and shook her, as a child who has cried itself to sleep continues to sob in its dreams.

She was young, with a fair, calm face, whose lines bespoke repression and even a certain strength. But now there was a dull stare in her eyes, whose gaze was fixed away off yonder on one of those patches of blue sky. It was not a glance of reflection, but rather indicated a suspension of intelligent thought.

There was something coming to her and she was waiting for it, fearfully. What was it? She did not know; it was too subtle and elusive to name. But she felt it, creeping out of the sky, reaching toward her through the sounds, the scents, the color that filled the air.

Now her bosom rose and fell tumultuously. She was beginning to recognize this   10 thing that was approaching to possess her, and she was striving to beat it back with her will—as powerless as her two white slender hands would have been.

When she abandoned herself a little whispered word escaped her slightly parted lips. She said it over and over under her breath: "free, free, free!" The vacant stare and the look of terror that had followed it went from her eyes. They stayed keen and bright. Her pulses beat fast, and the coursing blood warmed and relaxed every inch of her body.

She did not stop to ask if it were or were not a monstrous joy that held her. A clear and exalted perception enabled her to dismiss the suggestion as trivial.

She knew that she would weep again when she saw the kind, tender hands folded in death; the face that had never looked save with love upon her, fixed and gray and dead. But she saw beyond that bitter moment a long procession of years to come that would belong to her absolutely. And she opened and spread her arms out to them in welcome.

There would be no one to live for her during those coming years; she would live for herself. There would be no powerful will bending hers in that blind persistence with which men and women believe they have a right to impose a private will upon a fellow-creature. A kind intention or a cruel intention made the act seem no less a crime as she looked upon it in that brief moment of illumination.

And yet she had loved him—sometimes. Often she had not. What did it matter! 15 What could love, the unsolved mystery, count for in face of this possession of self-assertion which she suddenly recognized as the strongest impulse of her being!

"Free! Body and soul free!" she kept whispering.

Josephine was kneeling before the closed door with her lips to the keyhole, imploring for admission. "Louise, open the door! I beg; open the door—you will make yourself ill. What are you doing, Louise? For heaven's sake open the door."

"Go away. I am not making myself ill." No; she was drinking in a very elixir of life through that open window.

Her fancy was running riot along those days ahead of her. Spring days, and summer days, and all sorts of days that would be her own. She breathed a quick prayer that life might be long. It was only yesterday she had thought with a shudder that life might be long.

She arose at length and opened the door to her sister's importunities. There 20 was a feverish triumph in her eyes, and she carried herself unwittingly like a goddess of Victory. She clasped her sister's waist, and together they descended the stairs. Richards stood waiting for them at the bottom.

Some one was opening the front door with a latchkey. It was Brently Mallard who entered, a little travel-stained, composedly carrying his gripsack and umbrella. He had been far from the scene of accident, and did not even know there had been one. He stood amazed at Josephine's piercing cry; at Richard's quick motion to screen him from the view of his wife.

But Richards was too late.

When the doctors came they said she had died of heart disease—of joy that kills.

Eric Labbe (Annotations)

Knowing that Mrs. Mallard was afflicted with a heart trouble, great care was taken to break to her as gently as possible the news of her husband's death. . . .

> heart—literal or metaphorical?

She could see in the open square before her house the tops of trees that were all aquiver with the new spring life. The delicious breath of rain was in the air. In the street below a peddler was crying his wares. The notes of a distant song which some one was singing reached her faintly, and countless sparrows were twittering in the eaves.

> description— life

She did not stop to ask if it were or were not a monstrous joy that held her. A clear and exalted perception enabled her to dismiss the suggestion as trivial. . . .

> metaphor?

Josephine was kneeling before the closed door with her lips to the keyhole, imploring for admission. "Louise, open the door! I beg; open the door—you will make yourself ill.

What are you doing, Louise? For heaven's sake open the door."

"Go away. I am not making myself ill." No; she was drinking in a very elixir of life through that open window.

irony

Her fancy was running riot along those days ahead of her. Spring days, and summer days, and all sorts of days that would be her own. She breathed a quick prayer that life might be long. It was only yesterday she had thought with a shudder that life might be long.

irony

Some one was opening the front door with a latchkey. It was Brently Mallard who entered, a little travel-stained, composedly carrying his gripsack and umbrella. He had been far from the scene of accident, and did not even know there had been one. He stood amazed at Josephine's piercing cry; at Richards' quick motion to screen him from the view of his wife. But Richards was too late.

Kelly Leighton (Double-Entry Journal)

I was totally taken in, at the beginning, with Mrs. Mallard's grief. I expected the story to be one of loneliness and grief.

When her attitude changed—when she realized and savored her freedom—I was surprised, but pleased. My emotions turned with hers. I felt her freedom. When her husband shows up at the end, the story is written in such a way that the reader also feels her shock and disappointment.

She's more consumed with freedom than grief—great!

Chopin manipulates the reader in the most positive sense of the word. She plays upon the reader's expectations, and succeeds. The story has a teasing quality—and shock value.

Oh no—he's alive. I'd keel over!

Chopin's making a terrific statement about the difference between a woman's perception and how society perceives her. This ending plays on the notion; it's so sarcastically ironic. (Her joy was her freedom, not the resurrection of her husband.)

". . . of joy that kills." Irony is great!

Group Discussion

Eric: This story is a classic red herring but at the same time it works. How? We see Louise dealing with her husband's death and learning to actually like it and its ultimate freedom. She goes through a number of stages. She goes through stages from instant pain and grief to recognizing that there is something coming. She sees something on the horizon coming and then she tries to beat it back and tries to reject it, then she recognizes it as an approaching freedom and in the last stages she sort of embraces it and is really happy about it. Of course then in the end it's all turned around and it kills her. At the end I was taken by surprise by that whole ending.

Cinde: I was too.

Eric: Chopin sets us up by telling us Louise has a heart condition. This is how she sets it up so it's not completely out of the blue. Also I think the descriptions of nature are strange. They do a couple things. They're either indicating that despite the death of Brently life goes on, that may be one of the interpretations, or because of his death everything is now happy and free, or even though she thinks he's dead he really isn't. So she thinks he's dead but nature is telling us something else. There's a whole bunch of different interpretations, I think, about nature in that whole nature paragraph. I think the real one is that because he's dead she's now free and everything is pretty happy. I think that's what Chopin is trying to tell us. This could be a story not of death and dealing with death but of a woman's attempt to get out from under the domination of man only to be returned to it. Kind of a cyclical thing. It only takes her an hour to truly get over his death. She seems like she had been thinking about it for quite a while, getting rid of him, and his death gave her a chance to realize it. I think we have to read this story as a metaphor or allegory of a kind or the ending just doesn't work. It's kind of silly, kind of a dumb story if you don't read it as some sort of an allegory. If you read it as symbolic, certain things work I think.

Kelly: I liked her technique in writing the story and how she gets an emotion from the reader. What I was struck with most is how blind I was to the whole thing. I felt free and I felt good for her and then later when her husband shows up you feel shock and dismay at the character which I thought was kind of odd. I like the last line a lot: "She died of heart disease—of joy that kills." I think the whole statement is about the difference between the wife's perception of the position and how society perceives her. There is such a difference there that I think that it's a little conservative too.

Cinde: I wrote down something about the sister: Why does the sister think she's making herself sick? I think her sister's perception of how she was going to react to Brently's death was interesting. The title obviously is for our own interpretation. The line "the distant song" obviously is a reference to her newly found freedom. She heard the distant song. I liked that part when I read it. We talk about the style. Obviously it's very short. It's so short because that's what her freedom was. It was that short and that killed her.

Debbie: I was totally shocked when I read it. I thought it was powerful and I can't think of a happy marriage. I can imagine it better than I would when I was young, but it was still a shock to me. I think I might have been able to imagine it differently had I not gone through the same kind of situation.

Eric: So what are we going to do with that last sentence? What does it mean?

Kelly: You mean "of joy that kills?"

Eric: Yeah, what does it mean?

Kelly: They probably thought she's so overjoyed that her husband is alive that she has a heart attack. With the joy of her freedom being taken away, that's what killed her.

Cinde: I think it's a nice story. A really nice story up until the ending which is kind of a strange ending. Kind of a twilight zone type of ending.

Debbie: Would the message be as strong if the ending wasn't like that?

Cinde: It's a strange situation. But she had to do that.

Eric: What I'm saying is that if you don't read something into the story, there isn't anything here.

Debbie: Sure there is. Of course there is. She died over it, her disappointment. She feels free. She goes to the window, she's grieving.

Eric: Exactly, but that's not . . . well, I agree!

Kelly: No, you don't. You're outnumbered. We're not saying you're wrong. Tell us why. You mentioned a red herring. What does that mean?

Eric: I learned that last semester in Creative Writing class where the writer pulls this strange ending on you in that last minute which is completely unexpected.

Cinde: I think they want to add shock value to it.

Eric: Yeah, well that's a red herring.

Kelly: But isn't she shocked too?

Eric: I'm not sure what I was saying when I wrote this. Oh, this is what I meant. I think if you don't read this story metaphorically, the ending just doesn't work. The ending is kind of silly where her husband comes homes and she dies.

Cinde: Well, if she did have heart problems such a shock could kill her.

Eric: Yeah, but it's kind of a hokey ending. What I'm saying is that the ending is very powerful because it's set up in a metaphorical way by all of this dramatic stuff of her problem with her relationship with Brently.

Cinde: How else could you end it? You're set up from the beginning to know.

Eric: No, I'm not. All I'm saying is that it's a silly ending but it works. It works.

Kelly: I don't think it is. I think it's believable after you read this whole thing that she could have been so repressed the shock of seeing him again and knowing that she's going to have to go back to that kind of repression could have killed her.

Eric: Nah!

Debbie: Well maybe she'd rather die than go back to that anyway.

Cinde: But in the beginning they seem to make an awful big deal about her heart condition.

Kelly: Maybe she was a sick woman.

Cinde: Well she was sick because she was repressed. Also physically but more so because she was so emotionally repressed. That's the part I think that bothers me.

Eric: The only thing that I'm saying is that it's a strange ending, a difficult ending. It works, but it works only because of a certain dramatic shock that came before it.

Debbie: Well would you agree that her only way to absolute freedom was to die?

Eric: Maybe.

Kelly: Well, if we're done, I think this is my favorite of the group. I really liked it. I kind of liked the play, too. The ending is difficult but I think it works.

Cinde Veinot (Comments on Informal Research)

After I read this story, I came across a reference in another class to a scandal in the woman suffrage movement. It involved a supposed affair between Henry Ward Beecher and a married woman in his parish. But the big deal wasn't the affair so much as the fact that an activist named Victoria Woodhull published it in her paper [*Woodhull & Claflins Weekly*]. When I read about this woman, I started thinking of Mrs. Mallard—she reminded me of Mrs. Mallard a lot, because she said things like owning a person as a wife is just like owning them as a slave, and she said a lot about owning your own self. That seems to be what Mrs. Mallard is getting at—when she finds out she can't own herself, she dies. Woodhull wrote this stuff twenty years before Chopin wrote her story, so I wondered if maybe Chopin was influenced by that thinking. I felt it even more when I read *The Awakening*—the wife in that book isn't really like Mrs. Mallard, because Edna [in *The Awakening*] believes in free love and a single standard for men and women in sexual relationships, another thing Woodhull stood for, but Edna actually does kill herself when she realizes she can't be her own person. It seems like Chopin was saying the same thing in fiction that a lot of activists were saying in speeches and articles.

POLYGAMY

Ann Grace Mojtabai

Teheran, 1960. A warm evening. The courtyard in which we were sitting was not very beautiful. There was a narrow strip of ground that ran along the edge of the wall, spotted with shrubbery and some insignificant roses; the rest was flagstone surrounding the customary small pool of ablutions, set like a turquoise in the center.

I had come to Iran expecting nightingales and roses, but had not yet heard a nightingale above the sounds of street hawkers and traffic, and the famed rose gardens of Persia were nowhere in evidence; they remained out of sight, if they ever existed, sealed off by high proprietary walls.

But my interest of the moment was not in the garden; my eyes were fixed on my father-in-law. He was a large, imposing man in his mid-90's, with high color, still-black eyebrows and the scrub of a heavy beard. He might have passed for a much younger man and, in fact, claimed to be in his young, vigorous 70's.

"What do you think of this?" he asked, pointing to his wives, one large, one small, on either side of him. His wives smiled in my direction, then at each other. My father-in-law continued to stare at me and to wait; he really wanted to know what I thought.

For the few separate moments it took to translate his question and my reply 5 (with what distortion I shall never know), we gazed coolly at each other, each an anthropologist confronting opacity—the mind of a stranger. I thought I could hear him taking notes. I, for my part, was certainly jotting things down—but only impressions. I would see; I wasn't going to judge prematurely. My judgment, when it came, wouldn't be narrow, biased or culture-bound. "Customs differ," I said.

Long before meeting my father-in-law, I had been prepared for this—or, rather, I had been briefed, and imagined that I was prepared. It had been a briefing full of history (polygamy as a practical solution to the decimation of the male population in warfare and the resulting disproportionate preponderance of females over males); it had been a briefing on principle as well (the Koranic requirement that the husband distribute his affection equally among the co-wives).

But, of course, I was not ready to confront the live instance—three individuals who would bear an intimate family relation with me. Mother, father and what—aunt? mother-surrogate? I decided that the other party would simply be my Other

Mother-in-Law. At that moment, the language barrier turned out to be an opportune cover for, really, I did not know what I thought.

The happy threesome sat cross-legged on a takhte, a low wooden platform, covered with a rug. My particular mother-in-law, the tiny one, was the junior wife, chosen, I later learned, by the older woman as someone agreeable to herself, someone she thought the old man would like, too. The senior wife's passion was for talking, and her husband's silence had too long been wearing her down. She wanted someone in the house willing to hear her out and, she hoped, to respond from time to time.

I was left to imagine the precise formalities, but it seemed to me to be a marriage welcome to all the parties concerned. It was an arrangement not without its share of bickerings and quarrels, for however well-disposed the women were to each other, their respective children were rivals, and the wives were partisan for their children.

Still, as marriages go, theirs seemed to be a reasonably happy one.   10

When it grew chilly, we moved indoors. The sitting room was also my father-in-law's bedroom. He sat on a fine, ancient rug, with bolsters at his back, a bay of windows on his left and, in front of him, an array of small vials: vitamins, elixirs, purges. He didn't believe in modern medicine, but was taking no changes.

Stiff, wooden chairs of mismatching shapes were lined against the walls of the room. I eyed them, but, noticing that they were mantled in dust, furred with thin, unbroken velvet, decided they were not really for use, and sat on the floor instead. In fact, the chairs were chiefly ceremonial, a reluctant concession to the times, to the imposition of Westernization around the world. Not like the television set, which was an ecstatic testimony to the march of *universal* human progress, and which held, along with the samovar, pride of place among the old man's possessions.

The wives stepped out to bring refreshments. With a sinking sense, I noticed my husband getting up to speak to his mother in private. I was utterly adrift, alone with my father-in-law, a total stranger. The old man turned to me and said what I later learned was: "When hearts speak, no language is necessary." I recognized none of the words, but I guessed from his face and tone that whatever it was he had said was meant to be comforting and, trusting in a language of gesture and sign, I ventured a smile by way of reply.

Even today, I do not know what I think about polygamy. Or, perhaps, I know what I think—it's only that my feelings are mixed. Abstractly, I oppose the custom. These bonds ought to be reciprocal, one-to-one. Sexual favors *may* be distributed equally as required (a night with A, a night with B), but I doubt whether affection can be distributed so neatly. And, of course, the custom speaks of the poverty of opportunities for women.

On the other hand, the custom of mut'a, or temporary marriage, practiced by   15
Shiites, though not by Sunnites, seems to me to be possessed of some merits and, on the whole, somewhat more enlightened than prostitution, or the vaguely polygamous custom of balancing wife (with legal rights) with mistress (having no rights), which is so widely prevalent in the West.

In the mut'a marriage, a term is stipulated—a night, a year, a decade, an hour, whatever. A set term, a mehr—a wedding endowment for the woman—mutual consent and a contract specifying all this are required. The children of such unions are legitimate and entitled to share of the father's inheritance, although the sigheh, the temporary wife, has no claim to maintenance beyond the initial marriage endowment.

But polygamy is meant to be more than a mere alternative to such clearly deficient institutions as prostitution. And my feelings for polygamy as a true and viable form of marriage remain contrary, held in suspension. My opposition in theory is muffled by my observation of one palpable contrary fact. I saw a polygamous marriage work, and work well. That my mothers-in-law were deeply attached to each other, I have no doubt. I tend to question rather more their devotion to the husband who brought them together.

As for two mothers-in-law in one household, an old proverb would seem to apply: "Better two tigers in one cage than two mistresses in one household." But, in point of fact, the laws of addition don't always apply. After all, one shark and one codfish equal one shark; one raindrop and one raindrop equal one raindrop. The two women worked off their intensities on each other, with less energy left for me. So, actually, I had one mother-in-law, which, as all the proverbs of all nations attest, was quite sufficient.

Debbie Carlisle (Annotations)

... the rest was flagstone surrounding the customary small pool for ablutions, set like a turquoise in the center. ...

simile

He sat on a fine, ancient rug, with bolsters at his back, a bay of windows on his left and, in front of him, an array of small vials: vitamins, elixirs, purges. He didn't believe in modern medicine, but was taking no chances. ...

old vs. new

In fact, the chairs were chiefly ceremonial, a reluctant concession to the times, to the imposition of Westernization around the world. Not like the television set, which was an ecstatic testimony to the march of universal human progress, and which held, along with the samovars, pride of place among the old man's possessions. ...

personification

old vs. new

I was utterly adrift. ...

metaphor

Even today, I do not know what I think about polygamy. ...And, of course, the custom speaks of the poverty of opportunities for women.

old—metaphor—new

Kelly Leighton (Double-Entry Journal)

I think Mojtabai's voice is great. Maybe it's because her reactions and opinions are similar to my own. Maybe you could call it a "reader friendly" style of writing. Her talent is in gaining the reader's identification. She's easy to relate to, however foreign her sub-

The author's tone makes me feel badly for the wives and the daughter-in-law. It's surprising, no disgusting

ject may be. Now, I don't mean to be judgmental, but the whole idea of polygamy turns me off. The father-in-law was a creep to put her on the spot at the beginning. He must have known the situation would be uncomfortable for her. She handled it well. He seems arrogant.

that the senior wife chose the junior one.

I think it's interesting that this man was selective about the customs he chose to protect. Polygamy is one (perhaps due to the pleasure of having two women) sitting on the floor is another (perhaps out of stubbornness). However, television—the one object that poses the largest threat to preserving his culture—is embraced and worshiped. I don't get it!

Television should be smashed, not exalted, especially if they're trying to preserve their culture.

The concept of temporary marriage is interesting. Kind of like Western divorce without the pain. Perhaps this is something we should look into.

Temporary marriage sounds interesting.

Cinde Veinot (Double-Entry Journal)

Well, nightingales are free birds, singing. Romeo & Juliet. . . .

What significance do the nightingales hold?

This seems sort of unbelievable because they never really mention ages.

A 90-year-old man with several wives? Hmmm . . .

After reading the essay, I think she totally disappears—I don't buy the end!

By line 8, it seems as though she's already made a judgment about the situation.

She has definitely been Westernized. Perhaps that accounts for her bad attitudes towards polygamy.

Line 15 seems to be a jab at the West.

Group Discussion

Cinde: Do you believe this man of ninety claiming he was seventy? The poor daughter-in-law has no idea what she's getting herself into. What do you think? He puts her on the spot.

Kelly: I thought he was creepy. . . . I thought about the concept of temporary marriage. I said [in my journal] it was kind of a western version of divorce without the pain, and I said it was something we should look into.

Eric: For whom?

Kelly: What do you mean? For us, for everyone.

Eric: Do you really think Americans should consider temporary marriage?

Kelly: Well I mean if the partners both agree they want to be married for a year and that's it. Well it's just that the children you will have will be illegitimate children.

Cinde: I really didn't buy the essay at all. I bought the narrator. She was pretty believable. First a ninety-year-old guy who's still walking, talking and looking great and he had two wives and that he could be that clever. The funny thing about the narrator is that I thought she had already made a judgment by the first paragraph on the second page. It just seemed like her whole tone was completely negative. She just said, "Well I'm not really close to it but I don't know how I feel." I don't buy that. I really think that she had already made up her mind just by the way she said, "What do you think of this?" I think that maybe more than the TV the more threatening thing is her because you can tell by her reaction that she's very Westernized. It took a lot for him to say, "What do you think?"

Debbie: I thought it was interesting that he was selective about the customs he chose to protect or to keep. The thing about the chairs I thought was just stubborn. But the television. I think that would be the most threatening object or idea threatening to his culture.

Kelly: I find it sort of a joke.

Eric: I just read this recently . . . and it seems like a diary. It doesn't seem like she's making any kind of a decision either way. There's a decision right there. That's a decision in itself. She decided to be tolerant. I thought it was kind of interesting about the media culture and how that works and what the dynamic is there. It doesn't seem that the polygamy is all that bad for these people. It seems like culture. These two women are happy. They seem happy and there aren't a lot of cultural customs and overtones. If you're from Arabia and you're from a Nomadic culture that sort of thing is going to happen. You've got to have some sort of a legal attitude towards marriage; otherwise it just doesn't work. There have to be certain rules and laws to keep things together so I can see how we would complain in the West that this isn't a romantic, sharing, co-dependent relationship.

Debbie: Not only that, these women are subjected to this man.

Eric: But it doesn't bother them.

Debbie: It should.

Cinde: But that's us telling them what they should be bothered about.

Eric: What I mean by cross cultures is that you have this woman from the West with Western values going to an Eastern place and there's a clash there.

Debbie: So you think Eastern women don't value equality and respect as individuals.

Kelly: I'm sure they do.

Eric: No, they don't. I don't think they know about it.

Cinde: They may now.

Debbie: Don't you think there is something wrong with that?

Eric: To us but not to them because that's all they know.

Cinde: Were they aware that it was different anywhere else or aware of other options in life?

Kelly: But isn't there something wrong with that?

Eric: No. To you or to us but to a Buddhist? For us to say this is wrong and attempting to change that's forcing our cultural values on them. We don't agree with it. I don't happen to agree with the Australian Aborigines carving the cheeks of their young when they are going through the adolescent rites. We would call that scarification and that's bad, but it serves a purpose. Yes, we don't agree with polygamy.

Cinde: Do you think they should object more to it? Are you saying they are not believable enough?

Debbie: No. I'm just saying that he brought up that this is their culture and that ours is a Western culture and you should accept the culture for what it is. I'm saying no, dammit. Subjection is subjection—and very objectionable.

Eric: I think everybody should object to that. But this is different.

Kelly: Are these women dehumanized?

Eric: Is this a human rights issue? But for these women I don't know because with these women this is the way they see it and they've gone into it. You can't educate the whole world.

Cinde: No, you can't. It's nowhere near the same thing. You're talking about a set of cultural values that are based on Western tradition in the 50's.

Debbie: So you're justifying this? You don't think there is anything wrong with these women serving this man?

Eric: I don't think . . . there is any way we can change that. I don't think there is any way we can pass judgment on it.

Debbie: There is nothing wrong with it!

Eric: I don't agree with polygamy but I don't think that therefore we have to pass judgment on another culture.

Kelly: You don't necessarily have to agree with it.

Cinde: This is a very provocative piece of writing.

Eric: They're not objecting to it so it's not up to us to. It's fine that we don't agree with it.

Debbie: We feel sympathy for them.

Eric: I don't think any of us are arguing for polygamy here. For them it works.

Debbie: I don't like it at all.

Kelly: Maybe we can create meaning collaboratively.

Cinde: But we haven't reached consensus.

Debbie: It's political; that we can all agree on.

Eric Labbe (Comments on Informal Research)

This idea of imposing our standards on other cultures bothers me, because of course I agree with Debbie that polygamy really makes women seem like second-class citizens and all that, but I just can't get past the idea that there may have been some reason for it. I talked to my Comparative Religions prof from last year, and he lent me a couple of books on understanding Islam. It's interesting, Islam seems to have a lot of respect for women in many ways—property, custody rights, things like that. And the idea of temporary marriage is something they don't all agree on. Like, Khoumeni thought that short, temporary marriages would make things easier for kids at a co-ed college, where both sexes had to live together. But other Muslims say Muhammad changed his mind about temporary marriage and they forbid it.

[*in response to a question about polygamy in modern times*] It's interesting that most of the arguments about getting rid of polygamy are political and economic, not religious or human-rights oriented. The rules for polygamy were really strict—the men had to treat all the wives equally, and apparently the reasons for doing it had to do with things like a surplus of women in wartime and right after it—polygamy allowed repopulation and also allowed women to marry when there weren't enough men. But the reformers said that polygamy makes it hard for children to get the right education to become powerful citizens, and in these days it's too hard for one guy to be fair economically with up to four wives, so they'd like to get rid of it. But what's interesting is that the conservatives, the guys who want to keep it, say it keeps society from corruption because everybody knows that in places where monogamy is law, everybody has affairs. You know what else I didn't realize? Polygamy is OK'd in the Bible! David had more than one wife!

TO THE LADIES

Lady Mary Chudleigh

Wife and servant are the same,
But only differ in the name:
For when the fatal knot is tied,

Which nothing, nothing can divide: 5
When she the word *obey* has said,
And man by law supreme has made,
Then all that's kind is laid aside,
And nothing left but state[1] and pride:
Fierce as an Eastern prince he grows,   10
And all his innate rigor shows:
Then but to look, to laugh, or speak,
Will the nuptial contract break.
Like mutes she signs alone must make,
And never any freedom take: 15
But still be governed by a nod,
And fear her husband as her God:
Him still must serve, him still obey,
And nothing act, and nothing say,
But what her haughty lord thinks fit,   20
Who with the power, has all the wit.[2]
Then shun, oh! shun that wretched state,
And all the fawning flatt'rers hate:
Value your selves, and men despise,
You must be proud, if you'll be wise.

---

1. Pomp; "kind": natural.   2. Intelligence.

Kelly Leighton (Annotations)

<u>Wife and servant</u> are the same,
But only differ in the name:
For when <u>the fatal knot</u> is tied,
<u>Which nothing, nothing</u> can divide:
When <u>she the word obey</u> has said,   **images:**
And <u>man by law supreme</u> has made. . . .   **men—power-**
<u>Like mutes she signs alone</u> must make,   **ful**
And <u>never any freedom</u> take:
But still be governed by a nod,
And fear her husband as her God: **women—weak**
Him still must <u>serve, him still obey,</u>
And <u>nothing act, and nothing say,</u>
But what her <u>haughty lord</u> thinks fit,
Who with the power, has all the wit.
Then shun, oh! shun that <u>wretched state,</u>
And all the <u>fawning flatt'rers hate:</u>
Value your selves, and men despise,
You must be proud, if you'll be wise.

Debbie Carlisle (Double-Entry Journal)

Certainly, under these conditions, marriage would be hell. Giving over all self and power to any other person would be hell.

"Don't get married" poem. Man's innate rigor shows. Obey: husbands, God, the Word.

Marriage, for a woman, means being muted, repressed, governed, always fearful, subservient, passive, with no say. Marriage, for a woman, means a "wretched state."

Nuptial contract; death of laughter, free speech, joy!

Was it ever this bad? Was it the same as slavery? Isn't it coercion to allow oneself to be treated so wretchedly? What happens when someone else feels he or she owns a person, should control him or her "for their own good"? Is loss of self a kind of death?

Men before marriage are "fawning flatt'rers"! Marriage is dangerous; avoid it.

Kelly Leighton (Double-Entry Journal)

It's frightening to think that nothing much has changed since Chudleigh's time. There are still far too many people who'd agree that a wife is subordinate to a husband. It's depressing how many aspects of today's society are like those expressed in the poem.

Nothing (marriage, for instance) has changed in 300 years!

It is heartening to learn that feminism was alive 300 years ago. The views against marriage are amazingly contemporary. It's scary that, while feminist views predate the 20th century, our society's consciousness is still sexist! Will full equality take another 3 centuries?

Feminist reaction to the times?

I'm curious about Chudleigh's audience. Did they react positively? I think not. I'm surprised they didn't burn her at the stake!

How did her audience feel?

I don't like the title. It's inconsistent to all that seems positive. Perhaps she's being ironic. I don't know; there are too many questions raised by this title.

The title doesn't work for me.

Group Discussion

Eric: Here's proof that injustice doesn't always lead to great poetry. It's an interesting description of the way things were back then, even the way the hierarchical, patriarchal world view works today. I bet a lot of women looked at it and silently agreed with her. I can't really say much about it. It's pretty straightforward. The woman had guts to speak out that way back then, to let her voice be heard. But I wish she had written a better poem.

Kelly: Well I didn't really think about the merits of the poem. I feel good about it. I thought that because this was written three hundred years ago, or almost three hundred years ago, it was really surprising and a little frightening. I thought first it was surprising to hear a feminist view more than three centuries ago be brought out because the views on marriage are amazingly contemporary. This is also frightening because if they'd been around this long, they predate the 20th Century. Will it take three hundred more years for people to wake up? So I guess what I'm frightened of is just how little attitudes towards women have changed, and how today people relate, and how many men still see wives as their servants or their subordinates and I think that's kind of sad, too. I was curious about the reaction of her audience and what kind of reception she got. I'm surprised they didn't burn her at the stake. I was wondering about the title. Was that meant to be sarcastic or was that the way people titled such poems?

Debbie: Well it was interesting because I thought about the title and I thought that maybe it was not only directed towards just wives but maybe to people who are contemplating getting married, maybe like a warning or something. I just thought that it was harsh obviously, but there's a line in it that's kind of laid aside. Is that intended to mean that marriage is brutal because she goes on to suggest that in marriage you knew that there is never any freedom? Maybe she's trying to refer to a larger frame of reference?

Cinde: Are we at the point where questions might lead to further interpretations?

Kelly: I guess so.

Eric: I get the meaning of the poem and I see what it's saying. It's obvious. Everything that everybody has said is absolutely right. Well, no, what I'm saying is that the poem's strong, but simpleminded by today's standards.

Cinde: She's doesn't beat around the bush. It's very obvious. It's not even subtle.

Kelly: I still liked it.

Eric: Well the political statement is very interesting.

Debbie: I think that's what makes the poem.

Eric: Well, okay. I just didn't think it was a great poem.

Kelly: What did you think was wrong with it?

Eric: The rhyme scheme, the meter is just sort of blah.

Cinde: Yeah, it didn't really work well. Some of the words may be kind of overdone. The line, "Fierce as an Eastern prince he grows, / And all his innate rigor shows," might be overdone.

Debbie: We have to also consider the place of women at that time.

Cinde: Oh no. I just think the use of words, as in Eastern Prince, is kind of overstating the case just a little bit.

Kelly: I liked that. I thought that was perfect for the poem's time.

Cinde: There was good comparison in the poem, too.

Eric: I don't really object to the meaning of the poem. I think we all agree on that. It's just that I don't see it as a great poem.

Cinde: I wouldn't inscribe it in stone if that's what you mean. But how many great poems are there?

Eric: I suppose that's true.

Kelly Leighton (Comments on Informal Research)

I couldn't find out anything about her marriage except some reference to her unhappiness—at least that confirms our suspicions that the poem is in some ways autobiographical. What's really interesting, though, is the relationships she had with women. She was really into feminism—I couldn't believe it; in the eighteenth century! These women were writing all sorts of stuff to defend women's rights. What a crowd! I'd always thought the eighteenth century had only Pope and Jonson and those guys, but there was really a lot going on then that doesn't get into the major literature.

[*in response to a question about Chudleigh's feminist activities*] She heard a sermon at a wedding that talked about how morally weak women were, that they had to obey their husbands if they wanted to get to heaven. So Chudleigh wrote this dialogue-poem called *The Ladies Defence: or, The Bride-Woman's Counsellor Answer'd*. Apparently she published it at the urging of this group of literary women she belonged to, and she became famous as a result.

I also looked up Mary Astell, a woman who influenced Chudleigh. Astell is considered the first serious, educated feminist writer in England—she wrote two books called *A Serious Proposal to the Ladies*, and *A Serious Proposal to the Ladies Part II*. The titles are just like Chudleigh's, but she talks about more than marriage. She even suggests that unmarried women finance women's colleges with the money they would have used for their dowries . . . Maybe Eric's right; we ought to look at "To the Ladies" more as a political statement than as a poem.

7 Overview of Formal Presentations

Getting Started

"What will I write about?"

This question represents almost every student's nightmare, seeming to loom larger and to pose more difficulties than the "how to" questions that make up so much of the real work involved in writing a paper. A similar question often arises when the assignment is an oral presentation, a creative work of your own, or a group project instead of an individually authored paper.

Everything you do in exploring literature collaboratively empowers you to deal with that question. Annotating a text, keeping a journal, and especially discussing in groups can be seen as forms of seeking and testing topics for presentation to a wider community of readers. Think about your experience so far. You may have noticed already how frequently your group has started discussion of a literary work by talking about many aspects of the work; later the group identifies only a few of these aspects as promising for further thought and discussion. You've probably developed ideas about some of these "promising aspects," shared your ideas in your group, and gotten reactions to them. You've given your reactions when other members of your group have shared their ideas about these "promising aspects" with you. And everyone has probably come back to the group with more ideas, revised and new, to share. This informal sharing of your developing views and ideas among peers has probably been a rewarding experience in itself. It has also been serving you as a fast, fairly easy run-through of the major elements involved in presenting your views and ideas in writing—or even orally—to much wider groups that include strangers as well as fellow students.

You may have noticed also that sharing ideas with fellow students leads almost inevitably to a desire to share your views more widely. That's how it should be; writing about literature shouldn't be an artificial exercise separate from your exploration of literature. Acting on that desire to share, however, requires putting your views and ideas into a form appropriate for joining the conversation in a wider community of readers whether you do a paper, oral report, creative piece, or group project. It means essentially shifting from informal to formal presentation of your ideas.

Why are we calling presentations to wider communities "formal" presentations? Because the difference between sharing ideas in your group and sharing ideas in a wider community is essentially the difference between informal and formal communication. Although people sometimes think that informal means oral and formal means written, both informal and formal communication can be either written or oral. What sets apart informal from formal communication is a difference in purpose and style. In purpose, it's the difference between communicating to *explore ideas* (perhaps to discover new ideas) and communicating to *convey a chosen idea* so that it will be understood and accepted by other people. In style, it's the difference between *improvisation* and *premeditation*. When you share ideas in a small group, you enjoy the flexibility of being able to change anything on the spot, based on your feedback within this small group of readers. You can rely on immediate give-and-take to assist you in shaping your ideas, deciding what to say next, and modifying how you express points to eliminate misconceptions and clarify whenever necessary. In contrast, the opportunity for immediate give-and-take diminishes greatly as you approach larger and larger groups to share your ideas.

Consider a few examples. Suppose you are videotaping an oral presentation to be shown to your class later or you're submitting a paper or an exam to your instructor for credit. Would you be able to stop the videotape and alter it if your classmates began to look confused or impatient? Could you be there with your instructor to troubleshoot any problems that might turn up in your paper or exam? Would anything you could say afterward change your classmates' minds about your videotape or change your grade on that paper/exam? You would certainly get feedback after the fact that might help you to develop your ideas further or to do your next videotape/paper/exam differently, but you wouldn't often get a second chance to do your presentation. As you seek to share your views with groups larger than your class, you may find less opportunity to obtain any feedback, not just immediate feedback. Suppose you were to share your views by presenting them at a professional conference or by having your views printed in a published English journal. Time is often so short at conferences that the usual question and answer period must be cut to let people rush to the next event. Journals only occasionally print selected responses to pieces in their next issue, and many subscribers will get that next issue before even finding time to read your piece.

So formal presentations offer limited opportunity to obtain feedback from the wider community and usually no opportunity to modify your presentation based on that feedback. *That's why it is so important to seek feedback throughout the process of developing your formal presentation—because it must ultimately stand on its own without the possibility of your adjusting it further.* Your presentation must hold up your end of a conversation by anticipating and addressing in advance the wider community's reactions to what it says. It must present fully your ideas and reasoning instead of merely sketching them out to be expanded as feedback prompts. In addition, since your purpose now is to communicate a chosen idea rather than simply to test reactions to a variety of ideas, formal presentations require a *commitment* to your chosen idea. In other words, everything you present needs to be directed at (focused on) making your idea clear and credible. Consequently, one idea can't suddenly be abandoned in mid-presentation for a better idea unless you also revise the entire presentation to focus on that better idea from the start.

Since you can't rely on the give-and-take of questioning to produce— unanticipated—whatever clarification and development your audience requires in a formal presentation, you must anticipate and deal in advance with your audience's needs and reactions. Fortunately, you don't have to work blind. And you don't have to commit yourself immediately. You can continue to work with your small group to obtain feedback that will help you to develop your formal presentation.

When you share your ideas, plans, and drafts with your group, you can deal with these efforts informally. You can treat them as exploratory or experimental efforts, as evolving and open to revision, and as a focus for more of the active give-and-take that marks working in small groups. You can use your feedback there to represent the feedback you would expect from a larger audience. In this way you can develop—through the familiar, informal process of conversation in your peer group—a formal presentation that will bring you into the conversation of a wider community.

In sum, formal presentations differ from the informal conversation of your small group experience in two ways: They have the purpose of conveying a chosen idea, and they must be fully planned in advance to anticipate and address your audience's reactions, since you won't be able to adjust your presentation as it proceeds. The distinguishing features of a formal presentation are its

- restricted focus with some type of systematic organization,
- rhetorical strategy based on audience analysis, and
- extensive, in-depth presentation of both your ideas and your supporting reasoning.

Chapters 7 and 8 provide an overview of these features and an introduction to the process of developing formal presentations about literature by relying on informal conversation in small peer groups to help you with the process of development. We're going to speak here mainly in terms of written rather than oral presentation, partly for simplicity and partly because most formal, oral presentations about literature are written first and then revised to meet the special demands of being delivered orally. In the following chapters in this section, you'll find more detailed discussion of the most frequently encountered types of formal presentations (from those that focus upon literary works to those that use works only as starting points), as well as an introduction to the conventions of literary analysis.

RESTRICTING FOCUS BY FINDING A TOPIC AND DEVELOPING A PROPOSITION

Topics for papers are usually said to be either open (your choice) or assigned (chosen for you). But that's not the whole picture. Open topics routinely limit your choice at least to a particular literary work or works. Assigned topics may be so broadly inclusive that they demand further choices before you can handle them. And, when topics are collaboratively identified, they are in a sense both individually chosen and assigned. You participate in choosing topics, but then you have to abide by the group's decision.

We think you'll find that it makes better sense to envision a two-part process for finding a topic: first, the process of searching for a topic, and second, the process of refining a topic and developing a proposition. The first part concerns how to get started and how to keep going—either individually or collaboratively—in your search for a topic. The second part begins when you have a promising topic—whether individually chosen, collaboratively identified, or assigned by an instructor—and it concerns what's involved in refining that topic to develop it into a workable proposition. You can get an extra push forward in both parts of the process, in finding and refining a topic, by exploring possibilities through informal conversation with other people whenever you can.

Finding a Topic

You have a promising topic if more than one view of a matter can reasonably be held and you see a need for other people to be acquainted with one of those views. Look at it this way: If you can tell other people no more than what they already think or know, then you haven't much incentive to share your views, and no one else has much incentive to listen. So you need to be able to offer people something more—something that might add to their understanding or to their knowledge, even if it is simply more support for what they already think.

When you have been discussing a literary work in a small peer group of readers, you'll often find that one or more promising topics have emerged during group discussion. Of course, they don't usually come neatly labeled "paper topic" and ready to go. They are, in fact, more likely to be the opportunity for a topic or the makings of a topic when they first appear. So, to find a topic, you really need to learn to recognize where topics hang out and to look for them there. Those places are easy to spot. Sometimes topics lurk in what you disagreed about but found yourselves discussing at length or repeatedly coming back to discuss. Sometimes they lie in what none of you saw ahead of time but instead discovered and found interesting—maybe even exciting or challenging—as you talked. Sometimes they're waiting in annoying issues, questions, or quandaries that just couldn't be resolved in your group discussions. Consider how the following excerpt from discussion of "The Story of an Hour" turns the story's ending into an issue that could become a topic to follow up:

Eric: So what are you going to do with that last sentence? What does it mean?

Kelly: You mean "of joy that kills"?

Eric: Yeah, what does it mean?

Kelly: They probably thought she's so overjoyed that her husband is alive that she has a heart attack. With the joy of her freedom being taken away, that's what killed her.

Cinde: I think it's a nice story. A really nice story up until the ending which is kind of a strange ending. Kind of a twilight zone type of ending.

Debbie: Would the message be as strong if the ending wasn't like that?

Cinde: How else could you end it? You're set up from the beginning to know.

Eric: No, I'm not. All I'm saying is that it's a silly ending but it works. It works.

Kelly: I don't think it is. I think it's believable after you read this whole thing that she could have been so repressed the shock of seeing him again and knowing that she's going to have to go back could have killed her.

Eric: Nah!

Think of your search for a topic as similar to a rock hunter's search for mineral specimens or an autograph collector's quest for celebrity autographs. The key to success is recognizing where to look, then looking there to uncover something worth keeping. After a while, you'll become attuned to doing this. You'll begin to find yourself doing it—both individually and collaboratively—almost from the moment you start reading a work. For now, however, assume that the search for a topic is a separate task. Assume also that past group discussion has produced nothing that you can recognize as a promising topic or that has interested you enough to wish to pursue further. Where can you begin searching?

With other members of your group, try reviewing what happened in your earlier *group discussion* sessions. Even if those discussions didn't give you a ready-made topic, they're still your best lead to where promising topics might await. Start a new conversation. For talking points, ask yourself questions such as the following ones concerning your past discussions:

- What topics generated debate?
- Did you have strong views on any issue?
- Do you now see an answer to arguments or lines of reasoning that you couldn't answer before?
- Do you feel that a view you presented didn't get a full and fair hearing in the time available, or that you didn't have an opportunity to present it convincingly?
- Did your group identify any major questions about the work, major areas requiring interpretation, or problem areas that couldn't be resolved so far?
- Has anyone had a change of mind since you last talked?

Thinking along these lines can get a new discussion going and point you to areas where a promising topic might be found. Even when you don't have the opportunity for further group work and must search for a topic individually, you'll find that reviewing earlier group discussions will help you to start thinking more productively.

You can also use your *double-entry journal* and your *annotations* of the text to help you search for a promising topic. If you're searching for a topic collaboratively but without the benefit of earlier group discussion of a work, you can get discussion going by sharing portions of your double-entry journal and annotations. (That common part of beginning group discussion of a work won't be different just because you now have the objective of finding a topic.) If you're searching individually, use your double-entry journal and annotations to stimulate your thinking. In either case, begin by looking at places where your second entries differ greatly from your first entries:

- Where are those places?
- Why did your view change?
- What do you think produced the earlier impression that you later considered mistaken?

If you don't have places where your views changed, use your entries to identify which aspects of the work caught your interest. Do any of them still catch your interest, or do other points catch your interest now? You might simply read over your entries to identify what overall reaction to the work they represent, and ask yourself whether you feel the same way now. Again, you are searching for a starting point—not necessarily for a ready-made topic but for something to catch your interest so that you can use it to fire discussion or to send your own thinking in a direction that might lead to a topic.

For better results, take notes as you review your journal entries, think about them, and discuss them. Your notes will help you to be prepared to participate in discussion, and you may be able to see a prospective topic emerging more clearly when you reread your notes later. Similarly, take notes of your group discussions so that you can remember them more clearly and so that you can review the notes for signs of a prospective topic.

You might also try reconsidering the following:

- your research, if any, including critical views, historical-social conditions, accepted norms of the genre, and any other background materials;
- any special critical approach that might be applied, if your course has introduced you to critical approaches;
- your own experience or that of others known to you in circumstances similar to those presented in the work; and
- information you know about the author or the author's personal situation at the time the work was written.

These areas offer many opportunities for noticing connections, and points of agreement or disagreement. Here too you'll need to do some preliminary review and thinking to decide exactly what to share in your group or to follow-up on your own. The choice is easier when you remember that whatever you feel might open an interesting and insightful avenue of discussion will most likely have a similar appeal to others. Again, taking notes will help you to be prepared to participate in discussion, and you may be able to see a prospective topic emerging more clearly when you reread your notes later.

Finding a Topic

1. Find topics by looking where they hang out: in disagreements, annoying questions or issues, surprise discoveries, etc.
2. Review your small group discussions for leads.
3. Review your double-entry journal and annotations for leads and also to stimulate thinking and discussion.
4. Review other available information for leads: research, personal experience, biographical information, etc.
5. Talk through your ideas and potential topics in a small group or with a sounding board (a recruited listener).
6. Take notes as you review and discuss.

When you search for a topic collaboratively, you look in many of the same places you would look individually, and you have the additional advantage of being able to review your earlier group discussions as well. You also have the advantage of knowing you're not alone in your thinking about prospective topics. One of the greatest benefits of working collaboratively, however, is the assistance it provides you in assessing just how promising a prospective topic really is. You'll know already from group discussion whether a prospective topic would be likely to sustain additional conversation. You may also know from group discussion some of the key points to cover regarding your topic, alternative views to reconcile with yours, and special areas that require careful handling in order to communicate your ideas effectively. As a result, you probably have a head start on shaping your topic into a proposition and, ultimately, a paper.

Developing a Proposition or Thesis

What point will you make when you talk about your topic? What view or idea concerning a work will you try to share with a wider audience? Without a view, you have little to offer anyone regarding your topic—and nothing to keep your presentation from wandering aimlessly through assorted information and various competing views of your topic. Trying to share a topic without trying to share a view regarding it would be a pointless, purposeless exercise.

What makes a presentation worth your time and your audience's time is the view that you are offering through your treatment of the topic: your way of seeing or understanding your topic and, ultimately, the work. Thus, a formal presentation's point, commonly called the *proposition* or *thesis*, is defined as a view offered for the consideration or acceptance of other people concerning a matter on which rationally defensible, competing views can be held. (A rationally defensible view is one people can use facts and reasoning to present.)

You may find it helpful to recognize right away that this definition of proposition encompasses a range of possibilities. Consider two different kinds of views commonly encountered in presentations about literature. One is a view concerning what people ought to be discussing if they are to arrive at an understanding of a work. The other is a view concerning what that understanding should be. Remember, one reason people don't have all the answers about a literary work and can keep going back to talking about it—sometimes over many centuries—is that they come to realize that they probably should have been asking different questions about the work. The answers people find depend largely on the questions they ask. So a common, and important, focus for a presentation might be the view that a neglected or unrecognized issue related to your topic needs to be given attention and discussion. It might be the view that currently discussed issues would benefit by a refocusing on a specific new or reformulated question that the topic leads you to raise about the work. Or it might be the view that applying new information—perhaps about historical or social context—or applying new critical approaches—say, deconstruction or reader-response theory—would lead to better answers about a work. You may be more familiar with presentations that deal with what ought to be the answer rather than what ought to be the question since they are somewhat more common and more frequently discussed in textbooks. In these, the view which forms the focus of a presentation will be an insight that the topic provides for you about the work. The presentation will be essentially an argument making a case for the validity and value of this insight.

Proposition and purpose are closely related. When put into words, however, a proposition is usually stated as an idea and a purpose is usually stated as a course of action.

Proposition: *Frost's butterfly in "Tuft" functions as a catalyst.*
Purpose: *I plan to show how the butterfly functions in Frost's "Tuft."*

In this example, the difference between proposition and purpose lies in having to know the "how" in order to state the proposition. With a specific purpose like the one in the example (something general like, "I plan to discuss Frost's 'Tuft,'" wouldn't do), you could begin talking through your topic in your group or drafting your presentation with a reasonable expectation of developing a proposition.

How do you develop a proposition? The ways are as numerous as the ways of writing a paper. It's similar to driving from your home to a vacation spot in another state. You might travel back roads to gain as much as you can from the trip, or you might stick to the interstate highway to get there quickly. Even on the interstate, you might have a choice of routes: Traveling though a big city might be the most direct route from point A to point B, but it could also be much slower and more stressful than taking a longer, less direct loop around the city. You might even find reasons to choose different routes for different trips to the same destination. And shortcuts usually invite trouble. Writing isn't driving, of course, but in both activities different routes suit different people and different circumstances. Some people simply start writing with the expectation of discovering a proposition eventually and then revising drafts to fit it. Some people talk through or think through a topic until they have a working proposition that they can perfect while drafting and revising. Some people even work out their proposition and a detailed plan for its presentation before starting to draft. Many people do a bit of each of these in mixtures that vary each time. What stays the same, however, is the nature of the desired results. For a driver, it would be getting to the vacation spot—by car and with the gear necessary for a good time. For you in preparing a presentation about a literary work, it would be developing a proposition—actually a paper centered on a proposition—and surrounding it with all the "gear" necessary to lead other people to accept your view as credible.

So there's no single, right, all-purpose, foolproof way to go about developing a proposition. But we think that you'll find it helpful, whenever possible, to work collaboratively. Working with a group can play a major role in developing a proposition when the group serves as questioner and critic—

a role writers have to internalize when they work individually. Working in groups, you share your tentative propositions or your preliminary notes, ideas, or drafts. You use the give-and-take of group discussion as an opportunity to talk your way to a proposition. You start anywhere, even if you just begin talking about the literary work in relation to your topic. As the conversation proceeds, you may begin to see more clearly your topic and the issues it involves, and your proposition may come to you. You improve the odds for success by combining individual drafting with group discussion. To prepare for discussion, to follow up discussion, or to do both, try to write out your thoughts, tentative versions of your proposition, and even partial discussions of what you consider key parts of the literary work. What you get from the collaborative effort is likely to be in proportion to what you contribute; your peers will help to shape your thinking, but they aren't going to do your thinking for you.

Developing a Proposition

A proposition is an idea or view, not a topic, not a purpose, not a question.

1. Try talking your way to a proposition with a group or a recruited listener. Or draft your way to one by writing about your topic.
2. Put your proposition into words.
3. Try stating your topic as a question; the answer would be your proposition.
4. Try the "boil down" test.
5. Review your proposition collaboratively.

How do you know when you've arrived at a proposition? You'll know by trying to put your proposition into words and then seeing if it is recognizable as a proposition—seeing if it satisfies the requirements of a proposition and if other people are willing to consider it as one. Until you can put your proposition into words, you can't be entirely sure that you have a specific view to offer and that you are clear in your own mind about what it is. Simply having a feeling that you know what you want to say or a feeling about the point you want to make might be enough for you to begin talking informally about your topic or to begin drafting to explore your topic. But it's not enough to give your formal presentation the focus and organization it ultimately needs to succeed. For that, you'll need to have worked out your proposition, so that you can enter a process of revision (if you've begun drafting) or planning (if you've yet to draft) to center your paper on your proposition.

One technique that's helpful for getting your proposition into words involves restricting your topic to a specific issue and turning your topic into a question. The specific answer to your question could then be your proposition.

Topic:	The women's cover-up at the end of *Trifles*.
Topic as Question:	Why do Mrs. Hale and Mrs. Peters choose not to reveal Mrs. Wright's motive for murder?
Proposition:	Mrs. Hale and Mrs. Peters act out of empathy and guilt, having identified with her situation enough to feel that they are partially responsible for Mrs. Wright's desperate action.
Proposition: (alternative choice)	Mrs. Hale and Mrs. Peters choose not to speak because they realize that the men would laugh at their "evidence."

Another technique involves the "boil down" test. First, remember that a proposition will be an *idea* about something, not just an identification of purpose or topic. Then, try to boil your view down to about one sentence, a one-liner, even if you don't use that same one-liner in your paper. If you can, you'll be able to verify that you have a specific view to offer, and you'll be quite clear in your own mind about what it is. Group discussion of propositions and drafts frequently take the form of asking for boiled down versions of the proposition—so what's your point? What are you driving at? What do you mean? Why is this important? Consider the following examples of propositions:

Topic:	Use of language in "To the Ladies." Or nothingness in "To the Ladies."
Topic as Question:	Why does Chudleigh repeat the word "nothing" throughout "To the Ladies"?
Proposition:	Having equated married women with servants in "To the Ladies," Chudleigh identifies the defining characteristic of both as their *nothingness*.

Topic:	The oppression of women as a theme in "To the Ladies" and "Story of an Hour."
Topic as Question:	Has much changed in 200 years; is Mrs. Mallard less oppressed then her 18th century foremother?
Proposition:	Women are unequal partners in marriage as much in Chopin's "Story of an Hour" as in Chudleigh's "To the Ladies."

Topic:	Ambivalence as a rhetorical stance in "Polygamy."
Topic as Question:	Why does Mojtabai adopt a position of ambivalence toward polygamy in writing her essay?

| Proposition: | Mojtabai's professed ambivalence is dishonest—she communicates her deep revulsion toward the practice while refusing to admit that position explicitly. |
| Proposition: (alternative choice) | Mojtabai's professed ambivalence is a rhetorical stance calculated to get a Western audience to give the merits of polygamy a fair hearing by modeling for that audience a more open-minded attitude than might otherwise be expected and, at the same time, hiding her own acceptance of the practice. |

Whatever your topic, your proposition is your statement of what everything you have to say boils down to or adds up to. It's the answer to asking "what does it all mean" about the material presented in your paper. For that answer to emerge clearly for you and your audience, the material presented in your paper must all relate to your topic—more specifically, to your proposition. You will have shared your view effectively with others when their sense of what everything you have to say boils down to or adds up to is essentially the same as yours. That goal is well within your grasp when you have developed a proposition and put it into words so that you can use it as a guide in developing your presentation and as a basis for testing your latest draft.

ENVISIONING AUDIENCE

Who is your audience, and does it matter? For formal presentations, your audience is a wider community of readers with whom you want to enter into conversation and share your view of a literary work. That wider community could be any community larger than your small discussion group of several students within your class. It could be your class as a whole, your instructor as a representative of a larger community of scholars, other students of literature at your college or even across the country, any of several non-academic communities that might have or might be led to have an interest in the literary work, and so on. Each of these audiences will have different levels of familiarity with the work and the conventions of literary study, different perspectives from which to view the work and to think about your view, different reasons for being willing to enter into conversation with you. You'll want to avoid shutting your intended audience out of the conversation, so you'll want to match to your audience the way you plan to present your views. Otherwise, your real goal of communicating your view will not be accomplished. And you'll have monologue in place of a conversation.

Granted, working as a student in a classroom context makes it harder to appreciate the importance of adjusting your presentational style to suit your audience. You probably feel that your audience for most assignments is either your instructor or classmates—even when the assignment specifies a different audience. So you may feel that you've had little need to use what you know about your audience as the basis for deciding about exactly what and how much to include in your papers. Because an audience of other students or your instructor is probably one more like you in most respects than not, it is easy to lose sight of how specialized that audience really is. Think about it. You and your classmates and instructor are not just the "average" audience—not after at least twelve years of schooling and the pursuit of higher education. All of you are to a great extent representatives of a general class of well educated, academically attuned, literate readers who are likely to be familiar with both the literary work under discussion and, to some extent, the conventions of literary analysis. Thus, most assignments really involve your dealing with a special audience: the academic audience. Perhaps, without knowing it, you may already have been making choices to shape your papers for that audience. Recognizing that fact will help you to shape your formal presentations to increase their effectiveness.

Dealing with the Academic Audience

How do you match your presentation to the academic audience? You do it by observing the conventions of literary analysis, providing the solid organization and developed reasoning expected in academic writing, and learning where the line between familiar and unfamiliar can reasonably be drawn for such an audience. If you know that the instructor is your primary audience, try not to envision the instructor as an expert but as another reader interested in making sense of the work. Remember that literature serves to stimulate thought and to prompt discussion, not to pose readers a puzzle or to send them searching for a hidden meaning carved in stone. So envision your instructor, especially in a collaborative classroom, as another reader interested in being engaged in conversation about the literary work. Even instructors in traditional classrooms usually have more interest in the strength of the evidence and reasoning behind your view than in whether your view matches a preconceived "right" view. When you're writing for your instructor or your classmates, it's reasonable to envision your audience as familiar with materials covered in class, unfamiliar with materials not treated in class, and either receptive or unreceptive to your view on an issue (judging from what you have heard in group and classroom discussions).

You can also draw on your experience working in discussion groups. Your efforts to contribute your views to discussion in your group sessions have probably taught you something already about matching delivery to audience. You have probably recognized that not everyone in a group will catch on to an idea at the same time, that different facts or bits of reasoning will convince each person that an idea has merit, and that adjusting to the situation as it develops will prevent dead ends. You may even have learned enough about the people in your group to anticipate what they'll say or do and to be ready to handle the situation. Working on formal presentations involves developing this same kind of sensitivity to audience, both as a segment of the population like the academic audience and as a collection of individuals like those in your discussion group or literature class. Later, you'll be able to draw on your experience of matching your presentation to your academic audience to envision how to shape presentations for other, more fundamentally different audiences.

Dealing with Unreceptive Audiences

Unreceptive audiences pose a special challenge, as you may already have discovered in group discussion. Fruitful discussion requires an openness to new ideas and a willingness to engage in give and take. But everyone occasionally reacts to new ideas with a closed mind. Consider, for example, the conversation about "To the Ladies" transcribed in the Case Study. Eric Labbe and Kelly Leighton approach the poem from opposite directions:

Eric: Here's proof that injustice doesn't always lead to great poetry.

Kelly: Well I didn't really think about the merits of the poem. I feel good about it. . . . it was really surprising and a little frightening. . . . the views on marriage are amazingly contemporary.

Eric remains unreceptive later to his peers' interest in exploring the poem as a political statement: His position seems to be that the quality of the ideas can be no better than the quality of the poem. As the conversation continues, his peers remain equally unreceptive to his preoccupation with the poetic quality of the poem: Their position seems to be that poetic quality is secondary to the ideas handled in the poem. Each side acknowledges the other's view, but neither is willing to take it seriously:

Eric: I just think the use of words, as in Eastern Prince, is kind of overstating the case just a little bit.

Kelly: I liked that. I thought that was perfect for the poem's time.

Cinde: There was a good comparison in the poem, too.

Eric: I don't really object to the meaning of the poem. I think we all agree on that. It's just that I don't see it as a great poem.

Cinde: I wouldn't inscribe it in stone if that's what you mean. But how many great poems are there?

Everyone has a pet idea or a deep-seated preconception and may refuse to listen if it is challenged. When you believe in your view and wish others to consider it seriously, you *can* help people to think about your view on its merits. The key to success lies in keeping people's minds open long enough for them to pay attention to the evidence, so that the evidence can begin making them receptive to your view. If your audience's immediate reaction upon hearing your view would be a refusal to engage in conversation, keep silent about your view for a while. Focus discussion on those areas of the literary work that you believe most strongly substantiate your view, but don't state your view until later. Rely on your choice of evidence and on calling attention to its key features to prompt your audience to begin following a line of reasoning parallel to your own. If it really supports your view, the evidence will slowly lead your audience toward the same view. While it may be easy for someone to refuse to listen to a particular view, it is harder for a person to deny the supporting evidence that he or she has already heard and accepted. It's still harder for people to reject a view that they have begun to see on their own.

Compare the two following versions of Debbie Carlisle's draft paragraph on Mojtabai's "Polygamy." One version uses inductive reasoning and the other uses deductive reasoning:

Example A: Debbie's Draft Using Inductive Reasoning

Ann Grace Mojtabai starts her essay with a series of contrasts. She begins with what she says is a "not very beautiful" Iranian courtyard. It has a wall and "a narrow strip" of ground, sparse shrubbery, roses that she calls "insignificant," flagstone pavement, and a traditional pool "set like a turquoise in the center." Telling us that she expected "nightingales and roses," she says that she only heard "street hawkers and traffic" instead of nightingales and that the "famed rose gardens of Persia" must have been a myth or out of sight. She also tells us her father-in-law looks like a "vigorous 70's," but she knows he is "in his mid-90's." Over and over, we see her Western expectations clashing with Iranian reality. Her father-in-law is in better shape than she would expect for his age. Ordinary city life greets her instead of a romantic Persia straight out of the *Arabian Nights*. That courtyard with its wall, ground, shrubbery, roses, pavement, and jewel-like pool doesn't really

---

seem to fit her label of "not very beautiful" unless we won't settle for less than the "famed gardens of Persia." Over and over, Mojtabai presents a more negative and less realistic view than her facts seem to support. Given this start, the reader is introduced to the polygamists and asked along with Mojtabai, "What do you think of this?" Again she tells us that her expectations clashed with reality, for she "had been briefed" on polygamy but found that she "was not ready to confront the live instance." So the pattern of contrasts continues here. Does the pattern of unreliable narrative viewpoint also continue throughout her presentation of information about this polygamous marriage?

Example B: Debbie's Draft Using Deductive Reasoning

Mojtabai sets us up to take a more positive view of the Iranian custom of polygamy than most Westerners ordinarily would take. She does this by using a narrative voice that is attractive and unreliable at the same time. Her expectations are the same kind of storybook views that we probably have, so we can identify with her and even trust her for having a Western viewpoint. We can also sympathize with her when she is disappointed by the real Iran. On the other hand, we discover that we can't trust her judgments when she is willing to offer them. Instead, we learn to draw our own conclusions about the facts she provides. At the start of her essay, Mojtabai presents a more negative and less realistic view than her facts seem to support. We see this in a series of contrasts between reality and what she expects. She downgrades the Iranian courtyard as "not very beautiful" in spite of its storybook features. It has a wall edged with a garden containing shrubbery and roses, flagstone paving, and a pool "set like a turquoise in the center." The courtyard can't match, it turns out, the "famed rose gardens of Persia" that she expected. She got a real courtyard garden and ordinary city life instead of all "nightingales and roses." She also got living relatives to deal with instead of descriptions in an anthropology textbook. Even her father-in-law is in better shape than she would expect for his age; he looks in his "vigorous 70's" although he is really "in his mid-90's." By now we ought to be used to taking a more realistic view of the facts than Mojtabai does. That's when she introduces us to the polygamists and we are asked along with her, "What do you think of this?" After the introduction, we are ready to discount expectations, hers and ours, and ready to discover that the facts are more positive than she is willing to say.

Working through evidence to ideas is a form of *inductive reasoning*. You are probably more familiar with *deductive reasoning*, which involves presenting an idea first and then presenting the evidence that supports the idea. It's the basis of the traditional thesis-first essay. A decision to use deductive reasoning should be based on consideration of your audience, just as a decision to use inductive reasoning should be. Deductive reasoning is more appropriate than inductive reasoning for receptive audiences because it meets directly their desire to know your view and to have your evidence and reasoning revealed so that they can consider the merits of your view. In fact, inductive organization may actually antagonize receptive audiences by delaying this process; they often see it as thwarting their desire to get to the point and therefore seeming to waste time. Think carefully before deciding that you have an unreceptive audience. A genuinely unreceptive audience would refuse to listen as soon as it knew your view, whereas an audience that doesn't agree with you but would be willing to listen and converse is nevertheless a receptive audience. While the directness of deductive organization would be a disadvantage with an unreceptive audience—prompting a refusal to engage in conversation—that directness is an advantage with a receptive audience since just hearing a new idea can sometimes be enough to awaken a receptive audience to the idea's merits.

When you're certain that you have a genuinely unreceptive audience, try inductive reasoning. It has four parts, as follows. The first two parts are crucial to success; all except the second part can be very brief.

1. Identify the topic to be examined but don't reveal your view or even hint it. Don't reveal your view at the beginning. (In fact, try not even to hint about your view until as late as possible.) Instead, provide a focus for your discussion by identifying in neutral terms a specific aspect of the literary work that you'll be examining. The aspect might be a specific topic, such as "imagery" in "To the Ladies," or a specific issue such as "to what extent do the men and women interpret details differently in *Trifles?*" Choose this aspect carefully. Since the purpose of your discussion is to acquaint your audience with the basis for your view, your view must relate to this aspect of the work. Identify this aspect carefully too. You'll probably want to offer some reason why this aspect is worth examining in order to interest your audience in it, but keep the reason neutral in relation to your view. Similarly, if you identify an issue, choose one that won't automatically reveal your view. Remember that you are dealing in this situation with an audience that would refuse to listen if it suspected what view you wish it to consider.

2. Review areas/evidence that most strongly substantiate your view—maintain an objective/neutral approach. Select for discussion those areas which most strongly substantiate your view. But don't present this material in relation to your view, and don't draw conclusions that point directly to your view. Instead, adopt an objective/neutral viewpoint that essentially answers the question, "what can be observed here upon closer examination?" or "what seems to be worth noticing here?" For now, as far as your view is concerned, let your carefully selected evidence speak for itself. Your aims here are to focus your audience's attention on the "right" evidence (whatever you believe strongly substantiates your view), to help your audience to accept that evidence, and ideally to let the accumulating evidence for your view begin to move your audience to begin reasoning (on its own) from the evidence toward your view.

3. Reveal your view by beginning to reason from the evidence to your view. After covering several major areas and building up an accumulation of evidence which substantiates your view, you may reveal your view by beginning to reason to the view from the evidence already provided and from any remaining evidence as you present it. Introduce your view as a natural outgrowth of the evidence—not as a surprise or a stunt like a magician's pulling scarves and flowers from up the sleeve where they've been hidden. At this point, you can safely speak more directly about your view because you have already gained a partial hearing for it by leading your audience to give serious thought—possibly even acceptance—to the strongest evidence for your view. Equally important, you have thereby engaged your audience in a conversation that has gone too far to be easily broken off without further rational discussion. Now you can treat your originally unreceptive audience as you would a receptive, open-minded audience that disagrees with your view. Present any remaining evidence complete with the reasoning relating it to your view.

4. Conclude with an explicit expression of your view. Take the opportunity to leave your audience with a clear, complete statement of your view if you have not already done so in bringing your discussion of the evidence to a close.

Inductive and deductive reasoning can be used in conjunction with your choice of organizational plan (see Chapter 8) and can be applied to entire papers or to portions of them as short as single paragraphs. Say, for example, your proposition is one your audience would be willing to consider, but a major point to be offered in its support is one your audience would not be willing to give a hearing. You might use deductive reasoning in setting up your paper as a whole—presenting your idea and proceeding to examine the evidence for it—but then use inductive reasoning when you handle the problem point—going over the details of the point before mentioning what you believe they show. Similarly, you might decide that your audience would be receptive to a point which you plan to present in your paper, but unreceptive to the point of your paper as a whole. In that case, you could use inductive reasoning in laying out your paper as a whole, setting up a review of evidence relevant to your topic before mentioning how you view the evidence, but then using deductive reasoning when you handle the uncontroversial point—sharing your view of that point before examining its details.

Try to be aware of your audience. Use your knowledge of your audience to help you to make the choices which face you in communicating your views. Once you have formulated your proposition, thought about your reasoning process, and considered your audience, you'll be ready to develop and draft your formal presentation.

8 Overview of Formal Presentations

Developing and Refining

Where do I start? What do I talk about first? What do I talk about next? Your presentation has to start somewhere and to move in some sequence through the areas you wish to discuss. No one can talk about everything at once.

For generating an initial draft, you might try writing without paying attention to sequence, essentially moving in random order. If you feel comfortable proceeding at random, you'll find it a useful way to get started. Later, the random sequence will have to be replaced with an orderly one if only to assure your audience that your thinking is unmuddled. By arranging the content of a paper so that it presents a recognizable pattern of development, you help your audience to envision your presentation as a whole and to see your reasoning more clearly. For much the same reason, many writers feel uncomfortable working on even an initial draft without some plan for a reasonable sequence of content. They want to be able to envision where they are going and to review what they have written in relation to their sense of what will follow. We'll refer here to plans for the orderly sequence of content as *organizational plans*.

SYSTEMATIC ORGANIZATION

You can develop a unique organizational plan to suit any unique combination of proposition, audience concerns, and evidence. In practice, however, you'll probably find yourself doing what most writers do: relying on one of several common organizational plans—or some combination of them. You'll find here an introduction to three of the most useful plans.

1. **Derivative Organization.** Derivative organization follows a sequence established by the literary work. Two common forms of derivative organization are *spatial organization*, the order in which events appear in a work, and *chronological organization*, the actual time sequence of those events. When the order of appearance and the order of occurrence of events in a work are the same, spatial and chronological organization will be the same.

2. **Order of Importance.** A presentation organized by order of importance proceeds according to the level of importance that your selected aspects of

a literary work bear in relation to your proposition. (You select which aspects of the work to discuss, and you decide their level of importance.) A presentation organized by order of importance may proceed from the most important to the least important or from the least important to the most important aspects of the work.

3. Comparison/Contrast. Comparison and contrast involve viewing one thing in relation to another; for example, one character in relation to another within a work, one work in relation to another work, or even a work in relation to an external standard such as Freudian theory or Aristotle's definition of tragedy.

These organizational plans can be applied to entire presentations or to portions of them as small as individual paragraphs. Within an overall organizational plan, writers frequently combine a variety of organizational plans, choosing the plan best suited to each aspect of the work to be discussed. For example, a paper presenting a view of an event's significance might be organized in the order of most to least important supporting evidence, but it might, at one point, compare and contrast two characters' views of a situation and, at another point, present a chronological discussion of the outcome of the situation.

Imagine writing such a paper about Mrs. Mallard's discovery that Brently's death means freedom for her in Chopin's "Story of an Hour." What would you choose as your most important piece of evidence? Would it be that line from late in the story, "'Free! Body and soul free!' she kept whispering," or that earlier line, "free, free, free!" coupled with the comment following it about her racing pulse and relaxation? Would it be her view near the end that she's not ill but "drinking in a very elixir of life"? Maybe it would be her reflection on being able to "live for herself" or on how people insist on their "right to impose a private will upon a fellow creature". Whatever you choose, you would follow it with the next strongest of these pieces of evidence, and so on. Having established Mrs. Mallard's view, you might then contrast it with Richards' and Josephine's views as shown in the way they approach her at the beginning and end of the story. Finally, you might review the chronology of news, grief, gradual recognition of freedom, triumphal descent from her room, and shattering revelation to explain her extreme reaction to Brently's resurrection.

Derivative Organization: Spatial

Spatial organization follows the same sequence of presentation found in the literary work; in other words, you discuss aspects of the work in the order of their appearance in the work. You need not cover everything in the work— only whatever you consider relevant, as much or as little as that may be—provided that you cover your choice of items in the same order as they appear in the work. Because it is a "ready-made" organization requiring little additional planning, writers often find spatial organization an attractive choice. But it is a suitable choice only when your proposition and the order of appearance in the work are related. **Caution: Avoid merely retelling the story; what you have to say *about* the events is what's important here.** Spatial organization is the standard organization for explication, which attempts to explain how the work as a whole develops from its parts (see Chapter 9). An explication of Chudleigh's "To the Ladies," for example, would proceed through the poem from beginning to end, explaining the contribution each part makes to the whole:

> In "To the Ladies," Chudleigh emphasizes the powerlessness of the married woman by comparing her to a servant: "Wife and servant are the same, / But only differ in the name" (1–2). For servant and wife, the key word is "*obey*." Both have masters "by law supreme"; they are both subservient by divine and human law in the eighteenth century. Moreover, man is not just a master: he is as "Fierce as an Eastern Prince" (9) or virtually unlimited in his power. For both wife and servant, "to look, to laugh, or speak" (11) without permission is unacceptable. Both can "never any freedom take" (14), and both must be ready to be directed "by a nod" (15). No matter how unbearable, wife and servant are stuck in their roles: "Him still must serve, him still obey, / And nothing act, and nothing say" (17–18). For both it is a "wretched state" (21), but Chudleigh implies that it is even more wretched for the wife because women have a choice: the choice is up to "the ladies" to give up their freedom by choosing to marry.

When spatial organization is combined with deductive reasoning (as in the preceding example), the writer's view of the work as a whole is presented explicitly and each part is examined to show how it contributes to the emergence of that view. When spatial organization and inductive reasoning are combined, the writer's view of the work as a whole is not mentioned until after as many parts of the work as possible have been examined for what they have to offer in themselves and, perhaps, in relation to adjacent parts or a subsection of the work. **Caution: Avoid the pitfall of merely retelling the story; comment suitably on events.** Only after this narrower focus on the parts has built up evidence favorable to the writer's view does the writer reveal that view and discuss it directly. Consider the following inductive version of the paragraph on Chudleigh's poem:

> In "To the Ladies," when Chudleigh says "Wife and servant are the same, / But only differ in the name" (1–2), to what extent does the comparison hold up? Chudleigh refers to the permanence of marriage as the "knot . . . Which nothing, nothing can divide" (3–4), to the marriage ceremony's vow of obedience (5), and to marriage's making "man by law supreme" (6). In the eighteenth century, divorce was rare and the husband

was recognized in church and civil law as having legal control of his wife's person and property. In contrast, servants were not serfs legally bound to their masters, although economic and social conditions did limit their mobility and masters could physically punish disobedient servants. Chudleigh speaks further of power by comparing the husband to "an Eastern Prince" (9) and stating that it could be a violation of a wife's marriage contract for her "to look, to laugh, or speak" (11) without permission. Good servants were expected to fade into the wallpaper and never, without permission, to interact socially with the people they served; they were expected to "never any freedom take" (14) and to be ready always to be "governed by a nod" (15). In the relationship of servant to master, the servant in all circumstances "still must serve, him still obey, And nothing act, and nothing say" (17–18). These requirements of sub-servience and self-abnegation, however, Chudleigh applies directly to wives, not servants. Applied to wives, they seem extreme and objection-able. In developing her comparison of wives and servants, Chudleigh goes far beyond quibbling with the biblical designation of wife as helpmate and the biblical injunction to wives to be obedient to their husbands. She attacks marriage as a "wretched state" (21) because it legitimizes men's oppression of women.

Derivative Organization: Chronological

Chronological organization follows the time sequence of the events pre-sented in a work. When a work presents events in the order of their occurrence, chronological organization will be the same as spatial organiza-tion. When, however, the order of occurrence is broken by flashbacks or when events are revealed in a random order such as through a character's stream of consciousness, reminiscences, or investigation of past events, chronological organization will differ from spatial organization. Then fol-lowing the order in which events actually *occurred* would constitute chron-ological organization; whereas following the order in which events are actually *presented* to the reader would involve spatial, not chronological, organization.

For example, in Glaspell's *Trifles* the events which led to murder are revealed piecemeal as the women make new discoveries and fit them to-gether like scraps of material in a quilt. Following the order of discovery would be spatial organization, a method that might be more useful for focusing attention on the women's intelligence or their motivation for keeping silent at the end. Following the reconstructed, actual sequence of events leading to the murder would be chronological organization, a method that might be more useful for focusing attention on Mrs. Wright's character and motivation. Generally, chronological organization is suitable for discus-sions centered on process (gradual change over time), cause-effect (how one event leads to another), and clarification of time sequence. A discussion of William Faulkner's "A Rose for Emily," for example, would benefit from chronological organization because when the narrator's reminiscences about events in Miss Emily's life are put in proper time sequence, they suggest not only an answer to the central mystery behind the locked room's contents but also a psychological insight into Miss Emily herself.

When chronological order is combined with deductive reasoning, the writer's proposition is made explicit and each event is examined in turn for the contribution it makes in support of the proposition. When chronological organization and inductive reasoning are combined, the writer's proposition is not mentioned until after as many events in the work as possible have had their nature probed. Note: The emphasis is not on what happened but, instead, on what is worth noticing about what happened. Only after this narrower focus on the significant aspects of events has built up evidence favorable to the writer's proposition is that proposition revealed and discussed directly.

Caution: Inductive reasoning in combination with chronological order can be risky because it can too easily lead inexperienced writers to offer mere plot summary in place of a reasoned view of a work. Avoid this pitfall by always going beyond simply saying what happened next. Instead, offer something in answer to the question "so what?" about that event. If you look through your annotations, journals, and notes from group discussions, you'll find plenty of material to answer that question.

Order of Importance

Order of importance provides writers a freedom and degree of control in sequencing not available with derived organizations. Because you choose which aspects of a work or evidence from the work to discuss and you determine what level of importance to assign to them, you are able to skip around within a work, moving backwards and forwards and back again as your topic or line of reasoning invites you to move. As a result, a wide variety of different sequences of discussion can be set up to fit a wide variety of objectives, and organization by order of importance supports the construction of a strong chain of reasoning essential for effective analysis and argumentation. (Note: You can't arbitrarily assign levels of importance to aspects of a work; part of what makes organization by order of importance an effective organizational plan is your readers' recognition of the pattern.)

When organization by order of importance is combined with deductive reasoning, the writer's view is presented explicitly and each piece of evidence is examined to show how it supports that view. Consider the following paragraph from a character analysis of *Trifles*:

Glaspell helps us to empathize with Minnie Foster Wright by giving us an unattractive victim. No one has much that's good to say about John Wright. In fact, the more they think about him the less they can say that is good. The ugliest part of his personality is revealed in his killing of Minnie's canary. He has violently torn the door of the birdcage off its hinges (74) and "wrung" the little canary's neck (75). This senseless cruelty is magnified when Mrs. Hale follows up her earlier observation that Minnie "was kind of like a bird herself—real sweet and pretty, but kind of timid and—fluttery" (74–75). She realizes that Wright's killing the canary wasn't his only crime: "No, Wright wouldn't like the bird—a thing that sang. She used to sing. He killed that, too" (76). Wright killed his wife's spirit. Bits and pieces mentioned earlier about Wright now come to mean more than they did originally, like Mrs. Hale's comment that, despite no bad habits, "he was a hard man . . . Just to pass the time of day with him. [Shivers.] Like a raw wind that gets to the bone" (74). The first thing we heard about him in the play was that he was taciturn and insensitive to his wife: "I don't know as what his wife wanted made much difference to John" (68). In addition, the repeated comments that the Wright house isn't cheerful point back to John Wright. As Mrs. Hale says, "I don't think a place'd be any cheerfuler for John Wright's being in it" (71). It seems wrong to say anyone deserved to be murdered, but John Wright certainly earned the death penalty.

When organization by order of importance is combined with inductive reasoning, the writer's view is not mentioned until after as many pieces of evidence as possible have been presented and discussed. Consider the following inductive version of the paragraph on John Wright's character.

We learn a lot about the character of the victim, John Wright, in the course of the women's solution of the crime. He was capable of a violent cruelty since he killed his wife's pet canary, having torn the door of the birdcage off its hinges (74) and "wrung" the little canary's neck (75). Mrs. Hale recognizes this as part of a general pattern ingrained in his personality when she observes, "Wright wouldn't like the bird—a thing that sang. She used to sing. He killed that, too" (76). She has come to recognize that Wright is responsible for changing his wife into the wreck described at the opening of the play although as Minnie Foster she "was kind of like a bird herself— real sweet and pretty, but kind of timid and—fluttery" (74–75). Wright seemed okay on the surface—he was a "good" man in the sense of having no bad habits—but Mrs. Hale notes that "he was a hard man . . . Just to pass the time of day with him. [Shivers.] Like a raw wind that gets to the bone" (74). From the start of the play we're told he was a taciturn man, and he emerges as the root of his household's frequently mentioned cheerlessness. As Mrs. Hale says, "I don't think a place'd be any cheerfuler for John Wright's being in it"(71). No one has much that's good to say about John Wright. In fact, the more the other characters think about him the less they can say that is good. Glaspell helps us to empathize with Minnie Foster Wright by giving us in John Wright an unattractive victim, a man who deserves punishment if not killing.

Descending order of importance—from most to least important—generally produces more strongly persuasive argumentation than ascending order of importance. Why? If your audience finds your strongest evidence convincing, then every additional piece of supporting evidence becomes additional confirmation regardless of how minor that individual piece of evidence may be in itself. Working, instead, from least to most important runs the risk that your audience will find your first piece of evidence—the least important—unconvincing and, as a result, will listen with skepticism to your remaining evidence. Instead of moving your audience to increasing certainty about your view, you could simply be laboring to overcome a new-found skepticism. Avoid that pitfall by making certain that your least important point is nevertheless strongly convincing. Remember that organization by order of importance does not require you to use weak evidence or to discuss insignificant points; it only requires you to put in rank order what you do include in your paper. If you review any notes you've taken in group discussions, you should recognize areas in which you found yourself searching for the best evidence to support your views.

Comparison/Contrast

Comparison and contrast involve viewing one thing in relation to another, such as one character in relation to another within a work, one work in relation to another work, or even a work in relation to an external standard like biographical information, Freudian theory, or Aristotle's definition of tragedy. The urge to compare and contrast—often just to compare or just to contrast—seems to arise naturally and frequently as you discuss literary works. Sometimes the comparison/contrast is very brief, only a few sentences, and sometimes it's the organizational pattern for an entire presentation.

Extended comparison and contrast usually falls into one of two patterns. The first pattern involves discussing separately the two things to be compared and contrasted, then trying to pull the two discussions together to draw conclusions. For example, a comparison and contrast of the position of women in "Polygamy" and *Trifles* would discuss that issue in "Polygamy" until the issue is fully treated, then discuss that issue in *Trifles* (with or without reference to the preceding discussion), and finally try to pull the two discussions together by making connections in order to reach some conclusions. This pattern is best suited to brief presentations and to things that are not very complex. The longer the discussion and greater the complexity, the harder it is for your audience to remember the important points you've made long enough for you to use them in the concluding part of the presentation. For this reason, you may find yourself repeating what you've said earlier, and the presentation's conclusion can often be difficult to write.

The second pattern involves discussing together, on a point-by-point basis, the two things to be compared and contrasted, drawing conclusions as you go. For example, in this pattern a comparison and contrast of the position of women in "Polygamy" and *Trifles* would discuss the same aspect of the issue in both works, drawing conclusions, then move on to another aspect of the issue in both, drawing conclusions, until the relevant issues are covered. This pattern would then conclude by pulling together your various earlier conclusions as the basis for drawing overall conclusions. The second pattern is well suited to lengthy presentations and to things that are complex, but it doesn't give as strong a picture as the first pattern of what each of the two things being compared is as a whole. The presentation's conclusion, however, is far easier to write. Each pattern has its advantages and disadvantages, so choose wisely according to the nature and complexity of the comparison and contrast presentation you're planning.

When organization by comparison and contrast is combined with deductive reasoning, the writer's view is presented explicitly and the comparison and contrast is provided to support that view. The second pattern for extended comparison and contrast is well suited for this purpose, although both patterns can be used successfully. Consider the following example of a paragraph comparing and contrasting Mrs. Mallard's actual reaction to her husband's death with the reactions expected of her:

> From the start, Mrs. Mallard's reaction to her husband's death is not the conventional reaction expected of her. Josephine and Richards clearly expect the news to be a terrible shock, so they are careful to break it to her "as gently as possible" (81) because of her heart condition. We're told, however, that "she did not hear the story as many women have heard the same" (82). Instead of being paralyzed with shock, she weeps wildly. When she insists on going to her room alone, it seems like she's going into a conventional widow's depressed withdrawal. That's apparently what Josephine thinks as, filled with worry, she kneels "before the closed door with her lips to the keyhole, imploring for admission . . . [with the argument that] 'you will make yourself ill'" (83). In reality, Mrs. Mallard is the opposite of depressed, withdrawn, and ill. She's excited and happy about the future: "Her fancy was running riot along those days ahead of her . . . that would be her own" (83). The doctor's diagnosis of her cause of death at the end is just the last in a series of contrasts between reality and other people's expectations of Mrs. Mallard.

When organization by comparison and contrast is combined with inductive reasoning, the writer's view is withheld until the comparison and contrast is provided and conclusions are drawn that support and begin to reveal the writer's view. The first pattern for extended comparison and contrast is well suited for this purpose although both patterns can be used successfully. Consider the following inductive version of the paragraph comparing and contrasting Mrs. Mallard's actual reaction to her husband's death with the reactions expected of her:

> To what extent are we prepared for the unexpected ending beyond being told at the start that Mrs. Mallard has a heart condition? One of the first things we're told is that when Mrs. Mallard hears of her husband's death "she did not hear the story as many women have heard the same" (82). Instead of being paralyzed with shock, we're told, she weeps wildly. The next thing she does is insist on going to her room alone, and it seems like she's going into a conventional widow's depressed withdrawal. That's clearly what Josephine thinks as, filled with worry, she kneels "before the closed door with her lips to the keyhole, imploring for admission . . . [with the argument that] 'you will make yourself ill'" (83). We already know, however, that she's been experiencing a kind of joy. Instead of getting ill because she's depressed and withdrawn, she's getting excited because she's happy about the future: "Her fancy was running riot along those days ahead of her . . . that would be her own" (83). Throughout the story Mrs. Mallard does the unexpected, gives the unconventional reaction. The ending is a surprise only because we're buying into the conventional expectations held by Josephine, Richards, and the doctor. The doctor's diagnosis of her cause of death at the end is just the last in a series of contrasts between reality and other people's expectations of Mrs. Mallard.

When you consider an organizational plan for your presentation, do so with your proposition, audience, and evidence in mind. Think about whether that plan is likely to help or hinder your effort to show the reasoning behind your proposition and whether alternative plans are likely to be more effective. Would the plan, for example, steer you to the most relevant areas for discussion, or would it commit you to covering less productive areas? You can get help answering these questions by sharing your drafts with others.

SUBMITTING YOUR WORK FOR PEER REVIEW

As you develop and refine your draft, you can continue to test your ideas on your peers and to get feedback, as you work, on the outcome of your efforts. Usually, such peer response takes two forms: reading aloud and formal written review. You may be wondering how competent you may be to offer a critique of someone's work, or how another student's comments about your work may be of any help to you. But, as you have learned from Part I, collaboration with your peers is pretty helpful in making meaning of literary works. It can be equally constructive in helping to clarify your own work.

Sharing by Reading Aloud

Sometimes your instructor will arrange the classroom so that your completed draft may be read along with those of your classmates. In this kind of response, you're simply sharing your work with an audience as a kind of celebration of the process that helped you shape your piece. You may ask that your listeners focus their attention on specific parts of your draft, or you may request that they just listen attentively and receive your piece in the way you have delivered it—as a gift.

The reason for sharing your work and responding non-judgmentally at this stage of the writing process is to experience the conversational nature of writing as well as the social, collaborative nature of language. In the classroom, perhaps in a circle, you will feel the power that comes with owning words that you have arranged for your audience. Moreover, you will begin to *hear* both the harmonious and the discordant relationships among words that you and your classmates have put together. This awareness will add to your developing ability to make constructive judgments regarding language and literature.

Formal Written Peer Review

At times your instructor will ask that you engage in *formal written peer review* of your drafts. Depending on the size of the class, you'll find yourself discussing your work in small groups or receiving responses from the entire class. In either case, you provide copies of your draft for other students to read and respond to. Their responses will take three forms: descriptive, technical, and judgmental. Each formal written peer review offers a different type of useful feedback about your work. And each offers you a positive response first, then a more thorough investigation of your developing work that will help you to revise it into its final form.

Descriptive Peer Review

What you need from your readers is both reassurance and advice. When your reader *describes* what he or she sees in your draft, you'll be able to determine whether or not you've accomplished what you intended. In submitting your work to a **descriptive peer review,** you can be assured that, in this early stage of the writing process, your reader will not discuss the technical aspects of your writing, nor will he or she make any judgments about its content. You will receive, however, an outline in which your reader describes what each part (sentence, paragraph, essay) *does* (that is, how it functions: *it introduces, it explains, etc.*) and *says* (that is, its summary—what the sentence or paragraph or essay is all about).

Here is an example of the descriptive peer review for the first five sentences of the deductive reasoning paragraph that you read earlier in this chapter (p. 123):

The Passage

Glaspell helps us to empathize with Minnie Foster Wright by giving us an unattractive victim. No one has much that's good to say about John Wright. In fact, the more they think about him the less they can say that is good. The ugliest part of his personality is revealed in his killing of Minnie's canary. He has violently torn the door of the birdcage off its hinges (74) and "wrung" the little canary's neck (75).

What the Passage Does
The first sentence gives the reader the main point of the paragraph. Sentences two and three give the first reason in support of the paragraph's main point. Sentences four and five talk about the first reason some more, giving illustrations of why the first reason is convincing.

What the Passage Says
The writer states that Glaspell's sympathy in her portrayal of the character Minnie Foster Wright happens primarily because she has created an unpleasant character, John, who has hurt Minnie by brutally killing her canary.

It's important to note that, in telling what a passage **does,** the reviewer will not involve himself or herself in your passage's *content.* That's reserved for the **says** section of the outline. A detailed descriptive outline may provide you with a clearer picture of how a reader sees your piece, something you may be unable to do on your own because of your close involvement in it. How you respond to the description is your choice: You may make major revisions based on the response, or you may choose to leave the passage essentially as is.

Technical Peer Review

While a descriptive peer review will help you to affirm or clarify what you've written, you need to know a little more to prepare your work for submission. A **technical peer review** lets you know what your draft's technical strengths and weaknesses are. While your reader will still not comment on the content of the draft, he or she will provide you with narrative responses regarding its unity, coherence, development, style, and mechanics. In other words, your reader reviews the *way* your ideas are presented, not the ideas themselves. This kind of peer response should allow you to get closer to a finished product: You'll know whether or not your piece is headed in the right direction and you'll have advice that you can use for making the presentation of your ideas more effective.

A **technical peer review** is usually prepared during the early stages of the writer's draft so that the writer can benefit from the reviewer's comments about the draft's weaknesses as well as its strengths. However, even a relatively polished paragraph can benefit from a technical peer review. The writer of the deductive paragraph, for example, can benefit from the following review:

The Paragraph

Glaspell helps us to empathize with Minnie Foster Wright by giving us an unattractive victim. No one has much that's good to say about John Wright. In fact, the more they think about him the less they can say that is good. The ugliest part of his personality is revealed in his killing of Minnie's canary. He has violently torn the door of the birdcage off its hinges (74) and "wrung" the little canary's neck (75). This senseless cruelty is magnified when Mrs. Hale follows up her earlier observation that Minnie "was kind of like a bird herself—real sweet and pretty, but kind of timid and—fluttery" (74–75). She realizes that Wright's killing the canary wasn't his only crime: "No, Wright wouldn't like the bird—a thing that sang. She used to sing. He killed that, too" (76). Wright killed his wife's spirit. Bits and pieces mentioned earlier about Wright now come to mean more than they did originally, like Mrs. Hale's comment that, despite no bad habits, "he was a hard man . . . Just to pass the time of day with him. [*Shivers.*] Like a raw wind that gets to the bone" (74). The first thing we heard about him in the play was that he was taciturn and insensitive to his wife: "I don't know as what his wife wanted made much difference to John" (68). In addition, the repeated comments that the Wright house isn't cheerful point back to John Wright. As Mrs. Hale says, "I don't think a place'd be any cheerfuler for John Wright's being in it" (71). It seems wrong to say anyone deserved to be murdered, but John Wright certainly earned the death penalty.

Technical Peer Review

Everything in this paragraph really goes to prove one major point: "Glaspell helps us to empathize with Minnie Foster Wright by giving us an unattractive victim." Because of this, I think the paragraph is unified. Every description about Mr. Wright's insensitiveness to Minnie keeps on supporting and developing the main point, which makes the paragraph read clearly and hold together—and it's well developed. It seems like the writer has followed all the rules for quoting and documenting, and I can't see any mechanical weaknesses.

Judgmental Peer Review

Perhaps the most helpful peer review you will receive is a **judgmental peer review.** While your reader should, as always, begin by reassuring you that what you have written is worthwhile, he or she should focus on the draft's content as well as its point of view. The process here may be slightly more difficult for both you and your reader: Your reader has to be both honest and aggressive, offering you the kind of response you may not have even considered about your content and point of view. You, on the other hand, have to be able to take criticism in the constructive way that it's offered. Do realize that, in this stage of the writing process, your draft is getting closer to submission. Therefore, this kind of judgmental criticism is crucial: It assures you that all views about your proposition or thesis have been entertained.

Here is an example of a judgmental peer review on the preceding deductive paragraph:

> The writer has argued logically and thoroughly about how appropriate Glaspell's sympathy towards Minnie Wright is, but some people who read the play might find murder just too offensive to dismiss. The writer may want to at least think about the idea that Glaspell is being "politically correct" in trying to win our sympathy for Minnie's unusual (illegal? immoral?) stand against male oppression. Even if the writer later refutes such ideas, it might make for an even more compelling argument if views like this were brought into the open.

Why Peer Response Works

In working through the very complex process of interpreting literary texts, you and your peers were given a great deal of responsibility for making meaning of those works. You made observations about them by taking notes, summarizing, and paraphrasing; you evaluated them by looking closely at the words and the patterns those words shaped; you discussed literary works from a technical perspective, looking for figurative language (similes and metaphors) and symbols, for instance; and you judged whether or not you could respond sympathetically to some topic or issue raised by such works. In essence, you were practicing the very same kind of analysis that you may be asked to practice with your peers' written work. Since we believe that the judgments you have made about literature show a good deal of responsibility and insight, we also believe you will demonstrate that same kind of mature approach in helping your peers to refine their formal work.

In Chapters 7 and 8 you've been introduced to the various processes involved in moving from exploring literature to communicating your views. In the next two chapters you'll learn about the various types of presentations you may make (Chapter 9), as well as how to conform to the conventions associated with making literary presentations (Chapter 10).

9 Types of Presentations

Explication, Analysis, and Evaluation

Writing an explication involves showing how the meaning of a literary work gradually emerges as you read the work; it is your explanation of how what is in a work helps to shape and develop for you the work's meaning/purpose/point. Thus, the real emphasis in an explication is on the overall meaning of a work. In this respect explication differs from analysis, which focuses on a special aspect—a part—of a work, and from evaluation, which presents judgments about the quality of a work with reasoned support for those judgments. Of course, these neat divisions are more often observed in academic writing than in informal conversations about literature. Because of your familiarity with collaborative learning, however, making the transition from group discussion to presentations will be easier than you may expect.

Already in your groups and probably in your journals, you've done some explication, analysis, and evaluation. You've done explication when you've tried to make sense of a portion of a work, as you saw Eric doing in the Case Study chapter for a paragraph in "Story of an Hour."

I think the descriptions of nature are strange. They do a couple of things. They're either indicating that despite the death of Brently life goes on, that may be one of the interpretations, or because of his death everything is now happy and free, or even though she thinks he's dead he really isn't. So she thinks he's dead but nature is telling us something else. There's a whole bunch of different interpretations, I think, about nature in that whole nature paragraph. I think the real one is that because he's dead she's now free and everything is pretty happy. I think that's what Chopin is trying to tell us. This could be a story not of death and dealing with death but of a woman's attempt to get out from under the domination of man only to be returned to it. Kind of a cyclical thing.

You've done some analysis when you've begun to explore an aspect of a work, as in the group discussion of character and motivation in *Trifles*:

Cinde: I understand that he broke the canary's neck but is that reason to choke somebody? I understood that maybe she was . . . oh, I don't know.

Kelly: I don't know what you mean.

Eric: Well, wasn't that supposedly the reason she killed him?

Debbie: That was the straw that broke the camel's back.

Kelly: That was the breaking point. He broke the canary's neck and she killed him—and they really covered it up. He couldn't find a motive so obviously she would probably get off. First of all could she kill her husband and second of all could these women approve of it and sort of cover it up?

You've also done some evaluation when you've made judgments similar to these:

- I think if you don't read this story metaphorically, the ending just doesn't work. ["Story of an Hour"]
- What I'm saying is that the poem's strong, but simpleminded by today's standards. ["To the Ladies"]
- This is a very provocative piece of writing. ["Polygamy"]
- I really like this. I especially like the part where the women talk about what they saw going on and remembered her as a young cheerful girl who sang. [*Trifles*]

This chapter provides a closer look at each of these three types of presentations.

EXPLICATION

Writing an explication involves showing how the pieces of a work, as you encounter them, contribute to your understanding of the work. As this definition suggests, explications are usually sequential in organization, but their emphasis is not on what comes next in a work (summary does that). Their emphasis is on how each bit of the work contributes to your sense of the whole. Similarly, in an explication you'll often talk about the range of possible meanings that words, phrases, or passages might have, but the emphasis won't be on simply understanding what they mean (paraphrase does that). The emphasis will be on their implications for your overall understanding of the work—on how the various possibilities shape, modify, extend, or challenge that overall understanding.

In your journal entries and group discussions, you've engaged in a form of explication when you've explored the meaning of events and language as part of your effort to reach an understanding of a work. Consider the following journal entries:

Chopin's making a terrific statement about the differences between a woman's perception and how society perceives her. This ending plays on the notion; it's so sarcastically ironic. Her joy was her freedom, not the resurrection of her husband. ("The Story of an Hour")

I don't like the title. It's inconsistent to all that seems positive [about the poem]. Perhaps she's being ironic. I don't know; there are too many questions raised by this title. ("To the Ladies")

In the first excerpt, Kelly explains the ending of Chopin's story in terms of its relationship to what she has come to see as the story's theme. In the second excerpt, she records her effort to do the same with the title of Chudleigh's poem. She finds, however, that the title seems to work against her sense of the poem's strong message, revealing a puzzling ambiguity in the title. Explication would have Kelly go on to explore that ambiguity, identifying the "many questions" and trying to explain how each—or how the very existence of this ambiguity—fits with her sense of the poem. Both entries ponder a piece of a work not just to understand what the piece means in itself but in order to understand how it relates to other parts of the work, especially to the work as a whole. You can see how composing an explication might be a natural outgrowth of your usual activity in coming to terms with a literary work.

Instructors in literature courses frequently give explication assignments to provide students the opportunity to demonstrate both an understanding of a literary work and an ability to use the work to present supporting evidence and reasoning. The key features of explication as a type of formal presentation are these:

1. Emphasis throughout on the overall meaning, point, or purpose of the work.
2. Explanation of how everything discussed relates to the overall meaning, point, or purpose of the work. (No paraphrases or summaries without this explanation.)
3. Discussion of the work in sequence—minor deviations are acceptable if the discussion as a whole is sequential.
4. Attention to
   a. those parts of the work that most strongly demonstrate the basis for your understanding of the work as a whole, and
   b. the more complex or more puzzling parts of the work in order to show how they make sense or fit in relation to your understanding of the work (and to show they don't contradict your view.)
5. Discussion of other parts of the work, if you'll have enough space, with priority for inclusion given to the more significant, complex, or puzzling of the remaining parts. Every part need not be covered in an explication.

Following up briefly on that last point, the shorter the work explicated the greater the possibility for giving it detailed, in-depth discussion. For this reason, explication is generally considered most suitable for short works. But everything in a literary work is seldom worth detailed, in-depth discussion, so explication of longer works is possible. How short, how long? Consider the target length of your written presentation as the dividing line: a work of equivalent length or greater would be a longer work. You'll find that explications of very short works or very short excerpts from longer works will often give close attention to almost every line. At the other extreme, explications of long works will usually, by necessity, deal with much larger portions of the work at a time, pausing to give detailed discussion only to the most crucial of passages. (Note: **Explication of an excerpt from a longer work requires not only attention to how the parts of the excerpt relate to your understanding of the excerpt as a whole but also attention to how the excerpt relates to your understanding of the work as a whole.**)

What follows is a sample explication paper, composed after journal writing, group discussion, and class discussion of several works by the same author. Since explication presents an overall understanding of a work and we'd like to leave open, as much as possible, the opportunity for you to form your own view of the works used throughout this book, the paper deals with a different work. It's a popular work by Robert Frost, "Mending Wall," which you may find somewhat similar thematically to the Frost poem used in Chapter 1. (You'll find a copy of the poem following the essay.)

```
                   Frost's "Mending Wall"
                     by Heather Hussey

      Robert Frost uses his poem, "Mending Wall," as
an arena for the meeting of two opposing forces: the
spirit of rebellion and the belief in tradition.
These two forces are personified in the forms of the
two neighbors. While one is full of new ideas and
imagination, the other holds fast to a more old-fash-
ioned, traditional way of thinking. The two meet at
"spring mending-time" (11), as they do each year, to
repair the damage done to the wall during the winter.
As the two men meet, so do their opposing viewpoints.
      The poem opens with a thought from the more whim-
sical neighbor: "Something there is that doesn't love
a wall" (1). The speaker is taken with the notion
```

that there is some mysterious force at work that is
responsible for the deterioration of the wall--some-
thing more mysterious than nature's "frozen-ground-
swell" (2) and sunshine. He wonders who or what could
have made these gaps, for he has ruled out hunters as
the cause (5) and "No one has seen them made or heard
them made"(10). Regardless, the damage has been done
and both neighbors, each having his share of boulders
on his side, "meet to walk the line/And set the wall
between [them] once again" (13-14). It has become a
habit, and the neighbors stay divided even when they
meet: "We keep the wall between us as we go" (15).
While he picks up the fallen pieces of the wall, however, the speaker considers how unnecessary the wall
is and comments:

> He is all pine and I am all apple orchard
> My apple trees will never get across
> And eat the cones under his pines, I tell him.
> (24-26)

To this fanciful idea, the neighbor only answers, "Good fences make good neighbors" (27), and
continues to rebuild the wall. Once again, the
speaker entertains the idea that "Something there is
that doesn't love a wall, That wants it down" (35-
36). He considers sharing this thought with his neighbor but decides not to: I'd rather / He said it for
himself" (37-38). He realizes that it would be an exercise in futility. His neighbor has to develop such
ideas for himself, but he's not capable of going beyond the saying handed down by his father and thinking for himself. The speaker even describes him as
"An old-stone savage" (40) and adds, "He moves in
darkness" (41), to emphasize the brutish ignorance of
his viewpoint.
    The attitudes of the two neighbors toward the
wall are manifestations of two entirely different
ways of thinking: the old school of thought, with its

blind faith in tradition, and a more "new-fashioned"
idealism which challenges tradition. As the speaker
says, "Before I built a wall I'd ask to know / What I
was walling in or walling out" (32-33). Had the neighbor taken a bit of initiative and questioned the necessity of the wall he so faithfully rebuilds, he
might have realized that there is a whole big world
out there that he has been walling out for too long.

MENDING WALL

Something there is that doesn't love a wall,
That sends the frozen-ground-swell under it,
And spills the upper boulders in the sun;
And makes gaps even two can pass abreast.   5
The work of hunters is another thing:
I have come after them and made repair
Where they have left not one stone on a stone,
But they would have the rabbit out of hiding,
To please the yelping dogs. The gaps I mean,   10
No one has seen them made or heard them made,
But at spring mending-time we find them there.
I let my neighbor know beyond the hill;
And on a day we meet to walk the line
And set the wall between us once again.   15
We keep the wall between us as we go.
To each the boulders that have fallen to each.
And some are loaves and some so nearly balls
We have to use a spell to make them balance:
"Stay where you are until our backs are turned!"   20
We wear our fingers rough with handling them.
Oh, just another kind of outdoor game,
One on a side. It comes to little more:
There where it is we do not need the wall:
He is all pine and I am apple-orchard.   25
My apple trees will never get across
And eat the cones under his pines, I tell him.
He only says, "Good fences make good neighbors."
Spring is the mischief in me, and I wonder
If I could put a notion in his head: 30
"*Why* do they make good neighbors? Isn't it
Where there are cows? But here there are no cows.

Before I built a wall I'd ask to know
What I was walling in or walling out,
And to whom I was like to give offense. 35
Something there is that doesn't love a wall,
That wants it down!" I could say "elves" to him,
But it's not elves exactly, and I'd rather
He said it for himself. I see him there,
Bringing a stone grasped firmly by the top 40
In each hand, like an old-stone savage armed.
He moves in darkness, as it seems to me,
Not of woods only and the shade of trees.
He will not go beyond his father's saying,
And he likes having thought of it so well 45
He says it again, "Good fences make good neighbors."

Explication is frequently associated with new criticism (see Glossary) because it emphasizes close analysis of literary works, but in current practice explication is often broadened to permit discussion of elements outside the work *to the extent that* they help to reveal the implications and relationships of the parts of the work to each other and to the work as a whole. A reader's personal experience that parallels in some way an incident in the work might be introduced to clarify the nature and impact of that incident or to explain the depth of the reader's response to it. For example, you might use a personal experience with a domineering and insensitive friend to gain insight into Chudleigh's conception of the male role in marriage. Other works by an author, other treatments of the same theme, related earlier works known to the author, contemporary events, how part of the work makes you feel, or almost anything might be fair game for brief discussion in an explication if that discussion is used to explore the implications of a portion of the work and to relate that portion to your understanding of the work as a whole.

ANALYSIS AND EVALUATION

As you consider the responses of your group to the literature you're studying, you'll discover that your discussions range far beyond explication. As we mentioned in the beginning of this chapter, one of the things you will have done already in your groups is to begin *analyzing* the literature—that is, breaking it down into parts to see how the parts work together to make a coherent whole. Consider these comments on *Trifles* and "The Story of an Hour," for example:

Even Mrs. Peters, who's married to the law, tries to cover up the evidence. But she's not married to the law in just that way. Mrs. Hale is the real representative here for women's rights. She says, "We live close together and we live far apart." She knows that it's the years of loneliness that did Mr. Wright in, that Mrs. Wright couldn't handle it any more. (*Trifles*)

So she thinks he's dead but nature is telling us something else. There's a whole bunch of different interpretations, I think, about nature in that whole nature paragraph. I think the real one is that because he's dead she's now free and everything is pretty happy. I think that's what Chopin is trying to tell us. ("The Story of an Hour")

These bits of conversation reveal the beginnings of analytical thinking. The students here are focusing in on one element of the literary work in order to make meaning of the whole work. In the first excerpt, Debbie is discussing both *character* (Mrs. Hale) and *language* (Mrs. Hale's comment about living together). In the second, Eric is discussing both *symbol* (the freedom suggested by nature) and *setting* (the view from the closed room). Both students are looking at part of the work in an attempt to see how the whole fits together.

We also mentioned that in your groups you've probably begun *evaluating* the literature—that is, determining how well you think it works as literature. Consider, for example, the following comments on "To the Ladies" and "The Story of an Hour":

Eric: Well, okay. I just didn't think it was a great poem.

Kelly: What did you think was wrong with it?

Eric: The rhyme scheme, the meter is just sort of blah.

Cinde: Yeah, it didn't really work well. Some of the words may be kind of over done. The line, "Fierce as an Eastern prince he grows, / and all his innate rigor shows," might be overdone.

Debbie: We have to also consider the place of women at that time.

Cinde: Oh no. I just think the use as in "Eastern Prince" is kind of overstating the case just a little bit. ("To the Ladies")

I think if you don't read this story metaphorically, the ending just doesn't work. The ending is kind of silly where her husband comes homes and she dies . . . ; it's kind of a hokey ending. What I'm saying is that the ending is very powerful because it's set up in a metaphorical way by all of this dramatic stuff of her problem with her relationship with Brently. ("The Story of an Hour")

In the first excerpt Eric and Cinde are criticizing the poem *as a poem* by focusing on the *meter, rhyme scheme*, and *language*. In the second, Eric is criticizing the *plot* of the story. Both students are making judgments about the *quality* of the works rather than talking about what's in the works.

Formal presentations often involve analysis and evaluation of literature—especially if the writer of the presentation and the audience share a similar knowledge of the work(s) being discussed. While explication is used frequently to indicate to an instructor that a student understands the work, or by an instructor to help students understand it, analysis and evaluation are used to communicate between people on a more equal footing. In the rest of this chapter we will discuss various approaches that you can take in analyzing and evaluating literature. As you prepare to make a formal presentation, you should find that one or two of these approaches will work well with the observations, questions, and conclusions you have formulated in your reading, journals, and group discussions (and possibly your research). These approaches will help you shape the material you've gathered into a formal presentation that can communicate your interpretation to an audience clearly and coherently. The approaches we'll cover include analysis of:

- Character
- Setting
- Point of View
- Symbols
- Figurative Language (Metaphors and Similes)
- Theme

Evaluation often focuses on one or more of these elements; we will discuss evaluation in terms of supporting judgment.

Character Analysis

In fiction and drama (and sometimes in narrative poetry and essays as well), the personalities of the characters are usually essential to making meaning of a literary work. If you find that you have spent a good deal of time discussing a character (or characters), you may decide to use that material to construct a *character analysis*. Character analyses may take many forms: You may describe the personality of a character, explain the motivations of a character, trace the changes in a character, or investigate the relationships between characters. Consider the following excerpts from group discussions of "The Story of an Hour," *Trifles*, and "Polygamy":

Kelly: I like the last line a lot. "She died of heart disease—of joy that kills." I think the whole statement is about the difference between the wife's perception of the position and how society perccives her. ("The Story of an Hour")

Kelly: . . . she could have been so repressed the shock of seeing him again and knowing that she's going to have to go back to that kind of repression could have killed her.

Eric: Nah!

Debbie: Well maybe she'd rather die than go back to that anyway.

Kelly: Maybe she was a sick woman.

Cinde: Well she was sick because she was repressed. Also physically but more so because she was so repressed. ("The Story of an Hour")

In this excerpt, Kelly suggests a possible topic for a character analysis: "The real 'Story of an Hour' is the story of the great disparity between Mrs. Mallard's perception of herself and the world's perception of her." Cinde's comments suggest yet another topic: "Mrs. Mallard's illness is both physical and spiritual, with the heart representing both the primary engine that fires the body and the housing of the soul."

They are kind of set in their ways. The attorney and the sheriff feel there could be nothing of importance in the kitchen where women are used to worrying over trifles but they look everywhere but the important places for this case. What are they doing looking in the barn? It's kind of stupid looking in the barn but isn't that where a man would look for clues? The women with their careful attention to trifles and their knowledge of a woman's psychology were able to figure things out—the queer stitching, the separation, no kids, the frigid husband and the dead canary. They can put all these little tiny things together while the men are out looking in the barn. You can also see that because the women were concerned about Mrs. Wright as a person, they were able to discover things about her. By trying to bring her the quilt, they discover the bird. It's those trifles that solve the murder. But they don't give her away. They don't turn her in. In some way they feel that what happened was just. Even Mrs. Peters, who's married to the law, tries to cover up the evidence. But she's not married to the law in just that way. Mrs. Hale is the real representative here for women's rights. She says, "We live close together and we live far apart." She knows that it's the years of loneliness that did Mr. Wright in, that Mrs. Wright couldn't handle it any more. (*Trifles*)

In this excerpt Eric suggests a wealth of possible topics: "By refusing to pay attention to what they consider 'trifles,' men miss much of what goes on between people—even life-and-death struggles." Or, "In choosing between her husband (the law) and Mrs. Wright (her spiritual sister), Mrs. Peters is choosing humanity over legality." Or, "Mrs. Peters' comment that 'We live close together and we live far apart' speaks volumes about the plight of women at the turn of the century."

The funny thing about the narrator is that I thought she had already made a judgment by the first paragraph on the second page. It just seemed like her whole tone was completely negative. She just said, "Well I'm not really close to it but I don't know how I feel." I don't buy that. I really think that she had already made up her mind just by the way she said, "What do you think of this?" I think that maybe more than the TV, the more threatening thing is her because you can tell by her reaction that she's very westernized. It took a lot for him to say, "What do you think?" because if she objected when she gets there, she's going to upset the household. ("Polygamy")

Cinde's observations on the narrator of this essay might suggest the following topic: "Although the narrator of 'Polygamy' tries to convince us (and herself) that she's objective and neutral, her presentation of the situation reveals more about her own judgments than about her in-laws' lifestyle."

As you can see from these excerpts, the notion of composing a character analysis is not something that's superimposed on the material, but rather something that grows naturally out of a discussion of the literary work. One of the great values of exploring literature collaboratively is that you usually have material that will fit any number of standard presentation forms.

Analysis of Setting

The action in a literary work takes place in a particular environment—the location, the social and cultural environment, and the time all affect characters and their behavior. A focus on setting can heighten awareness of the various influences on characters' behavior and can help readers understand the action. If you have made comments about locations, time periods, or social/cultural issues in your preparation, you may be able to use those comments in an analysis of *setting*. Consider the following comments about "To the Ladies," *Trifles*, and "Polygamy":

> I was curious about the reaction of her audience and what kind of reception she got. I'm surprised they didn't burn her at the stake. ("To the Ladies")

Kelly's observation calls up questions about both the time period and social environment in which the poem takes place. Her question might suggest the following topic: "Eighteenth century England was singularly unreceptive to Lady Mary Chudleigh's ideas about women's rights; her poem represents a threat to a closed, ordered world."

> That kitchen! It's so dismal and cold. I grew up in a rural area, and I remember how—oh, I don't know, how *warm* the kitchen always was. It was big and had a big stove and in the winter you'd have hot cocoa after coming in from playing. I mean, this kitchen seems so cramped and dirty and cold. That just did something to me from the beginning. (*Trifles*)

Eric had commented on the kitchen as early as his preliminary reading of the play; it's not surprising that he returns to the topic in group discussion. His observation might lead to the following topic: "The atmosphere of the kitchen in *Trifles* suggests that the murder of John Wright is the result of some fundamental evil in the house."

> I thought it was kind of interesting how the cultures—how that works and what the dynamic is there. It doesn't seem that the polygamy is all that bad for these people. It seems like culture. These two women are happy. . . . If you're from Arabia and you're from a Nomadic culture that sort of thing is going to happen. You've got to have some sort of a legal attitude towards marriage otherwise it just doesn't work. . . . I can see how we would complain in the west that this isn't a romantic, sharing, co-dependent relationship. ("Polygamy")

Eric's observation here calls attention to the fact that polygamy is *natural* in parts of the Arab world of 1960. His comments might suggest the following topic: "To consider the morality of polygamy from an exclusively western perspective is to ignore the culture that produced the practice and in which it flourishes." (In fact, Eric did pursue this idea further in group discussion.)

You may have noticed overlapping of analyses of character and setting; there's nothing wrong with such overlapping. While it's possible in an analysis to pull out part of a literary work, it's impossible to isolate that part from everything else in the work. Thus a setting analysis of "Polygamy," for example, will also involve a discussion of the narrator's biases and how they reflect her character as much as they reflect the culture she's commenting on. Literature cannot be broken down into pieces like tinker-toys; each element of the literature is integrally related to every other element.

Analysis of Point of View

The narrator of the story always influences the way the story is told. If you find yourself assessing the reliability of the character from whose viewpoint the story is told, examining the narrator's knowledge, prejudices, position in the story, or relationship to other characters, then you may be able to use your material to construct an analysis of *point of view*. Consider the observations made here on *Trifles* and "Polygamy":

> The women with their careful attention to trifles and their knowledge of a woman's psychology were able to figure things out—the queer stitching, the separation, no kids, the frigid husband and the dead canary. They can put all these little tiny things together while the men are out looking in the barn. (*Trifles*)

This excerpt from Eric's longer observation on character could conceivably lead to an analysis of point of view. (After all, point of view is closely connected to character.) Eric's comments might lead to this topic: "While we hear the opinions of both men and women in *Trifles*, our sympathies are clearly intended to lie with the women."

> The funny thing about the narrator is that I thought she had already made a judgment by the first paragraph on the second page. It just seemed like her whole tone was completely negative. She just said, "Well I'm not really close to it but I don't know how I feel." I don't buy that. I really think that she had already made up her mind just by the way she said, "What do you think of this?" I think that maybe more than the TV, the more threatening thing is her because you can tell by her reaction that she's very westernized. It took a lot for him to say, "What do you think?" because if she objected when she gets there, she's going to upset the household. ("Polygamy")

This is another excerpt from the section on character, and again the observations can serve more than one purpose. Eric's assessment of the narrator's biases might suggest the following topic: "Ann Grace Mojtabai's characterization of polygamy is clearly biased; her immersion in western values prevents her from judging the practice objectively." (You may also notice here that Eric's observations on setting would be relevant to this topic.)

You're probably aware by now that the same observations can be used to develop topics that move in different directions. Character is closely related to point of view, but sometimes setting is related as well. Interrelationships between various elements of literature help make it such a fascinating area to explore.

Analysis of Symbols

Without even being aware of it, we all use symbols when we tell stories. We might focus attention on a ring, for example, in telling the story of a failed romance. In literary works symbols work to focus readers attention on issues involved in the story, and an analysis of those symbols can help readers make meaning from the work. If you notice that you have commented on the significance of particular objects or places in a literary work, you may well have material that will contribute to an analysis of *symbols*. Consider the following comments on *Trifles* and "The Story of an Hour":

> I especially like the part where the women talk about Mrs. Wright before she was married and the women saw what was going on and remembered her as a young cheerful girl who sang. . . . She loved the bird. It was all the joy she had and he killed it. (*Trifles*)

Kelly's comment on the bird is interesting because without even realizing it, she actually says that the bird is a symbol: "It was all the joy she had. . . . " Thus a topic comes naturally from her observation: "In Susan Glaspell's *Trifles*, the bird symbolizes Mrs. Wright's joy. When he kills the bird, her husband has symbolically killed Mrs. Wright herself."

> So she thinks he's dead but nature is telling us something else. There's a whole bunch of different interpretations, I think, about nature in that whole nature paragraph. I think the real one is that because he's dead she's now free and everything is pretty happy. I think that's what Chopin is trying to tell us. ("The Story of an Hour")

Eric's observation, like Kelly's, points directly to a symbolic use of nature. He's convinced that nature doesn't just exist for its own sake in the story. His topic might go something like this: "In 'The Story of an Hour,' nature represents the freedom and joy that Mrs. Mallard thinks she'll experience now that her husband is dead."

You may have noticed that Eric's comment was used at the beginning of the chapter to illustrate setting as well as symbol. Once again, the same observation can lead to a different topic. In fact, symbols are often so subtle (even in life) that they can be characters, parts of the setting, even seemingly insignificant objects. The fact that something is a symbol in a literary work does not prevent it from serving other purposes as well.

Analysis of Figurative Language (Metaphors and Similes)

A literary work is important in part because of the story it tells, but the way in which the story is told is what makes the work memorable. When you analyze *metaphors* and *similes* (see Chapter 2) in a work, you develop a feel for the author's (and sometimes the character's) sensibilities. The metaphors an author uses can help readers understand the perspective from which he or she is writing. (For example, an author who refers to a love affair using the metaphor of a stormy sea has a quite different perspective from an author who uses the metaphor of a calm lake.) If you find that you have commented on comparisons made by a writer, you may be able to expand those comments into an analysis of figurative language. Debbie, for example, made the following comments on "Polygamy" and "To the Ladies":

> She seems to be creating a picture for us—the pool in the center of the flagstones is "set like a turquoise." That's an interesting image, given how dreary her description of the yard is. ("Polygamy")
>
> She carries that comparison of servant to master—that's how the poem opens—throughout the poem. That's why I think the "Eastern Prince" line works. She even calls the husband the wife's "God" at one place. I think she's really consistent in her comparisons. ("To the Ladies")

Debbie's comments on these two selections illustrate that even the figurative language can be effective in all types of writing. The essay and the poem probably constitute for most people the two extremes of literary genres: one is straightforward, usually not considered "imaginative" literature, while the other is considered the epitome of imagination. And yet metaphor and simile are used to advantage in each.

Analysis of Theme

Most literary works can be classified according to a theme—a central idea or purpose found in the work. As you read a selection, you try to incorporate it into your experience of the world; in order to do that, you have to have a sense of what the work means as a whole. Very few literary works can be reduced to a single theme; because different readers come to a selection with different perspectives, most worthwhile literary works support several themes. If you notice mention of general ideas or statements about a whole work, you may be able to use that material to compose an analysis of theme. The following comments on *Trifles* and "The Story of an Hour" suggest the beginnings of thematic analysis:

> In some way they feel that what happened was just. Even Mrs. Peters, who's married to the law, tries to cover up the evidence. But she's not married to the law in just that way. Mrs. Hale is the real representative here for women's rights. She says, "We live close together and we live far apart." She knows that it's the years of loneliness that did Mr. Wright in, that Mrs. Wright couldn't handle it any more.
>
> The attorney and the sheriff feel there could be nothing of importance in the kitchen where women are used to worrying over trifles but they look everywhere but the important places for this case. What are they doing looking in the barn? It's kind of stupid looking in the barn but isn't that where a man would look for clues? The women with their careful attention to trifles and their knowledge of a woman's psychology were able to figure things out—the queer stitching, the separation, no kids, the frigid husband and the dead canary. They can put all these little tiny things together while the men are out looking in the barn. You can also see that because the women were concerned about Mrs. Wright as a person, they were able to discover things about her. By trying to bring her the quilt, they discover the bird. It's those trifles that solve the murder. (*Trifles*)

In the first excerpt, Kelly suggests that the play is offering an interpretation of justice that's at odds with our legal system. She might be able to expand on that in an essay, stating as a tentative theme: "Although in the eyes of the law Mrs. Wright is simply a murderer, the women in the play are convinced that a higher justice has been served by Mr. Wright's death." But later Kelly focuses on an alternative theme: "In dismissing the women's concerns as trifles, the men reveal their total ignorance of the essential elements of life." She's still looking at the same play, but she moves in different directions as she makes meaning of it. The specificity of her comments indicates that an analysis of the play can support these two themes (and probably others as well).

> [*Responding to a question about the apparent equation of death and freedom*] There's a whole bunch of different interpretations, I think, about nature in that whole nature paragraph. I think the real one is that because he's dead she's now free and everything is pretty happy. I think that's what Chopin is trying to tell us. This could be a story not of death and dealing with death but of a woman's attempt to get out from under the domination of man only to be returned to it. Kind of a cyclical thing. It only takes her an hour to truly get over his death. She seems like she had been thinking about it for quite a while, getting rid of him, and his death gave her a chance to realize it. ("The Story of an Hour")

Eric's observations led him to state this tentative theme for the short story: "When our surroundings become so oppressive that we see no way out, then death becomes an expression of freedom or liberation." Even though the theme is stated rather vaguely at this point, Eric's conclusions about the story are based on solid evidence, particularly the imagery in what he calls the "nature paragraph." His reading of the story will support his statement of theme.

In discussing theme in a literary work, you will find yourself making reference to many of the other elements covered in this chapter—character, setting, point of view, symbols, and figurative language. Since theme deals with the work *as a whole*, your observations concerning certain features or parts of the selection become relevant in your analysis of theme.

Evaluation (Supporting Your Judgments)

In several of the comments discussed earlier in the chapter, you may have noted students making judgments about the quality of the literature. That a work has been published is no reason to assume that all readers will find it worthwhile; it's perfectly acceptable to evaluate the literature you read. However, readers should always remember that evaluation is more than simply a statement of taste. Just as in any other form of argument, the reader arguing for or against the quality of a literary work is obliged to support that argument with specific evidence. We find the beginnings of supporting evidence in the criticism of "To the Ladies" and "The Story of an Hour," parts of which appeared at the beginning of the chapter:

Eric: Well, okay. I just didn't think it was a great poem.

Kelly: What did you think was wrong with it?

Eric: The rhyme scheme, the meter is just sort of blah.

Cinde: Yeah, it didn't really work well. Some of the words may be kind of overdone. The line, "Fierce as an Eastern prince he grows, / and all his innate rigor shows," might be overdone.

Debbie: We have to also consider the place of women at that time.

Cinde: Oh no. I just think the use of words as in "Eastern Prince" is kind of overstating the case just a little bit. ("To the Ladies")

Kelly: You mentioned a red herring. What does that mean?

Eric: I learned that last semester in Creative Writing class where the writer pulls this strange ending on you in that last minute which is completely unexpected.

Cinde: I think they want to add shock value to it.

Eric: Yeah, well that's a red herring.

Kelly: But isn't she shocked too?

Eric: I'm not sure what I was saying when I wrote this. Oh, this is what I meant. I think if you don't read this story metaphorically, the ending just doesn't work. The ending is kind of silly where her husband comes home and she dies.

Cinde: Well, if she did have heart problems such a shock could kill her.

Eric: Yeah, but it's kind of a hokey ending. What I'm saying is that the ending is very powerful because it's set up in a metaphorical way by all of this dramatic stuff of her problem with her relationship with Brently. ("The Story of an Hour")

Both Cinde and Eric are challenged by others in the group to defend their judgments. (This, by the way, is one of the beauties of collaborative learning—by the time you begin making a formal presentation you've already marshaled some support for your views.) While their evidence from the wording of the poem and the realism of the ending of the story would be insufficient for a formal presentation, they have nevertheless begun to think about how to justify their judgments. As they prepare formal evaluations, they know where to look to find supporting evidence.

As we mentioned earlier, evaluations can involve analysis of character, setting, point of view, symbols, figurative language, and theme. The difference between an analysis and an evaluation lies in the writer's purpose: The writer who analyzes a selection is interested in communicating a particular reading of the selection to the audience, while the writer who evaluates is interested in using that analysis to communicate a judgment of the quality of the literary work.

The following is a paper Kelly Leighton composed from her observations on and conversations about *Trifles*. Following the paper is a brief discussion of its evolution, from Kelly's initial notes through her journal entries and discussions with other students.

One Man's Trifle Is Another Woman's Evidence

by Kelly Leighton

Susan Glaspell's play <u>Trifles</u> is appropriately named, for it is the things that men consider useless observations that result in the women's solving the murder of John Wright. As the men move self-importantly through the house and barn, the women look at the little things that truly indicate what has gone on in the house. Not only do Mrs. Peters and Mrs. Hale solve the murder, but they show an understanding of what is important in life as well. In dismissing the women's concerns as trifles, the men reveal their total ignorance of the essential elements of life. This theme of male ignorance runs through the entire play.

The county attorney, Mr. Henderson, and the sheriff, Mr. Peters, feel there could be nothing important in the kitchen where women are used to worrying over "trifles." At the beginning of the play, when the men are deciding where to look for clues, the attorney asks Sheriff Peters if there's anything important in the kitchen. The sheriff replies, "Nothing here but kitchen things" (70). So they turn their attention to the more "important" places, the barn, for example. What could they be looking for in the barn? It is while the men are in the barn that the women find the first clue: the quilt. When the men laugh at them for wondering if the quilt was being quilted or knotted, the sheriff's wife explains,

---

"apologetically," that "they've got awful important things on their minds" (73). But it is a woman, Mrs. Hale, who notices that the square Mrs. Wright has been working on is poorly stitched, while the others are all perfectly done. And both she and Mrs. Peters realize the significance of the quilting, because they look toward the door where the men have just left. Mrs. Hale even goes so far as to rip out the bad sewing and redo the square, as if she knows that the evidence might be bad for Mrs. Wright. Their attention to "trifles" has uncovered a clue that the men, with "awful important things on their minds," have not only missed, but have not even looked for.

While the men are searching all over the place for the kind of clues they would look for, the women find the one piece of evidence that would prove the county attorney's case. Mrs. Peters has explained to Mrs. Hale that what the men are looking for is "a mo-tive; something to show anger, or--sudden feeling" (72). That is just what the women find when they dis-cover the bird cage with its door hinge broken "as if someone must have been rough with it" (74). Anger and sudden feeling are certainly evident in the condition of the bird cage. And, of course, the bird with its wrung neck in the sewing box is clear proof of anger. Mrs. Peters, the sheriff's wife, is quick to point out that in strictly legal terms, "We don't know who killed the bird." But Mrs. Hale, who relies on women's ways of understanding things rather than the legalistic ways men use, replies, "I knew John Wright" (76). Both women then realize what it would have meant for Mrs. Wright to lose the canary. Mrs. Hale says, "If there's been years and years of noth-ing, then a bird to sing to you, it would be awful--still, after the bird was still," and Mrs. Peters adds, "I know what stillness is. When we homesteaded in Dakota, and my first baby died—after he was two years old, and me with no other then--" (76). The men are too busy searching for clues to think about what life must have been like for Mrs. Wright. They consider such speculation, like the women's attention to the preserves, to be merely "trifles." But lives are made up of trifles, and the women know that.

How is it that the women are able to solve the case while the men are not? The women, with their careful attention to trifles and their knowledge of a woman's psychology, put little things together—the messy kitchen, the uneven stitching, the isolation, the frigid husband, and the dead canary. They put all these "trifles" together while the men are out looking in the barn. Because the women are concerned about Mrs. Wright as a person, they are able to discover things about her. It is only by accident that they discover the bird, but that accident results from their trying to bring Mrs. Wright things that she might want while she is in jail. It is those trifles that solve the murder.

The women do not stop once they solve the crime, however. They actually remove the evidence that might lead the county attorney to find the motive he is looking for. Why do they do this? I think that the play suggests that a higher justice was served when John Wright died, that he, like the men we meet in the play, could not appreciate the trifles that make a woman's life meaningful. The women decide that if men are so blind to what is really important in life, then they do not deserve to have the evidence. The county attorney does not even bother to look at what the women are bringing to Mrs. Wright, because he cannot imagine anything important in the things. The final irony comes when Mr. Henderson sarcastically congratulates "the ladies" on the only discovery he thinks anyone has made in the house:

> COUNTY ATTORNEY [facetiously]. Well, Henry, at least we found out that she was not going to quilt it. She was going to--what is it you call it, ladies?

> MRS. HALE [her hand against her pocket]. We call
> it--knot it, Mr. Henderson. (77)
>
> This last line of the play, with its suggestion of
> the knot that was tied around John Wright's neck,
> brings home clearly the theme that in their blindness
> to "trifles," men miss the true meaning of life.

You may recall from the sample annotations in Chapter 2 (pp. 29–34) that Kelly's initial interest in the play lay in the images of conversation and communication, and not in the differences between men's and women's perceptions. In her journal, however, Kelly asked herself what the title of the play meant, and wrote the following:

> The women pay careful attention to trifles—the stitching of the quilt piece, the canary cage, while the men can't imagine anything of importance in the kitchen. The men don't pay attention to "trifles" like how the Wrights lived either. They go off to the barn to find clues.

In group discussions, Kelly listened to Cinde's and Eric's objections to the play's portrayal of men (p. 80), considering those observations in light of her journal entry and her lengthy statement reproduced earlier in this chapter (p. 145). Cinde's questions about the impact of John Wright's killing the canary (p. 80) also seems to have influenced Kelly's interpretation of women's sensitivity, and Eric's comments about the "cramped and dirty and cold" kitchen (p. 141) seem to have contributed to Kelly's analysis of the women's attention to "trifles." (If you think back to Part One and Chapter 6, Case Study, you'll notice that these students' comments in group discussion reflect their annotations and journal entries.) In the paper, Kelly has synthesized these observations and formalized many of her comments, adding evidence from the play to support her conclusions.

CONCLUSIONS

As you develop your informal observations into formal presentations, you'll find that your annotations, journal entries, and notes from discussion and research are invaluable to you. Rather than sitting down and staring at a blank page, wondering what to write, you will sit down to sift through a collection of material that offers you possible directions to move in, possible topics to consider, and evidence to support the statement you ultimately choose to make about a literary work. The explication, the formal analysis, and the evaluation are the culmination of the work you began to do when you made your first marginal note on the page.

10 Conventions of Literary Analysis

WHY MAKE REFERENCE TO SOURCES?

As you have learned in the previous chapters, in the collaborative classroom there is no single correct interpretation of a literary work; rather, the meaning of a work can differ in different social settings, or for different readers within the same setting. You have also learned that if you want to reach consensus about an observation, you must direct attention to the reasons for considering one interpretation or another. *What* you think will be more likely to interest—and possibly convince—people when you can also tell them *why* you think so. Even in initial group discussions of a work, members are asked to justify their positions. For example, in the discussion of Chudleigh's "To the Ladies," Eric makes the following observation:

> Here's proof that injustice doesn't always lead to great poetry.

During the discussion that follows, Cinde expresses her agreement with Eric, and then Debbie and Kelly ask the two what they mean. Cinde's reply is as follows:

> Some of the words may be kind of overdone. The line, "Fierce as an Eastern prince he grows, / And all his innate rigor shows," might be overdone.

This quotation may or may not convince the others that Chudleigh "overdoes" things in her poem, but it provides a focus for the discussion and offers possible support for Eric's initial observation. The group discussion becomes more meaningful as members support their observations. Once you've decided upon an interpretation and prepare to present it formally, the responsibility for supporting your interpretation becomes even more serious. If your readers are to accept your interpretation as valid, then you must make the connection between your ideas and what appears in the literary work (and possibly in other sources). After having worked through Chapters 2–4 of this book, you're probably aware that most interpretation begins with just the reader and the author, then moves through annotating the text, writing in a journal, and discussing in groups. As you discovered in Chapter 5, you may sometimes choose (or be required) to make use of other writers in your presentation, engaging in research. When you prepare a formal presentation, whether you're referring to the literary work itself (called a *primary source*) or to a related work (called a *secondary source*), you will find it necessary to *document* sources, that is, to tell your reader where you found certain types of information.

When you make a formal presentation in a literature class or write an article for a literary journal, you are participating as a member of a specific literate community. This community, recognizing the importance of documentation, has developed a system that provides readers with the necessary information to identify a source without unnecessary disruption of the writer's message. The literary community's guidelines for documentation might be more appropriately called "rules," since they are fairly rigid. You may want to consider documentation guidelines as "rules of the road" for writers—while they're not always necessary for clear communication, they create a comfortable sense of familiarity for readers. Thus, while you were assured in earlier chapters that there is no single "right" interpretation of a literary work, you will be told in this chapter that there are indeed right (and wrong) ways to use and to document sources. Your exploration of literature so far has prepared you to join the literature community, sharing with others your formal presentations about the works you read. This community has agreed upon certain guidelines, or conventions, so that all readers and writers recognize the appropriate signals for quotations or documentation of sources.

Many of you may be familiar with documentation from other courses in which you wrote research papers. If so, then you should find the material in this chapter familiar. But even if you are unfamiliar with documentation, the common-sense rules that apply to literary analysis should pose no great problem for you.

A final note before getting on with the chapter: While conventions apply to both oral and written presentations, the actual documentation formats refer only to written analyses. For this reason, and to avoid unnecessary confusion, most of this chapter will refer to written presentations.

WHEN SHOULD REFERENCE BE MADE TO SOURCES?

If you are like most students, sometimes you are uncertain about when to refer to a literary work. You may have been told that in college, you are to assume that the audience is familiar with the work being discussed. You also may have been cautioned to avoid writing plot summaries in place of literary analyses. How, then, are you supposed to know when to refer to the work? The purpose of your paper will often dictate both the need to refer to a source and the nature of the reference. The ways in which you can refer to a literary work can be divided into three categories:

- *Summary/general mention*, or briefly referring to a scene, incident, or idea;
- *Paraphrase*, or repeating something the author has written in your own words; and
- *Quotation*, or copying directly the words of the author.

Whether you choose to summarize, to paraphrase, or to quote depends on your purpose in presenting the material. (Only paraphrase and quotation require full documentation; the method of documentation will be discussed later in the chapter.)

Summary

At times you will want to remind your reader of a particular scene, bit of dialogue, or description. For example, assume that in discussing Mrs. Mallard's transformation in "The Story of an Hour" you want to remind the reader of the moment when she first recognizes the profound impact of her husband's death. All your reader needs in this case is a general mention of the scene; you might write something like this: "When Mrs. Mallard looks out the window and sees the fullness of spring in the world outside her house, she begins to understand the freedom she's gained." In this case you are referring to a scene that any careful reader will recall; therefore, you need not go into any more detail when mentioning it, nor do you need to pinpoint exactly where the scene appears in the story. Furthermore, since you are only offering the reader a reminder rather than calling attention to the scene, there is no reason to quote. Unless the wording of the scene is crucial to your point, or the reader might have trouble recalling the scene, there is no need for you to present a quotation. A mention of the scene is sufficient for your purpose.

In longer works, brief summaries or even mention of where in the work a scene occurs is necessary to orient the reader. In discussing a scene from a novel, for example, you may want to help the reader recall the scene by mentioning the chapter in which the scene appears, the point in the narration/plot, or the page number(s). In this case, you are offering the reader some assistance, not calling special attention to the scene itself, so you can simply make a reference without quoting anything from the scene.

You may also find summarizing useful when dealing with secondary sources. Suppose that you want to provide your reader with some interesting biographical information on Chopin—for example, that it was not until after her husband's death that she began her professional writing career. The information is relevant to your purpose, but not crucial. In this case you can simply refer to the information in the most general way. As in the other examples, your purpose here is not to call special attention to the information, but merely to provide it for the reader's benefit. Thus a general mention or summary is all you need.

Paraphrase

Suppose that you want to call the reader's attention to a line in the story that is sometimes overlooked, or that is relevant but not crucial to your interpretation. When describing Mrs. Mallard's grief, Chopin's exact words are, "She knew that she would weep again when she saw the kind, tender hands folded in death; the face that had never looked save with love upon her, fixed and gray and dead." You want to remind your readers that Mrs. Mallard does indeed feel grief, but your focus is her newfound freedom. Furthermore, it is the *idea* of Mrs. Mallard's grief, not Chopin's *words*, that are important to your presentation. Thus rather than quoting the lines, you *paraphrase* them, expressing Chopin's idea in *your own words*. Your paraphrase might read something like this: "When Mrs. Mallard imagines seeing her husband's kind hands and loving face in the casket, she knows that she will cry." Your purpose is served because you remind readers of the line without distracting them from your primary focus.

When using secondary sources, you will find yourself choosing to paraphrase frequently. The guidelines for paraphrasing from secondary sources are roughly the same as those for paraphrasing from primary sources. Assume, for example, that you want to refer to a notion put forth by Carrie Chapman Catt, founder of the League of Women Voters. You don't feel that it's necessary to use Catt's words; the presentation is quite straightforward and not especially memorable. But you do want to refer to her *idea*. Catt says the following about objections to woman suffrage:

> In the United States, at least, we need no longer argue woman's intellectual, moral and physical qualification for the ballot with the intelligent. The Reason of the best of our citizens has long been convinced. The justice of the argument has been admitted, but sex-prejudice is far from conquered.

Presenting this idea in your own words, you might write,

> Carrie Chapman Catt felt that while Americans were intellectually reconciled to women's equality, their prejudices had not yet been eliminated.

Direct Quotation

In key parts of your presentation you will want to direct the reader's attention to specific parts of the literary work. Since *quoting* involves incorporating an author's exact words into your text, a discussion of quotation is necessarily more complicated than a discussion of summary or paraphrase. In this section you will learn about issues involved with quoting:

- Reasons for quoting
- Quoting exactly
- Integrating quotations

Reasons for Quoting

There are several reasons why you might choose to use a quotation rather than a paraphrase or a summary:

- *Key passage*—If you refer to a passage that is essential to the purpose of your paper, chances are you'll want to use a direct quotation from that passage.
- *Powerful language*—If the author's wording is so powerful that a paraphrase would be ineffective, then direct quotation is a wise choice.
- *Distinguished reputation*—If a source for your paper is well respected and his or her words will lend credence to your analysis, then it's beneficial to use a direct quotation from that source.
- *Concise statement*—If the description (often of a theory or school of thought) is so concisely stated that a paraphrase would be ineffective, then reproduce the exact description.

Key Passage:

Perhaps there is a key passage that figures prominently in your analysis. For example, if you want to point out the irony of Mrs. Mallard's death—that it represents her ultimate freedom, you will probably want to quote the last lines of the text: The doctor claims that she died of "joy that kills." These three words epitomize the irony of the story; a simple mention of the final scene will not highlight the irony, nor will a paraphrase of the line. The words themselves are essential. (Even if all the words in a passage are not essential, you may wish to quote an entire passage if you will be referring to specific words later as you discuss the passage in detail.)

Powerful Language:

There may be times when the author's words are so powerful, so crucial to your analysis that you simply must reproduce them. For example, Chopin's description of Mrs. Mallard as she emerges from her room is very powerful: "There was a feverish triumph in her eyes, and she carried herself unwittingly like a goddess of Victory." You may wish to reproduce that description verbatim, even though a paraphrase would adequately reflect your point.

The quotation in this instance makes the point all the more compelling because of its power.

Distinguished Reputation:

Perhaps one of the sources you are using has a distinguished reputation, and you feel that using this person's actual words will strengthen your position. In this case, it can be helpful to use a quotation rather than a paraphrase. Elizabeth Cady Stanton is recognized as one of the great feminists of the nineteenth century; thus in a paper on women's rights, her own words would carry more weight than a paraphrase:

> According to Elizabeth Cady Stanton, "Whatever the theories may be of woman's dependence on man, in the supreme moments of her life, he cannot bear her burdens."

Concise Statement:

On occasion you will find a quotation that is so concise that paraphrasing would make the idea lose some of its clarity, or would take up more words than the original quotation. Often descriptions of technical terms or schools of thought are better presented in quoted form rather than in paraphrase. Ann Grace Mojtabai, for example, describes the Shi-ite custom of temporary marriage concisely:

> In the mut'a marriage, a term is stipulated—a night, a year, a decade, an hour, whatever. A set term, a mehr—a wedding endowment for the woman—mutual consent and a contract specifying all this are required.

A paraphrase of this description might well take more space than the quotation itself, and would likely lose some of the clarity of Mojtabai's words.

Quoting Exactly

The preceding discussion indicates that the decision to use a quotation is not a casual one. Because of the power of quotations, it is necessary that they be reproduced *exactly* as they appear in the original. If you choose to quote rather than to paraphrase or summarize, then you obviously think that the writer's wording is crucial. It only makes sense, then, to be certain that the quotation is an exact duplicate of the original. Perhaps it's best to consider yourself a human copy machine when you are quoting: you will reproduce what the writer has said in the same way that a copier would reproduce it. If any changes are to be made—and often changes are necessary—they are made *after* you have written out the quotation in its exact form. (Making changes within quotations is covered later.)

Integrating Quotations

Once you have decided to use a quotation, you will have to determine how to fit it into your text. Just as convention dictates how to present a quotation, is also dictates how to integrate quotations into your text. If you have invested a good deal of time and effort into your presentation, you want your audience to be able to follow it smoothly. Thus it's important to present quotations in such a way that they do not disrupt the presentation; specifically, quotations must be introduced and altered appropriately.

Introducing Quotations:

One of the few "rules" of using quotations that most people agree upon is that a writer should not simply "shove" a quotation into the text. A quotation must be anchored to the writer's own text; to suspend it is to give the reader no indication of how the quotation fits into the presentation as a whole. If you find yourself tossing quotations out, like darts on a game board, chances are you haven't thought about how those quotations fit with your text. It's likely that such quotations will end up suspended in your paper. The following passage illustrates a suspended quotation:

> In Susan Glaspell's *Trifles*, Mrs. Hale's opinion of men is not very positive. "Men's hands aren't always as clean as they might be."

If you think back to your group discussions of literary works, you should recall that on occasion a student would use a quotation to support his or her point. It's doubtful that in conversation anyone would suspend a quotation as in the preceding example; instead, it's more likely that the quotation is made a part of the statement. In a group discussion of *Trifles*, Kelly makes the following observation:

> Mrs. Hale is the real representative here for women's rights. She says, "We live close together, and we live far apart." She knows that it's the years of loneliness that did Mr. Wright in, that Mrs. Wright couldn't handle it any more.

Even in casual conversation, then, where conventions of literary analysis do not apply, speakers sense the need to integrate quotations into their text rather than simply suspending them. It's all the more important in a formal presentation, where there is little or no feedback from the audience, for quotations to be smoothly integrated into the text. The preceding suspended quotation might be integrated into the text in the following way:

In Susan Glaspell's *Trifles*, Mrs. Hale's opinion of men is not very positive. Her comment, "Men's hands aren't always as clean as they might be," could be taken metaphorically, indicating her observations of men involved in "dirty" business.

This quotation is now integrated into the text by an introductory comment, but it is also followed by an explanation of precisely how the writer interprets the quotation. A follow-up comment calls attention to what the writer wants noticed in a quotation, making clear the logical connection between the quotation and the rest of the text. This writer has clearly thought a good deal about the quotation; it hasn't simply been shoved in because the instructor requires the use of quotations.

There are a number of ways of integrating quotations into your text; here are a few examples of introductory (or concluding) expressions:

[She] says,
[He] writes,
[She] concludes,
[He] observes,
[She] suggests,
According to [him],
In the words of [her],

If you find it impossible to integrate a quotation into your text—perhaps because it is too long or difficult, you may introduce the quotation with a complete sentence of your own, ending with a colon. In the following example, a complete introductory sentence both introduces the quotation and indicates its importance:

Charlotte Perkins Gilman uses the symbol of the wedding ring in order to highlight the limitations of women's opportunities at the turn of the century: "Wealth, power, social distinction, fame,—not only these, but home and happiness, reputation, ease and pleasure, her bread and butter,—all, must come to her through a small gold ring."

Altering Quotations:

One of the problems that arises when you integrate quotations into your own text is that often the structure of the quotation doesn't quite fit the structure of your sentence. If you're quoting, you're obliged to repeat the author's exact words, so what can you do to make the quotation fit? There are several ways of integrating quotations smoothly:

1. Use only a phrase rather than an entire sentence.
2. Use ellipses to indicate omissions.
3. Use brackets to indicate substitutions.

Phrases are far more easily integrated than complete sentences. If only a part of a passage is necessary to your purpose, then you may want to consider integrating a phrase into your own sentence:

Gilman feels that women's achievements are limited to those gained "through a small gold ring."

Ellipses are used when you eliminate unnecessary words that may distract a reader or interfere with smooth reading. To do this, you simply substitute ellipses, a series of three spaced periods, for the omitted material—regardless of whether you've omitted one or ten words. Suppose that in using the Gilman quotation, for example, you want to eliminate the phrase "to her" in order to be consistent with the plural "women" in the introduction to the quotation. The altered quotation would look like this:

Charlotte Perkins Gilman uses the symbol of the wedding ring in order to highlight the limitations of women's opportunities at the turn of the century: "Wealth, power, social distinction, fame,—not only these, but home and happiness, reputation, ease and pleasure, her bread and butter,—all, must come . . . through a small gold ring."

When omitting the end of a sentence, or when omitting more than one sentence, use a period first and then ellipses—a total of four spaced periods. Suppose you wished to eliminate the last four words of the following quotation: "But all that she may wish to have, all that she may wish to do, must come through a single channel and a single choice." The altered quotation would look like this:

"But all that she may wish to have, all that she may wish to do, must come through a single channel. . . . "

Brackets can be used to add to or change something in a quotation. Perhaps the tense of a verb is different from the tense of your presentation, or the author uses a pronoun and it's necessary for your reader to know who the author is talking about. In such cases, include the substituted material in brackets, as in the following example:

"But all that [a woman] may wish to have, all that she may wish to do, must come through a single channel and a single choice."

On rare occasions you will find an error in a quotation. Convention dictates that you repeat the author's words exactly as they appear in the original, but you don't want the error to appear to be your own. In such cases, insert the Latin word *sic*, meaning *so*, in brackets following the error. This insert alerts the reader to the fact that the error appears in the original. For example, if an author has referred to Charlotte Perkins *Gillman* rather than *Gilman*, you would present the quotation this way:

> "Charlotte Perkins Gillman [*sic*] was an outspoken proponent of women's rights."

Indicating Quotations:

Integrate into your text quotations of fewer than three lines of poetry or four lines of prose. Use double quotation marks around the quoted material, as in the preceding examples. For a quotation within a quotation, use double marks for the larger quotation, and single marks for the internal quotation:

> When her father-in-law asks what she thinks of his two wives, Grace Mojtabai tells us that she is careful in her response: "My judgment, when it came, wouldn't be narrow, biased or culture-bound. 'Customs differ,' I said."

For longer quotations (more than three lines of poetry or four lines of prose), set off the quotation by indenting it ten spaces from the left margin. Do not use quotation marks, since the indentation signals the reader that this is a quotation :

> Charlotte Perkins Gilman uses the symbol of the wedding ring in order to highlight the limitations of a woman's opportunities at the turn of the century:

> > But all that she may wish to have, all that she may wish to do, must come through a single channel and a single choice. Wealth, power, social distinction, fame,—not only these, but home and happiness, reputation, ease and pleasure, her bread and butter,—all, must come to her through a small gold ring.

Punctuating Quotations:

At the end of a quotation, place periods and commas inside quotation marks, regardless of whether or not the periods or commas appear in the original:

> Lady Mary Chudleigh warns that a woman must "fear her husband as her God."

When Lady Mary Chudleigh says that a woman must "fear her husband as her God," she is criticizing men's power in marriage.

Place semicolons and colons outside the quotation marks:

Lady Mary Chudleigh warns that a woman must "fear her husband as her God"; she knows that women have no power in marriage.

Lady Mary Chudleigh warns that a woman must "fear her husband as her God": for a woman, there is little difference between God and man.

The placement of other punctuation marks (question marks, exclamation points, dashes) depends on whether or not they are part of the quoted material.

A Note on Parenthetical References:

Most literature instructors will ask you to use the "new MLA style" of documentation, which consists of parenthetical references rather than footnotes or endnotes. A complete discussion of this style appears later in the chapter. However, the use of parenthetical reference has an impact on punctuation. These brief rules should cover most situations:

1. When the parenthetical reference immediately follows a quotation, do not place the final period inside the quotation marks. Instead, place the period after the parenthetical reference.

"My judgment, when it came, wouldn't be narrow, biased or culture-bound. 'Customs differ,' I said" (88).

2. For indented quotations, place the final period immediately after the passage, followed by the parenthetical reference.

But all that she may wish to have, all that she may wish to do, must come through a single channel and a single choice. Wealth, power, social distinction, fame,—not only these, but home and happiness, reputation, ease and pleasure, her bread and butter,—all, must come to her through a small gold ring. (327)

3. When quoting two lines of poetry (integrating the quotation into your text rather than indenting it), use a slash (/) preceded and followed by single spaces to indicate the break between the two lines

Lady Mary Chudleigh warns women, "Value your selves, and men despise, / You must be proud, if you'll be wise."

WHEN SHOULD REFERENCES
BE DOCUMENTED?

When you make reference to a source, you face the decision of whether or not you are obliged to *document* the source (or tell the reader where the words or ideas came from). Sometimes the question of whether or not to document can be tricky. On the one hand, papers cluttered with footnote numbers and/or parenthetical references are annoyingly hard to read and provide little indication of what the writer thinks; on the other hand, papers that present all words and ideas as the writer's own arouse suspicion and lack the force of expert opinion that supports the writer's ideas. How can you determine when it's appropriate (or necessary) to document a source?

It might help to start with the easy decisions. First, convention dictates that almost every time you quote a source, you must document it. When you write "joy that kills" in your paper, you must tell the reader that it comes from Kate Chopin's "The Story of an Hour." (Later in the chapter you will see how to provide the reader with this information.) On the other hand, information that is common knowledge—even if it appears in a text that you're reading—does not have to be documented. For example, the fact that women had very few rights at the turn of the century is well known. Even if a critic of Chopin mentions this in a literary analysis of her work, you need not credit the critic.

The two cases mentioned here are straightforward; the decision to document or not is relatively easy. But there are other cases in which you will find yourself exercising judgment. Sometimes it's necessary to distinguish between things that are common knowledge to any educated reader (e.g., Mr. Mallard is not an abusive husband, even though he is apparently domineering) and interpretations (e.g., Mrs. Mallard's heart attack can be considered a form of suicide). Making such distinctions is not as difficult as it may appear from this explanation, however. Remember that in the collaborative classroom, you take part in many conversations about a literary work. In the course of those conversations you begin to see what each reader or group accepts as true about the work and what readers and groups disagree on. Thus by the time you write about a literary work, you should have a pretty good idea of the difference between common knowledge and interpretation. (Later in the chapter you will find advice on acknowledging the help and ideas of fellow students in your paper.) Furthermore, if your presentation involves research, you will come to understand what other writers consider common knowledge, as well as what ideas are subject to dispute.

A NOTE ON PLAGIARISM

These days the issue of plagiarism is a thorny one, both inside and outside the classroom. Many colleges and universities are reviewing their policies on academic honesty, and in the public arena incidents of plagiarism receive a good deal of media attention. In the 1988 Democratic primary campaign, Senator Joseph Biden had to withdraw from the race because it was discovered that he had used the same phrasing in one of his advertisements that a British politician had used earlier. In 1991, the Dean of Boston University's School of Journalism, Joachim Maitre, resigned his deanship after it became known that he had presented a film critic's ideas as his own in a commencement address. And again at Boston University, a research team discovered that Martin Luther King had presented someone else's ideas as his own in his doctoral dissertation.

Our culture's concept of property rights extends itself to words and ideas; individuals obtain patents on their ideas and copyrights on their words. Thus a person can be said to "own" ideas that were first expressed by him or her, and to "own" the words used to express those ideas. In the public sphere, legal action can be taken if one writer "steals" another's ideas or words; in the academic world, punitive action can be taken if a student does the same thing. As a result, everyone who makes public presentations, whether oral or written, has to consider the issue of plagiarism. But this issue should not be considered only in terms of "intellectual property rights." When you make presentations to others, you should also be mindful of intellectual honesty, and acknowledge the contribution that others have made to your presentation.

Unfortunately, so many ideas seem new to students that it's hard to determine what needs to be documented. In addition, people new to a field often learn the language and ideas of that field by "trying on" what the experts have said and written. So how do you avoid getting caught in the plagiarism trap? Fortunately, the guidelines regarding plagiarism are fairly straightforward in most college courses—and many instructors are aware of the pitfalls awaiting students, especially in introductory courses. What follows is a discussion, including a few guidelines, of how to present your material without risking the penalties associated with plagiarism.

Summary and Plagiarism

Some people might argue that there is no such thing as a truly new idea—and they may be right. But in this society, ownership of ideas is taken seriously. If you want to find out whether or not a specific idea is the "property" of a particular writer, you can use your research to help you come up with an answer. As you read about a subject, you will find writers referring to each other; if one writer credits another with originating a certain idea—about polygamy in Islamic cultures, for example—then you should probably refer to that idea as the property of its originator. If, however, you discover in your reading that most writers refer to an idea as common knowledge in the field—that the oppression of women in Islamic cultures results in part from fear of female sexuality, for example—then you can assume that there's no need to attribute that idea to any specific writer. You will find yourself having to make judgment calls on occasion, because you are uncertain whether an idea is exclusive to one writer or common knowledge. In such cases it's wise to consult your instructor. (Note: Writers are not expected to document facts that are generally known or easy for anyone to check in widely available reference works. If a fact is in dispute, however, the source should be acknowledged.)

Paraphrasing and Plagiarism

Sometimes it's difficult to put another writer's ideas into your own words, especially if the writer expresses himself or herself effectively. But convention holds that a paraphrase cannot repeat too many words from the original and cannot repeat the structure of the original. How many words are too many? Often this is a judgment call. If a passage contains key words or phrases that cannot be substituted (such as *polygamy* or *woman suffrage movement*), then you have no choice but to use the author's words. In general, it's a good idea to repeat from the original only terms such as those mentioned above and words for which there are no synonyms. An effective way to paraphrase an author's ideas is to put the book aside while you write out your paraphrase. Unless you have a photographic memory, you will have to rephrase the material in your own words. After writing the paraphrase you can check the original to see if you have captured the idea adequately. It's also helpful to ask a friend or classmate to read the original, and then listen to you present the idea in your own words. The friend can let you know whether or not you are presenting the idea clearly and whether or not you sound too much like the original. The following is an example of what might be considered a plagiarized passage, followed by an example of appropriate paraphrasing (from an earlier section of this chapter) according to current convention. (Note: Even if you paraphrase a passage, convention dictates that you document it. Documentation form is covered later in the chapter.)

Original Passage:
In the United States, at least, we need no longer argue woman's intellectual, moral and physical qualification for the ballot with the intelligent. The Reason of the best of our citizens has long been convinced. The justice of the argument has been admitted, but sex-prejudice is far from conquered.

Plagiarism:
Carrie Chapman Catt believed that in the United States people no longer needed to argue woman's moral, intellectual and physical capabilities for voting. The logical minds of the most important citizens had for a long time been assured of this. The rightness of the argument had been conceded, but prejudice based on sex was a long way from being overcome.

Acceptable Paraphrase:
Carrie Chapman Catt felt that while Americans were intellectually reconciled to women's equality, their prejudices had not yet been eliminated.

In the plagiarized passage, a few of Catt's words and phrases are repeated, but more significant is the fact that the writer used sentence structures identical to Catt's, apparently simply looking up key words in a thesaurus and substituting synonyms. The appropriately paraphrased passage is handled in the way that a translation from a foreign language would be: The general idea of the passage is conveyed in structures and words common to the translator's own language. (The futility of this kind of plagiarism should also be apparent in the awkwardness and lack of clarity of the plagiarized passage. Just as a literal, word-for-word translation from a foreign language is usually hard to follow, so is this passage.)

Direct Quotation and Plagiarism

Probably the easiest type of plagiarism to avoid—and to understand—is that involving direct quotation. The conventions regarding presenting another's exact words are clear: Whenever another writer's words are presented, those words must be enclosed in quotation marks and the author of the words must be credited. (Note: **According to convention, it is not enough to attribute a quotation to a writer; the words themselves must be placed in quotation marks as well. This guideline is designed to allow readers to distinguish between paraphrase and quotation.**) The Carrie Chapman Catt passage can be used to illustrate plagiarized quotations as well.

Plagiarism:
Carrie Chapman Catt argued that in the United States, at least, we need no longer argue woman's intellectual, moral and physical qualification for the ballot with the intelligent.

Appropriate Quotation:
Carrie Chapman Catt argued, "In the United States, at least, we need no longer argue woman's intellectual, moral and physical qualification for the ballot with the intelligent."

HOW SHOULD REFERENCES
BE DOCUMENTED?

Sometimes student writers (and professional writers as well) become frustrated when faced with page upon page of rules for proper documentation of sources. The rules are fairly rigid, and it's necessary to check the rule for different kinds of documentation (short story vs. novel, article in an anthology vs. article in a periodical, and so on). Precisely because of these rules, however, using proper format is the easiest part of documentation. While writers often have to exercise judgment regarding whether to summarize, paraphrase, or quote, as well as whether or not to document a source, they rarely have to exercise judgment regarding how to document a source. Usually, all they need to know is where to look up the appropriate documentation form. This section will cover several issues involved in properly documenting sources:

- Reference to Authors' Names
- Reference to Titles
- Parenthetical Documentation (in-text citation)
- Footnotes/Endnotes
- Manuscript Format

Reference to Authors' Names

When you refer to an author in your text (not in parenthetical references, which will be covered later), you should consider that your audience may not have followed the same path that led you to your conclusions. Thus it's necessary to provide readers with the full names of authors you refer to. The first time you mention an author in your text, use the author's full name (and title, if appropriate). Thereafter, as is customary in public discourse, refer to the author by last name—without any accompanying title. Referring to an author by first name suggests a familiarity that is normally inappropriate in public discourse.

> Charlotte Perkins Gilman dealt with the oppression of women in fiction as well as in essays. Gilman's story "The Yellow Wallpaper" is a frightening account of a woman driven mad by her overprotective husband.

Reference to Titles

Just as you refer to an author by full name first, titles should be presented fully, at least the first time they are used. If a long title will be used frequently in your text, and you are fairly certain that readers would understand an abbreviation, then abbreviating is appropriate. For example, you might refer to the full title of Alice Walkers *The Temple of My Familiar* the first time, and later refer to the novel as *Temple*.

Parenthetical Documentation
(in-text citation)

The Modern Language Association is responsible for setting documentation guidelines for papers in literature and language. A complete guide to documentation can be found in the association's publication, *The MLA Handbook for Writers of Research Papers*. What follows are examples of the more common references found in student papers.

According to the MLA guidelines, a writer provides minimal information on sources in the text itself, and complete publishing information at the end of the paper in a "Works Cited" (or "Works Consulted") page. These citations conform roughly to old footnote/bibliography citations. The basic purpose of parenthetical references is to provide the reader with the necessary information to find the source in your Works Cited page and then to find the quoted material in the source. The standard parenthetical reference includes the author's last name and the page number of the reference.

Mrs. Mallard dies "of joy that kills" (Chopin 83).

Often, however, you will have introduced the quotation with the author's name. In such cases, all you need include in parentheses is the page number.

Chopin's heroine dies "of joy that kills" (83).

Sometimes you will find yourself quoting from two works written by the same author. If the context does not make clear which work is being referred to, then you can use an abbreviated title along with a page number. For example, if you are writing a paper on two different Toni Morrison novels, *Song of Solomon* and *Beloved,* you may need to use a parenthetical reference like this:

(Morrison, *Song* 257)

in order to clarify for the reader the source of the quotation. The key here is to use common sense. How much information will your reader need in order to find the entry in your "Works Cited" page (where you provide full publishing information for the source)? If you include only a page number, will the reader be certain of the author and title? If so, then all you need is a page number. If not, then you need to include more information.

The Works Cited page itself includes, in alphabetical order by authors' last names, a list of all works cited in your text. (Authorless works are alphabetized according to title.) Author's names appear last name first, followed by the name of the work and the appropriate publishing information. Some instructors may ask that you include works that were helpful to you even though they are not actually cited in your text, in which case you might end your paper with a "Works Consulted" page. Typical entries for a Works Cited or Works Consulted page will look like this:

Morrison, Toni. *Beloved*. New York: Knopf, 1987.

Note that the title of the novel is italicized (underlined on a typewriter). Titles of longer works (books, plays, magazines, newspapers, films, and television programs) are italicized, while titles of shorter works (essays, stories, articles, and poems) are placed in quotation marks. Examples of parenthetical references and works cited entries for a number of types of references appear at the end of this section.

Footnotes/Endnotes

Even though MLA has abandoned the footnote/endnote style of documentation, you may find such references helpful. Occasionally you will want to provide your reader with additional information about sources or ideas in your text (in a *textual note*). In such cases, you use the traditional footnote/endnote form. At the end of the section requiring the note, insert a raised numeral (notes are numbered consecutively throughout the paper). A corresponding numeral will appear either at the bottom of the page (footnote) or at the end of the paper (endnote). Here is an example of a textual footnote:

Charlotte Perkins Gilman uses the symbol of the wedding ring in order to highlight the limitations of women's opportunities at the turn of the century: "Wealth, power, social distinction, fame,—not only these, but home and happiness, reputation, ease and pleasure, her bread and butter,—all, must come to her through a small gold ring."[1]

---

[1] Gilman creates a chilling account of her own marriage in the short story "The Yellow Wallpaper."

SAMPLE WORKS CITED ENTRIES

Although the following list may seem confusing, with a different format for each type of source, each entry includes the same essential information, in the same order:

Books: Author, title, place of publication, publisher, and date.
Periodicals: Author, title of article, name of periodical, date, pages.
Other Sources: Author or speaker, title of presentation, date, and place of presentation.

Anonymous Work

Beowulf. Trans. David Wright. Baltimore: Penguin, 1972.

Book by One Author

Morrison, Toni. *Beloved.* New York: Knopf, 1987.

Book by More than One Author

Horton, Rod. W., and Vincent F. Hopper, *Backgrounds of European Literature.* New York: Appleton, 1954.

Edited Book

Gates, Henry Louis, Jr., ed. *Bearing Witness: Selections from African-American Autobiography in the Twentieth Century.* New York: Pantheon, 1991.

Selection from an Anthology

hooks, bell. "Black is a Woman's Color." *Bearing Witness: Selections from African-American Autobiography in the Twentieth Century.* Ed. Henry Louis Gates, Jr. New York: Pantheon, 1991. 339–348.

Introduction to Primary Source

Carpenter, Richard C. Introduction. *Far From the Madding Crowd.* By Thomas Hardy. New York: Bantam, 1967.

Translation

Camus, Albert. *The Plague.* Trans. Stuart Gilbert. New York: The Modern Library, 1948.

Work from a Collection

Welty, Eudora. "Clytie." *The Collected Stories of Eudora Welty*. New York: Harcourt, 1980.

Article in Scholarly Journal

Winterowd, W. Ross. "The Purification of Literature and Rhetoric." *College English* 49 (1987): 257–273.

Article in a Monthly Publication

McCorkle, Jill. "Departures." *The Atlantic* Dec. 1991: 84–89.

Article in Weekly/Biweekly Publication

Lacayo, Richard. "Shadows and Eye Candy." *Time* 30 Sept. 1991: 72–74.

Article in newspaper

Montgomery, M. R. "Redrawing the Native American image." *Boston Globe* 28 Feb. 1991: 69+.

Material from Class Notes

English 209A: "Approaches to Literature." Merrimack College, 3 Oct. 1991. Class notes.

Interview

Sunstein, Bonnie. Personal interview. 17 Nov. 1987.

Videotape/Film

Garland, Patrick, Dir. *A Doll's House*. With Claire Bloom, Anthony Hopkins, and Sir Ralph Richardson. South Gate Entertainment, 1989.

or

A Doll's House. Garland, Patrick, Dir. With Claire Bloom, Anthony Hopkins, and Sir Ralph Richardson. South Gate Entertainment, 1989.

Lecture

Graham, Joyce L. "Freeing Maya Angelou's *Caged Bird*." National Council of Teachers of English 81st Annual Convention. Seattle, 24 Nov. 1991.

ACKNOWLEDGING CONTRIBUTIONS OF FELLOW STUDENTS

A paper written for a collaborative class—even if that paper is individually authored—can truly be considered a collaborative effort. From the moment when students begin discussing a work until the last peer response is received, the writer is receiving support from his or her peers. Thus it is appropriate to acknowledge the contributions of those who helped you formulate your proposition and present your ideas clearly, logically, and coherently. Often instructors in collaborative classrooms will ask you to include (after the title page) an acknowledgments page that cites the contributions of your fellow students. (Kelly Leighton's paper, reprinted here, includes an acknowledgments page. You might also look at the end of the Preface for our acknowledgment of those who assisted us in writing this book.)

MANUSCRIPT FORMAT/SAMPLE PAPER

Instructors often provide their own guidelines for formatting your final copy. Ordinarily, a cover page will include the title of your paper (capitalizing the first letters of each major word, with no underlining or quotation marks highlighting your title), your full name, your instructor's name, the name of the course, and the date. The title is normally repeated on the first page of your paper, and pages are numbered consecutively. At the end of the paper, the "Works Cited" or "Works Consulted" page appears.

What follows is an expanded version of Kelly Leighton's paper from Chapter 9. The paper illustrates appropriate documentation of sources and a widely accepted manuscript form.

One Man's Trifle Is Another Woman's Evidence

Kelly Leighton
EN155A
Dr. K. S. Cain
November 14, 1990

Acknowledgements

I would like to thank the following people for their
contributions to this paper:

> Debbie Carlisle, for her consistent focus on re-
>   lations between men and women—she gave me
>   a new "lens" to see through;
> Eric Labbe, for his refusal to bow down at the
>   altar of literature—he taught me that it's
>   OK to question even the great authors; and
> Cinde Veinot, for her skepticism about
>   Glaspell's portrayal of men—her questions
>   kept me from taking any interpretation for
>   granted.

One Man's Trifle Is Another Woman's Evidence

Susan Glaspell's play *Trifles* is appropriately named, for it is the things that men consider useless observations that result in the women's solving the murder of John Wright. As critic C. W. E. Bigsby says, ". . . while the men wander around the house baffled as to motive, the women slowly piece together the reason for the crime from the trifles which they find—a poorly stitched quilt, a song bird with a broken neck in a fancy box" (25). Not only do Mrs. Peters and Mrs. Hale solve the murder, but they show an understanding of what is important in life as well; in Bigsby's words "they recognise [*sic*] the pain out of which the crime had come . . ." (25). In dismissing the women's concerns as trifles, the men reveal their total ignorance of the essential elements of life. This theme of the destructive force of male ignorance runs through the entire play.

The county attorney, Mr. Henderson, and the sheriff, Mr. Peters, feel there could be nothing important in the kitchen where women are used to worrying over "trifles." At the beginning of the play, when the men are deciding where to look for clues, the attorney asks Sheriff Peters if there's anything important in the kitchen. The sheriff replies, "Nothing here but kitchen things" (70). So they turn their attention to the more "important" places, the barn, for example. However, instead of shifting to follow the men, the action remains in the kitchen, highlighting its importance in the drama (Dymkowski 92). It's while the men are in the barn that the women find the first clue: the quilt. When the men laugh at them for wondering if the quilt was being quilted or knotted, the sheriff's wife explains, "apologetically," that "they've got awful important things on their minds" (73). But it is a woman, Mrs. Hale, who notices that the square Mrs. Wright has been working on is poorly stitched, while the others are all perfectly done. And both she and Mrs. Peters seem to recognize that the uneven sewing "reflects the tensions which finally turn [Mrs. Wright] from a creative to a destructive force" (Bigsby 25), because they look toward the door where the men have just left. Mrs. Hale even goes so far as to rip out the bad sewing and redo the square, as if she knows that the evidence might be bad for Mrs. Wright. Their attention to trifles has uncovered a clue that the men, with "awful important things on their minds," have not only missed, but have not even looked for.

While the men are searching all over the place for the kind of clues they would look for, the women find the one piece of evidence that would prove the county attorney's case. Mrs. Peters has explained to Mrs. Hale that what the men are looking for is "a motive; something to show anger, or--sudden feeling" (72). That is just what the women find when they discover the bird cage with its door hinge broken "as if someone must have been rough with it" (74). Anger and sudden feeling are certainly evident in the condition of the bird cage. And, of course, the bird with its wrung neck in the sewing box is clear proof of anger. Mrs. Peters, the sheriff's wife, is quick to point out that in strictly legal terms, "We don't know who killed the bird." But Mrs. Hale, who relies on women's ways of understanding things rather than the legalistic ways men use, replies, "I knew John Wright" (76).

Both women realize what it would have meant for Mrs. Wright to lose the canary. Mrs. Hale says, "If there's been years and years of nothing, then a bird to sing to you, it would be awful--still, after the bird was still," and Mrs. Peters adds, "I know what stillness is. When we homesteaded in Dakota, and my

first baby died--after he was two years old, and me
with no other then--" (76). The men are too busy
searching for clues to think about what life
must have been like for Mrs. Wright. They consider such speculation, like the women's attention to the preserves, to be merely "trifles."
But lives are made up of trifles, and the women
know that. Through these trifles they discover
what Christine Dymkowski calls "the clues to
the desperation and loneliness of Minnie's
life" and achieve an "understanding that
. . . goes beyond the mere solving of the
crime to a redefinition of what the crime was"
(92).

How is it that the women are able to solve the
case while the men are not? The women, with their
careful attention to trifles and their knowledge of a
woman's psychology, put little things together--the
messy kitchen, the uneven stitching, the isolation,
the frigid husband, and the dead canary. They put all
these "trifles" together while the men are out looking in the barn. Because the women are concerned
about Mrs. Wright as a person, they are able to "acknowledge the shared experience which . . . breeds the
compassion which they offer . . ." (Bigsby 25). It is
only by accident that they discover the bird, but
that accident results from their trying to bring Mrs.
Wright things that she might want while she is in
jail. It is those trifles that solve the murder, and
more importantly, that allow them to understand "the
more violent psychological aspects of women trapped
in loveless marriages" (Sutherland 323).

It is this new understanding that causes the
women to go beyond solving the crime. They actually
remove the evidence that might lead the county attorney to find the motive he is looking for. Why do they
do this? I think that the play suggests that a higher

justice was served when John Wright died, that he, like the men we meet in the play, could not appreciate the trifles that make a woman's life meaningful. Furthermore, according to Christine Dymkowski, the women gain a new perspective, asking themselves which was the worse crime, Mrs. Wright's murder of her husband or his murder of her spirit (92). They decide that if men are so blind to what is really important in life, then they do not deserve to have the evidence. The county attorney does not even bother to look at what the women are bringing to Mrs. Wright, because he cannot imagine anything important in the things. The final irony comes when Mr. Henderson sarcastically congratulates "the ladies" on the only discovery he thinks anyone has made in the house:

> COUNTY ATTORNEY [facetiously]. Well, Henry, at least we found out that she was not going to quilt it. She was going to--what is it you call it, ladies?

> MRS. HALE [her hand against her pocket]. We call it--knot it, Mr. Henderson.

This last line of the play, a "subdued, ironic, and grisly reminder of the manner in which a stifled wife has enacted her desperate retaliation" (Sutherland 322), brings home clearly the theme that in their blindness to "trifles," men not only miss the true meaning of life, but crush the life out of women who struggle to keep that meaning alive.

Works Consulted

Bigsby, C. W. E. *A Critical Introduction to Twentieth-Century American Drama.* vol. 1: 1900-1940. New York: Cambridge UP, 1982.

Dymkowski, Christine. "On the Edge: The Plays of Susan Glaspell." *Modern Drama* 31 (1988): 91-105.

Evans, Sara M. *Born for Liberty: A History of Women in America.* New York: Macmillan, 1989.

Glaspell, Susan. *Trifles. Exploring and Communicating About Literature—A Collaborative Approach.* Kathleen Shine Cain, Albert C. DeCiccio, and Michael J. Rossi. Boston: Allyn and Bacon, 1993. 68-77.

Sinclair, Andrew. *The Emancipation of the American Woman.* New York: Harper, 1965.

Sutherland, Cynthia. "American Women Playwrights." *Modern Drama* 21 (1972): 319-336.

11 Personal and Creative Pieces

In working through this book you have joined the community of people who know and value literature. Perhaps the best way to celebrate your membership in this community is to write your own literary work. Of course, not everyone is a budding William Shakespeare or Alice Walker. But every piece of imaginative writing is significant, simply because it has been written to be enjoyed. Your instructor may ask you to go beyond making meaning of literary works and approach literature from within—by doing it yourself. And in the process of creating your own literary work, you'll probably find that the activity can be enjoyable. This chapter, then, may be considered a kind of celebration. In fact, it is in the spirit of celebration that we include several works written by our own students. Moreover, we hope that you and your fellow students will share your own works in a celebratory way to demonstrate what we've been saying throughout this book—that literature is a conversation.

DEVELOPING A PERSONAL STORY: ARRANGED CHRONOLOGICALLY

Being asked to write "creatively" is a bit like being asked to bare your soul before strangers. But before you panic, consider this cliche: Everyone has a story to tell. If this is true for you, then you may find it interesting to work first on a personal story. In starting from home, so to speak, you have the opportunity to take advantage of the information you may have collected through close observation, formal research, and personal contact with others. In the exercise sequence that follows (first developed by Kenneth Bruffee in his book *A Short Course in Writing*), you will be asked to narrate a personal story.

EXERCISE 1

In about 500–750 words, write a non-fictional account of something that happened to you once that deeply affected you. This account may involve something that scared you, elated you, pleased you, angered you, humiliated you, satisfied you, or changed you. Write in language that fits the experience and that expresses, in the most powerful way you know, how you feel about what happened. Give plenty of physical and emotional detail—even use dialogue—so that your readers get a sense of what the experience was like. But write only as much as you need in order to tell this story as you feel it must be told. Don't pad it, and arrange your story chronologically, just as it happened.

As you can see, the only real requirement for this piece of writing is that you write honestly about something that happened to you that deeply affected you. In other words, answer the following questions: *What happened to you and how do you feel about it?*

You may feel a little overwhelmed at first, thinking about what the phrase "deeply affected" means. But this is a normal reaction; few people have had life experiences that sound as intriguing as the phrase initially suggests. Almost everyone, however, has a story or two that tells about something that has shaped who he or she has become. Narrating that story will prove interesting to both you and your readers, as you will discover in the student example that follows.

```
                    The Fire
                  Angela Fusco


     "Let's have one last fling in Montreal over Memo-
rial Day weekend," said Susan. We were co-workers in
the tax department in Boston, and wedding bells would
be ringing for the both of us within the year. Nei-
ther of us had been out of Massachusetts, let alone
flown before, and "one last fling" could be an educa-
tional experience for, shall we say, two non-worldly
individuals. Our newly bought honeymoon suitcases
were packed with enough clothes for two weeks, even
though we were just staying for three days. We wanted
to be ready for whatever we may encounter on our trip
away from home.
     Montreal turned out to be an exciting city with
so much to take in. To Susan's dismay, I insisted we
see, what seemed like the entire city, on foot. I
turned a deaf ear to her groans and complaints, even
though she pleaded that her tender, little feet were
killing her. I must admit that when I look back now,
```

---

that I was past recognition of pain because of the euphoric high that I was floating in. Shopping always
does that to me, and we had just discovered
Montreal's world renowned, massive underground mall.

Dusk was upon us when we suddenly realized that
our tired feet took us to a part of the city that AAA
would never recommend to their young novice travelers. The hungry eyes and repulsive attitudes of this
section's clientele, miraculously cured Susan's feet.
Her slow pace quickly accelerated and we unhesitat-
ingly ran like hell until our hotel was in view.

The Sheraton Mt. Royal was a welcome sight to
these two hungry and weary travelers. We decided that
our first evening in town would be best spent going
right to sleep. We put our dancing shoes aside for
the next night's adventure, and within minutes our
pulsating bodies quickly fell asleep.

During the middle of the night a nightmare awoke
me. I knew I shouldn't have seen that crazy movie
Clockwork Orange last week. It had so much violence,
noise, and crazy creatures. What the heck time is it?
I'm so tired. Wait a minute. Why am I still hearing
screams and crashes? "Susan, wake up! I think there
is a riot outside. Susan, I can't find my glasses—get
up!" "Oh my God, Angela; there are fire engines out
there and people everywhere."

When I opened our hotel door, we were quickly informed by the barricade of smoke that we were in a
full-fledged fire. I dashed out of the room to see if
there was any way to escape our fifth floor inferno.
The broken window with the completely vertical and
narrow fire escape at the end of the hall was our
only escape left. Susan, a fireman's daughter, insisted on packing her new clothes, in her new suitcase, before she would leave. I pleaded with her but
her stubborn nature wouldn't budge. I decided to grab
my empty suitcase and pocketbook while I frantically
paced and pleaded with my so-called friend. She told

me emphatically not to leave her and I stupidly
obeyed.

Long nightgowns and clumsy suitcases impeded us
further as we tried to make our way down the ladder
which took us back into the hotel. We later found out
that we were in the mezzanine, one floor below the
fire. French speaking firemen scampered about oblivious to Susan and me.

How we found our way out is still a mystery to
both of us. The next thing we knew it was 3:00 a.m.,
and we were shaking and sitting on our suitcases
across the street from the fire. Out of nowhere, two
young handsome Canadians greeted us and expressed
their deep concern for our ill-fated ordeal. One of
them beckoned us to accept his invitation to relax
and get refreshed at his sister's apartment. Susan
and I looked at each other and managed to smile. Was
this supposed to be it? Our one last fling?

SHARING BY READING ALOUD

When your story is completed, your instructor will probably arrange the
class so that the story may be read along with those of your classmates. In
this setting, as you may recall from Chapter 8, you're simply giving your
work to an audience; such sharing is a kind of celebration of the process that
helped you shape your piece.

THE PERSONAL STORY: ARRANGED
IN MEDIAS RES

Upon overcoming your initial fears about narrating a story that "deeply
affected" you, you probably found that the task posed in Exercise 1 was not
so hard to accomplish. After all, you were asked to write about what only
you know about. A little more challenging task is to emulate the classic
writers like Homer and Milton. Such writers told their stories by starting *in
medias res,* or in the middle of the action. By completing Exercise 2 below,
you'll overcome a significant challenge, and exhibit the kind of creativity
that'll lead you to compose the more literary artifacts proposed for you in
the later parts of the chapter.

EXERCISE 2

Rearrange the personal story you have written for Exercise 1 *in medias res*—in the middle of the action. One way to proceed is as follows: In the first part, perhaps in one paragraph, take up your story at a point just before the most exciting part or at the most important point. Give plenty of details, such as sights, sounds, things people said, and so on. Try to make the reader live through the experience exactly as you did. Then, just as you get to the climactic point, break off. In the second part, again perhaps in one paragraph, go back to the very beginning of the story. Tell us what led up to the experience you described in the first part of your story. Try to leave off just prior to the moment you chose to begin the first part with. In the third and final part, also perhaps in one paragraph, start with relating to us the climax of the story and end by telling us how the experience concluded. (*Your instructor may ask you to share by reading aloud.*)

You're probably aware, after having read through this new task, that this assignment will involve a little more work and a little more creativity, especially regarding the arrangement of your story. So, perhaps the best way to proceed in rearranging your story is to split the final stages of your original, chronologically ordered-story into two sections: The first section should serve as the opening of the story in the new arrangement. It should make your readers part of the action immediately and should provide them with the motivation for continuing their reading. The second section should be delayed until the end, and it should contain your newly arranged story's climax—its most memorable moment—as well as your conclusion to the story.

If you can proceed in this fashion, then your second part, according to the new arrangement, should provide the background information you offered throughout the early stages of your chronologically arranged story. An example of how the same personal story can be retold in this manner is evident in the following account: Angela draws the reader right into the story, builds suspense, breaks off and provides background, and then gives us the climactic moment and her conclusion.

```
                    The Fire
                  Angela Fusco


    My first night's sleep at the Sheraton Mt. Royal
was disrupted by what I thought was a dreadful night-
mare. I felt like I was living through the violent
```

and weird movie <u>Clockwork Orange</u> that I had seen a couple of nights ago. Crash! Bang! Boom! I heard the smashing of glass everywhere, and my heart pounded with fear because of the cries that I was forced to listen to. "Help!" "We're trapped up here." "Help me!" They never stopped screaming. My head was spinning and I finally realized that I wasn't dreaming after all. I frantically called out to Susan in the next bed and desperately tried to invade her deep sleep. "Susan! Susan, wake up. I think there's a riot outside!" Without my glasses on, everything was a blur to me. I dragged her to the window where she exclaimed, "Oh my God, Angela, there are fire engines and people screaming everywhere!" I ran to open our door and was immediately informed by a barricade of choking smoke that we were indeed in a hotel fire. The grayish clouds instantly spread their unwelcomed arms around us. I dashed out of the room to see if there was any way to escape our fifth floor inferno. At the end of the hall there was a broken window with a steep and narrow fire escape attached. I ran back to get Susan but she stubbornly refused to leave. "I'm not leaving this room, Angela, until I pack all my clothes in my new suitcase. You better not leave me alone and I mean it." Clad in my long nightgown, I deliriously paced and pleaded with Susan to leave our room.

Susan and I worked together in Boston and had been friends for about three years. Since we were both getting married within the year, Susan suggested we have one last fling in Montreal over Memorial Day Weekend. I agreed, plans were made, and before we knew what hit us, the beautiful city was before us and waiting to be explored. To Susan's dismay, I insisted we see the sights on foot. I turned a deaf ear to her groans and complaints, even though she threatened to take a bus and return to our hotel. She said her feet were killing her and that she was really ex-

hausted. I must admit that I was past recognition of
pain because of the euphoric state I was in. Shopping
always does that to me, and we had just discovered
Montreal's world renowned, massive underground mall.
Unhappily, she continued to shop with me until both
our weary bodies could shop no more. All we longed
for was to reach our hotel room. Our lifeless shells
instinctively gave into sleep as soon as we saw our
beds.

"Susan, for God's sake, we have to leave now!
There's nobody left on this floor and the air's so
thick I can hardly breathe!" Her persistent cries to
me somehow won out and I nervously but reluctantly
helped her pack. Our escape window took us back into
the hotel, one floor below the fire. "Susan, look
where we are! We're in the mezzanine. How the hell do
we get out of here?" We frantically ran down the
smoke-filled room, desperately searching for a way
out. All the doors we kept opening led to private
rooms that had already been evacuated. God must have
been with us because we saw a red EXIT sign. The door-
way led us to the hotel's pitch black back alley. We
made our way across the street, where we sat huddled
together on her suitcase, coughing and shaking. As I
tearfully watched attendants covering bodies with
sheets, I wondered what Susan was thinking.

Note that in this version, Angela is more a *literary* storyteller than she
was in her first version. She's more conscious of the language she uses;
consider, for instance, the words that describe the frenzy of the fire: *Crash!*
Bang! Boom! (Words like this, that resemble the sound they represent, are
called *onomatopoeia*.)

NOTES ABOUT WRITING STORIES

In both of Angela's stories, time—the sequence of events in the storyline—
is important, for it builds suspense. This suspense leads to the pleasurable

anxiety a reader feels as he or she is directed to the story's climax. Also in both stories, you'll note that tense is important; Angela uses the past tense consistently. Sometimes writers confuse this notion, thinking that the way to get their writers to feel a part of the experience is to use the present tense (*feel, walk, think*). However, since the personal story has already been experienced, the temptation to use the past tense (*felt, walked, thought*) is overwhelming. Thus, some writers end up switching tense throughout the story (I *feel* the cool breeze on my face, and as I *walked* through the park I *think* about what life *meant* to me). Now while this may work well for some situations, switching tense usually causes the reader confusion, and it is probably best that you check with your instructor before doing so. Finally, *dialogue* is used in both of Angela's stories. Dialogue is an especially clever way to give your story *verisimilitude,* or a sense that is it immediate and lifelike. Writers sometimes get confused with how they should set up dialogue, and this confusion is understandable. In an academic environment, the opportunity to use dialogue is not often presented. We suggest, first of all, that you make your dialogue as natural as possible. If this means using contractions or slang, go ahead and do so. Secondly, we suggest that you follow the general rule of using quotation marks around the dialogue. Third, we recommend that, in an extended conversation among your speakers, you arrange each speaker's dialogue as if it were a paragraph. Lastly, we suggest that you consult with your instructor about punctuation with dialogue, as well as about how to introduce or explain particular lines of dialogue.

WRITING CREATIVELY: FOLLOWING THE AUTHOR'S LEAD

Another way of getting the feel of what it's like to write creatively is to imitate those you have read. Instructors sometimes like to ask their students to rewrite conclusions to stories, lines in a poem, scenes in a play, etc. In so doing, they are asking their students to approach literature from *within*, that is, from the perspective of the author. Working through such an assignment, you may begin to feel comfortable with the notion of literature as a conversation: You will, in essence, be talking back to the author whose work gave you the cue for rewriting it, or extending it. Quite naturally, then, such an exercise also demonstrates that literature is alive, and it may help you to see that authors struggle to produce finished products that say something to their readers in much the same way as you do with your own written works. Revising is a big part of the literary author's composing process. In completing this exercise, you will be adding your voice to that of the original author, making new meaning of the work you choose to revise.

EXERCISE 3

Write a short piece—story, dramatic scene, poem—based upon one of the selections you have studied. You may choose to have your piece speculate about a character or scene several years after the conclusion of the literary text you studied. Or you may want to emulate a particular genre, say poetry, and write a different perspective on the subject in question. (*Your instructor may ask you to share by reading aloud.*)

In the example that follows, the student is working with a play (*A Doll's House*, 1879) by the great Norwegian dramatist, Henrik Ibsen. In the play, Nora comes to find out that her love for humanity is not appreciated by a society in which honor and male pride dominate. She has a confrontation with her husband of eight years, Torvald, during which she explains to him that she will no longer live a lie. She leaves him and their three children, a tremendously risky move for a nineteenth century woman. Many readers today—just as they did, but more bitterly, in the late 1800s—question her motives and wonder about what will happen to her children. In the following student example, the writer attempts to provide answers.

<u>A Doll's House:</u> Continued
Cinde Veinot

    It is fifteen years after Nora left Torvald and the children. Nora lives alone in a nice section of town in her own apartment. She has learned a lot during the past fifteen years and has become a mature, intelligent, and self-supporting woman. She is not wealthy, but has been able to fashion a comfortable way of life for herself.

    Nora's daughter Emmy comes to see her for the first time since she left fifteen years ago. Emmy is about eighteen and has grown up to be an attractive young woman.

Scene: Nora's apartment.

    Emmy stands in the hall outside Nora's apartment looking around and hesitantly rings the doorbell.

Nora: Company? Who could it be? (*Nora walks over to the door and opens it.*) Hello, may I help you?

Emmy: (*Speaking with uncertainty.*) I am looking for a Nora Helmer.

Nora: I am Nora Helmer.

Emmy: I am Emmy, your daughter.

Nora: Emmy! Emmy, my darling daughter. (*Nora hugs her—Emmy does not hug her back.*) You're all grown up! You're beautiful! Come in. Come in. (*Nora takes Emmy's hand and leads her into the living room.*)

Emmy: Anne Marie, my nurse, told me where you lived. I need to know the real reason you left home. Papa said you committed a crime and could no longer live with us. He said you could not be a good mother to us, so you went away. How could you just leave us? What did you do that was so terrible?

Nora: Oh, Emmy! Leaving you and your brothers was the most difficult thing I have ever done. But you must understand; I'll explain it all to you. I didn't commit a terrible crime. I was just trying to help and protect two people I loved very much.

Emmy: But why haven't you come to see us? Why haven't you written? What did you do that made you leave?

Nora: I *did* write and I *did* try to see you but . . . your father became very bitter and would not allow me to see you. He kept all the letters I wrote to you. When I tried to see you and your brothers, your father said you were doing fine and were better off without me. I couldn't argue. He is a powerful man in town with his position at the bank. What could I have done for you children?

Emmy: You could have been our mother!

Nora: But Emmy, I had to learn to be my own person, to have my own thoughts and opinions before I could be a good mother. Emmy, please sit down; I'll explain it all to you. I'm so glad you came!

Emmy sits down and Nora begins to explain what took place fifteen years ago and why she had to leave.

WRITING CREATIVELY: FOLLOWING
YOUR OWN LEAD

We began this chapter by writing, "Perhaps the best way to celebrate your membership in [the literature] community is to write your own literary work." That time has now arrived. Completing the following exercises should give you an awareness of what the creative process entails. You'll find yourself working through the same kinds of steps you followed in completing the other writing tasks in Part II: generating information that will become part of the dramatic scene, poem, or story; then focusing, structuring, developing, and clarifying that information for the reader's benefit. As exploring literary works and presenting your conclusions formally made approaching literature a richer undertaking, so too will creating your own work.

THE SHORT POEM

Many people find poetry frightening because it's sometimes difficult to understand. You may have figured you could never even attempt to write a poem. But many people have tried writing a poem at least once in their lives—to wish someone a happy birthday or for a special occasion. The kind of poem that you may just be willing to undertake is called a lyric poem, so named because the poem was usually sung to the accompaniment of a stringed instrument referred to as a lyre. It is a short piece that captures feelings with a few familiar words carefully arranged.

NOTES ABOUT WRITING POETRY

Most people who are inexperienced with poetry think that a poem has to have a rhyme scheme and a rhythmical beat. It is true that many poems have these qualities. But there are many that do not. Some poets feel more comfortable writing in a more open form, sometimes called *free verse*. Other poets are more inclined to paint pictures with words, creating what they hope are images that become etched in the reader's mind. The best advice we can offer you as you try your hand at poetry is to go with what feels natural to you. If you find yourself looking in the thesaurus often for rhymes, then perhaps you're trying too hard to fulfill the notion you may have about poems needing a rhyme. Thus you may end up with a poem that's referred to as *doggerel*, one that the reader notices you've struggled with because of its irregularities. Asking your instructor (and your classmates) for advice may be a remedy to you should you become bogged down by the attempt to write a poem.

EXERCISE 4

With a few familiar words, write a short poem that may suggest a multitude of meanings. If you want, base your poem on a characteristic of a poem you have studied in class. (*Your instructor may ask you to share by reading aloud.*)

The authors of the first two poems that we've reprinted were fascinated by Sylvia Plath's short poem "Metaphors" (1960):

I'm a riddle in nine syllables,
An elephant, a ponderous house,
A melon strolling on two tendrils.
O red fruit, ivory, fine timbers!
This loaf's big with its yeasty rising.
Money's new-minted in this fat purse.
I'm a means, a stage, a cow in calf.
I've eaten a bag of green apples,
Boarded the train there's no getting off.

Plath's piece is a riddle about her pregnancy that may be solved by looking carefully at the many hints she provides: For example, there are nine letters in m-e-t-a-p-h-o-r-s; there are nine syllables in each line; there are nine lines; and each line metaphorically describes Plath's condition. The author of "Life" presents a riddle, too: When you read it, note how cleverly she has arranged words and created a voice to indicate that the poem is being spoken by a baby about to be born. In "Peace Keeper," the author chooses another approach to indicate that his poem is for his newborn daughter R-E-B-E-C-C-A; her name means "peacemaker" and the first letter of each line spells out her name. In the final poem, the author writes (in free verse) to express her feelings as she mourns over the body of a young girl taken from the world far before her time.

```
                        Life
                    Mary Massa


    Yin and Yang have met.
    The union makes me one,
    A lonely navigator. . . .
    Lost in a darkened sea,
    Thrust by fate and nature
    Toward an unknown destination.
```

No Ulysses am I, but
A mariner lost. . . .
A silken cord my only anchor.
My heart resounds with rhythm,
Echoed by another, and. . . .
Feeling that protection,
I find comfort in my world.
Yes, my world is dark,
But something is coming,
Something is coming. . . .
Bringing me toward the light.

Peace Keeper
Michael Damphousse

Round ready rose budding:
Entrance to life. Quiet. Proud.
Beautiful. Three months before solstice
Embellished with drops of warm rain.
Could smoke or fire rise some day to
Choke this fresh, serene flower?
Abide. Keep peace. It is your name.

God's Littlest Angel
Jane Galante

I remember your red hair flying in the breeze,
your long legs running and dancing across the lawn.
Exhausted you fall and then, slowly, pick yourself
   up and run again.
Always laughing, never crying.
Now you are sleeping so quiet and still.
Your once tanned face so white,
your once warm body so cold and stiff.
Why do they cry? why do they wail?

I miss you as the roses miss the
    warmth of spring,
as the autumn trees miss their vibrant
    colored coats,
as the snow falls and freezes all beneath,
as others play in the warmth of the sun
    you once loved.

Your pain and hurt are over; your soul is
    free at last.
Too long I had watched you suffer.
Too long I had watched you wither.
Forgive me, my child; I cannot cry for you.

Go now, my beloved cherub, into God's hands.
It is only a short time we will be apart.
I will be with you again one day when there
    will be no hurt or pain or sorrow,
where I will again watch your red hair flying
    in the breeze,
your long legs running and dancing across the lawn.

THE DRAMATIC SCENE

As you saw earlier in Cinde Veinot's *A Doll's House:* Continued, drama involves dialogue which serves to provide an audience with the motivation for characters' actions. It would be too demanding to ask you to write an entire play, but you can try out a scene. To proceed, you may want to imagine a scene in which people are discussing a matter of concern, either serious or trivial. Try to describe the scene and then to recreate their conversations. Then, arrange the scene in a manner similar to the way the dramatists you've studied have arranged their plays.

NOTES ABOUT WRITING
DRAMATIC SCENES

Once you're prepared to write your dramatic scene, you'll want to be sure to give the reader a list of characters and a description of the scene in which the action takes place before the characters actually begin speaking. Wherever you give emphasis to a speech, or wherever you highlight what may be happening while a speech is being delivered, try to do so in present tense. If you interrupt a character's speech with editorializing, do so in italics and inside parentheses. If you editorialize in this way after a character's speech, do so in italics so that the reader will know it is not part of the dialogue. Sometimes when people engage in a conversation, they interrupt one another. To show such interruptions in your dramatic scene, use the ellipsis (three spaced periods, four if the interruption comes at the end of a speech) or the dash. Should you require further assistance with these technical aspects, be sure you consult with your instructor.

EXERCISE 5

After examining the student sample that follows, try to write a brief dramatic scene focusing on two characters which shows the motivation behind each character's actions. (*Your instructor may ask you to share by reading aloud.*)

Lesson in Quill
Michael Damphousse

Characters: Younger:
A young man, restless.
Older: An old man, peaceful and firm.

Scene: *The action takes place in an overgrown pasture. A crisp day with the sun ducking in and out of clouds, currently in. Two men sit on a dilapidated rock wall which blends an overgrown pasture with a row of hemlocks to the left. One, noticeably older than the other, is carving the spent ashes from a pipe with the artistic accuracy of a jeweler. The younger cuts a crumbling piece of chocolate, about the size of a deck of cards, with the same level of intensity, losing a good portion to the ground. Two pheasants, a bright cock and a smaller hen, rest on a large rock next to the two shotguns, dead.*

Younger: This damned chocolate is crumbling every time I cut a piece from it. At the rate it's going,

---

I'll go hungry or give up to the cold before I get a big enough piece to enjoy.

Older: Patience. Besides those crumbs will warm some squirrels tomorrow, while we burn some of our own energy today.

Glances along the rock wall and taps his pipe on the nearest rock.

Have you guys decided if you'll go over to the Nana's for dinner next week? You know how much she loves to see the baby.

Younger: We haven't really talked about it. Every night seems to go by so fast with me doing my thing and she doing hers. I wonder why we. . . . We'll probably go—that is, if she hasn't planned anything else. She was a little disturbed that I decided to go hunting today, although week after week I seem to win the argument.

Older: Arguments. Did you ever think that the two of you are learning something from each other, not arguing? Sooner or later, as you chip to the middle of that hunk of chocolate, what was once a good thing to be enjoyed in small sweet bits will have withered away to a tiny mass, not quite as perfect as first viewed, yet worthy to be considered a treat. As time goes on, you'll eventually enjoy it for what it's worth. Until then, a better future will always be in your sights.

Younger: I guess so.

Studies the small piece of chocolate, now half the original size, disapprovingly . . . hums satisfaction.

Older: Shh! Son, I think I heard something.

Both sit deathly still, the younger's eyes occasionally glancing at his mentor's. Slowly, upwind, a small brown creature rounds a rock and waddles toward a downed hemlock. A porcupine. The younger lurches for his gun. As he turns and raises the barrel with his finger on the trigger, he catches his father's disapproving eye. Bashfully, he lowers the gun, pride at hand.

Younger: Well, my reflexes are still good. If they aren't tested, they may go on me . . . I . . . read that somewhere.

Older: That look's been on your face before. Porcupine quill soup, did you? Not the type of meal you could put on the table for approving mouths at home.

Younger: *(Ashamed, looks upwind again. Exclaims at a whisper. . . .)* Look! There's another—came out and went back in.

Older: *(Quietly, almost in a rhythmic song, enjoying the sight.)* A family of porcupines huddled together, trying to stay warm and keep the chill off. But soon they feel one another's quills and move apart. Day after day the need for warmth brings them closer together, their quills forcing them apart again.

As he packs his pipe quickly in one motion, a small one pops its head out to see the sun peek through the heavens only to turn her nose up to the cold.

Older: They are constantly driven back and forth, measuring their discomforts until they find the distance from one another that provides maximum warmth and minimum pain.

Glances back to his son, who stares intently into his eyes, seeking. Lights a match and holds it to his pipe. Talks between puffs, the working flame exploding in the air as each breath ignites.

(Puff) People, like all of God's creatures, are brought together in the same way, but their many quirks and intolerable quills drive them apart.

(Puff) The distance they finally find that permits them to coexist consists of politeness, respect, and good manners. Because of this finely tuned distance between us, we can only partially satisfy our need for warmth (puff) but, at the same time, we are spared the stab of one another's quills.
Exhales a large breath of smoke to extinguish the light.

Younger: I see.

The older picks up his gun and walks toward the hill, turns. . . .

Older: Don't think of that as a lecture; it was simply a tired hunter solving our world's problems.

THE SHORT STORY

What you did earlier in the chapter with the personal story, especially arranged in *medias res*, prepared you to write an imaginative short story. In addition to following the advice we offered about writing stories, what you'll need to do for this kind of piece is fictionalize, or make up the situation, the characters, their speech, and their actions. In the personal story, you were simply describing what you knew to be true, for you lived through the situation, you knew the characters, you were aware of what they said and did. In the fictionalized short story, you'll be creating these things; however, you'll probably find it worthwhile to base your creation upon what you know. In your story, the situation, the characters, their speech and their actions should be recognizable to your readers simply because they were recognizable to you in creating them. Finally, because it is short, the short story can be considered "language under pressure." With the right amount of effort, your story should strike your reader just this way.

EXERCISE 6

Write a short story that imaginatively imitates circumstances in life and that includes characters who move and speak as real people might if they were to be placed in such circumstances. Tell your story as best you can, remembering that the short story is language under pressure. (Review the section "Notes about Writing Stories" [p. 186] as you go about writing your short story.) (*Your instructor may ask you to share by reading aloud.*)

Winter Weather
Babette Duncan Wilson

". . . by the footprints in the butter!"

Skip Wainwright was telling another one of his silly jokes to a customer. Karen could never understand why people continued to pretend he was funny. He always made a fool out of himself by laughing so hard that people were forced to join in out of nervousness. "He does look comical," Karen thought, "with his horrible toupee which didn't match his gray overly long sideburns." Skip was her boss on these afternoons, though, and Karen was willing to put up with him because she needed the money to pay for clothes and entertainment. Ye Olde Butcher Shoppe, better known as Joe's Place, was close to home and paid better than Pizza Hut.

Joe was Skip's older brother who opened the store over thirty years ago. Initially, Joe worked eighty hour weeks to keep the place going. Now that Skip was around, Joe was able to take the afternoons and weekends off to spend with his family. Skip became a junior partner only eight years ago when he lost his job at the Nashua television station—after over twenty years of being known as "Skippy the Weatherman." Skip was replaced by a much younger and better looking college graduate. Not many of the newer customers recognized Skip from his broadcast days, but the regulars still feigned interest in Skip's knowledge of the weather.

Karen hated days when big snowstorms were predicted. Skip would really drive her crazy, talking about the barometer and the wind chill factor and the incompetence of the new breed of forecasters. Today was one of those cold and snowy New England February days that Karen dreaded on her walk from school to her job as cashier. As she expected, Skip spent all afternoon reminiscing about the Blizzard of '78.

"Well, Karen," he said turning down the radio, "I think those newfangled weathermen are full of it! Do you call this a storm?"

Karen merely shrugged and looked at him indifferently. She hated it when there were no customers around and she was reduced to having to listen to the old man.

She walked over to the window, rubbed a spot of frost off with her apron, and gazed out at the snow. It seemed to be falling rather heavily, four or five inches already on the ground.

"I don't know," she said. "There's a lot of snow out there. Since it just started at one, and there's half a foot out there already, I think this could be a big one."

Karen was an attractive sixteen-year-old, but she dressed a little bit too outlandishly for the older generation to understand. Skip liked to tease her about her pink streaked hair and was always reminding her that her earrings never matched. Karen would usually ignore him, knowing that he was the last person on earth to criticize anyone in his polyester pants and silly bow ties.

"You kids," said Skip, "you know nothing of bad weather. This is merely a dusting. You probably don't even remember '78—now those were storms! I was the only forecaster in the area, including Boston, who accurately predicted both those blizzards. These new meteorologists are always crying wolf. With all their new computers, they lack good old Yankee common sense. . . ."

Luckily, a customer walked in and Karen was spared the rest of his monologue. Mrs. Angus was a regular and would keep Skip busy for a while. Karen walked over to the refrigerator and pretended to straighten the milk cartons. While there, she also took advantage of the opportunity to straighten her hair, looking at her reflection in the glass door. On her way back to her post, she glanced at the clock—it was only 4:15, and she had an hour and fifteen minutes before she could leave.

When Skip finished wrapping Mrs. Angus' hamburger and chops, and the small talk was over, Karen rang up the order. The lady disappeared out the door into the snow outside.

Skip now listened to the radio, and Karen was happy to spend the time day-dreaming about the suede coat she had put on lay-away at the mall. "It's been unusually quiet, today," Karen thought. "It's probably 'cause of the storm." Karen began hoping she might be allowed to leave a little early. "Fat chance," she thought. "It would be easier having an Eskimo for a boss."

Skip decided to go out and shovel the walk. After he left, she took the opportunity to turn the radio to her favorite rock station. She sang along and swayed to the beat of Madonna's newest hit. Eight minutes later, Skip returned and loudly stomped the snow off his feet.

"It's coming down strong out there now," Skip said hesitantly. "I still think it will taper off soon, though. The roads are deserted. Nowadays everyone is afraid of snow. We've had such mild weather over the last few years that people react as if they've lived in Florida and fall apart at the. . . ."

Karen interrupted him to ask if she could leave early. Skip gave her an annoyed look and proceeded to go off on another tirade. When he was finished, he walked over to the radio and turned the station back to the news—just in time to hear a weather update.

". . . looks like we could easily have two or more feet, with winds gusting upwards of fifty miles an hour. Again, I urge everyone to stay put—traffic is at a virtual standstill and this blizzard could be the worst of the decade. . . ."

Skip turned off the radio and told Karen that she could go on home. Karen immediately went out back to grab her things.

When she returned, Skip was standing in front of the window, peering through a place he had cleared in the glass. The storm was raging beyond and white was all one could see. She saw his face reflected in the glass. He had a tortured expression and was as pale as a ghost. Skip seemed oblivious to Karen who was standing beside him. Suddenly, hurrying home was no longer important to Karen. She cared more about this old butcher than she had realized.

After a moment, he noticed her beside him in the reflection. It was an instant neither would forget; the gap between them was closed.

He was the first to turn around. The blood returned to his face and he smiled and asked, "How can you tell if an elephant has been in your refrigerator?"

The moment was gone, but the bond would remain.

CONCLUSIONS

To claim that literature is a conversation that all people are invited to take part in, and then to talk only about reading, responding, and making meaning of literary texts, is to ignore the value of creative responses. No matter how actively engaged in the works you now become, unless you try to understand the creative process, to see it as not unlike the process you use in writing about literary texts, you have an incomplete picture of literature. One way to acquire this understanding is to try your hand at making literature. Think about the following: Suppose you've read and studied Shakespeare's *Romeo and Juliet*, but have never seen it performed. Though you may have gained a great deal in the process of making meaning of the play, you have not experienced the immediacy of seeing the words in action. You may need both experiences to have the complete picture of what Shakespeare was attempting. Now that you have tried to fashion your own literary work, you may have a more complete picture of what it's like to be a literary author. And, with your classmates, you should celebrate this entrance into the ongoing conversation called literature.

12 On Your Own
Additional Readings

GROUP 1

"GIRL"
Jamaica Kincaid

Wash the white clothes on Monday and put them on the stone heap; wash the color clothes on Tuesday and put them on the clothesline to dry; don't walk barehead in the hot sun; cook pumpkin fritters in very hot sweet oil; soak your little cloths right after you take them off; when buying cotton to make yourself a nice blouse, be sure that it doesn't have gum on it, because that way it won't hold up well after a wash; soak salt fish overnight before you cook it; is it true that you sing benna in Sunday school?; always eat your food in such a way that it won't turn someone else's stomach; on Sundays try to walk like a lady and not like the slut you are so bent on becoming; don't sing benna in Sunday school; you mustn't speak to wharf-rat boys, not even to give directions; don't eat fruits on the street—flies will follow you; *but I don't sing benna on Sundays at all and never in Sunday school*; this is how to sew on a button; this is how to make a buttonhole for the button you have just sewed on; this is how to hem a dress when you see the hem coming down and so to prevent yourself from looking like the slut I know you are so bent on becoming; this is how you iron your father's khaki shirt so that it doesn't have a crease; this is how to iron your father's khaki pants so that they don't have a crease; this is how to grow okra—far from the house, because okra tree harbors red ants; when you are growing dasheen, make sure it gets plenty of water or else it makes your throat itch when you are eating it; this is how you sweep a corner; this is how you sweep a whole house; this is how you sweep a yard; this is how you smile to someone you don't like too much; this is how you smile to someone you don't like at all; this is how you smile to someone you like completely; this is how you set a table for tea; this is how you set a table for dinner; this is how you set a table for dinner with an important guest; this is how you set a table for lunch; this is how you set a table for breakfast; this is how to behave in the presence of men who don't know you very well, and this way they won't recognize immediately the slut I have warned you against becoming; be sure to wash every day, even if it is with your own spit; don't squat down to play marbles—you are not a boy, you know; don't pick people's flowers— you might catch something; don't throw stones at blackbirds, because it might not be a blackbird at all; this is how to make a bread pudding; this is how to make doukona; this is how to make a pepper pot; this is how to make a good medicine for a cold; this is how to make a good medicine to throw away a child before it even becomes a child; this is how to catch a fish; this is how to throw back a fish you don't like, and that way something bad won't fall on you; this is how to bully a man; this is how a man bullies you; this is how to love a man, and if this doesn't work there are other ways, and if they don't work don't feel too bad about giving up; this is how to spit up in the air if you feel like it, and this is how to move quick so that it doesn't fall on you; this is how to make ends meet; always squeeze bread to make sure it's fresh; *but what if the baker won't let me feel the bread?*; you mean to say that after all you are really going to be the kind of woman who the baker won't let near the bread?

NAMING OF PARTS

Henry Reed

Today we have naming of parts. Yesterday,
We had daily cleaning. And tomorrow morning,
We shall have what to do after firing. But today,
Today we have naming of parts. Japonica
Glistens like coral in all of the neighboring gardens,   5
      And today we have naming of parts.

This is the lower sling swivel. And this
Is the upper sling swivel, whose use you will see,
When you are given your slings. And this is the piling swivel,
Which in your case you have not got. The branches   10
Hold in the gardens their silent, eloquent gestures,
      Which in our case we have not got.

This is the safety-catch, which is always released
With an easy flick of the thumb. And please do not let me
See anyone using his finger. You can do it quite easy   15
If you have any strength in your thumb. The blossoms
Are fragile and motionless, never letting anyone see
      Any of them using their finger.
And this you can see is the bolt. The purpose of this
Is to open the breech, as you see. We can slide it   20

Rapidly backwards and forwards: we call this
Easing the spring. And rapidly backwards and forwards
The early bees are assaulting and fumbling the flowers:
     They call it easing the Spring.

They call it easing the Spring: it is perfectly easy   25
If you have any strength in your thumb: like the bolt,
And the breech, and the cocking-piece, and the point of balance,
Which in our case we have not got; and the almond-blossom
Silent in all of the gardens and the bees going backwards and
     forwards,
     For today we have naming of parts.   30

"TREATISE ON MANNERS"

Jonathan Swift

Good manners is the art of making those people easy with whom we converse.
     Whoever makes the fewest persons uneasy is the best bred in the company.
     As the best law is founded upon reason, so are the best manners. And as some lawyers have introduced unreasonable things into common law, so likewise many teachers have introduced absurd things into common good manners.
     One principal point of this art is to suit our behaviour to the three several degrees of men; our superiors, our equals, and those below us.
     For instance, to press either of the two former to eat or drink is a breach of   5 manners; but a farmer or a tradesman must be thus treated, or else it will be difficult to persuade them that they are welcome.
     Pride, ill nature, and want of sense, are the three great sources of ill manners; without some one of these defects, no man will behave himself ill for want of experience; or of what, in the language of fools, is called knowing the world.
     I defy any one to assign an incident wherein reason will not direct us what we are to say or do in company, if we are not misled by pride or ill nature.
     Therefore I insist that good sense is the principal foundation of good manners; but because the former is a gift which very few among mankind are possessed of, therefore all the civilized nations of the world have agreed upon fixing some rules for common behaviour, best suited to their general customs, or fancies, as a kind of artificial good sense, to supply the defects of reason. Without which the gentlemanly part of dunces would be perpetually at cuffs, as they seldom fail when they happen to be drunk, or engaged in squabbles about women or play. And, God be thanked, there hardly happens a duel in a year, which may not be imputed to one of those three motives. Upon which account, I should be exceedingly sorry to find the legislature make any new laws against the practice of duelling; because the

methods are easy and many for a wise man to avoid a quarrel with honour, or engage in it with innocence. And I can discover no political evil in suffering bullies, sharpers, and rakes, to rid the world of each other by a method of their own; where the law hath not been able to find an expedient.

As the common forms of good manners were intended for regulating the conduct of those who have weak understandings; so they have been corrupted by the persons for whose use they were contrived. For these people have fallen into a needless and endless way of multiplying ceremonies, which have been extremely troublesome to those who practise them, and insupportable to everybody else: insomuch that wise men are often more uneasy at the over civility of these refiners, than they could possibly be in the conversations of peasants or mechanics.

The impertinencies of this ceremonial behaviour are nowhere better seen than 10 at those tables where ladies preside, who value themselves upon account of their good breeding; where a man must reckon upon passing an hour without doing any one thing he has a mind to; unless he will be so hardy to break through all the settled decorum of the family. She determines what he loves best, and how much he shall eat; and if the master of the house happens to be of the same disposition, he proceeds in the same tyrannical manner to prescribe in the drinking part: at the same time, you are under the necessity of answering a thousand apologies for your entertainment. And although a good deal of this humour is pretty well worn off among many people of the best fashion, yet too much of it still remains, especially in the country; where an honest gentleman assured me, that having been kept four days, against his will, at a friend's house, with all the circumstances of hiding his boots, locking up the stable, and other contrivances of the like nature, he could not remember, from the moment he came into the house to the moment he left it, any one thing, wherein his inclination was not directly contradicted; as if the whole family had entered into a combination to torment him.

But, besides all this, it would be endless to recount the many foolish and ridiculous accidents I have observed among these unfortunate proselytes to ceremony. I have seen a duchess fairly knocked down, by the precipitancy of an officious coxcomb running to save her the trouble of opening a door. I remember, upon a birthday at court, a great lady was utterly desperate by a dish of sauce let fall by a page directly upon her head-dress and brocade, while she gave a sudden turn to her elbow upon some point of ceremony with the person who sat next her. Monsieur Buys, the Dutch envoy, whose politics and manners were much of a size, brought a son with him, about thirteen years old, to a great table at court. The boy and his father, whatever they put on their plates, they first offered round in order, to every person in the company; so that we could not get a minute's quiet during the whole dinner. At last their two plates happened to encounter, and with so much violence, that, being china, they broke in twenty pieces, and stained half the company with wet sweetmeats and cream.

There is a pedantry in manners, as in all arts and sciences; and sometimes in trades. Pedantry is properly the overrating any kind of knowledge we pretend to. And if that kind of knowledge be a trifle in itself, the pedantry is the greater. For which reason I look upon fiddlers, dancing-masters, heralds, masters of the ceremony, &c. to be greater pedants than Lipsius, or the elder Scaliger. With these kind of pedants, the court, while I knew it, was always plentifully stocked; I mean from the gentleman usher (at least) inclusive, downward to the gentleman porter; who are, generally speaking, the most insignificant race of people that this island can afford, and with the smallest tincture of good manners, which is the only trade they profess. For being wholly illiterate, and conversing chiefly with each other, they reduce the whole system of breeding within the forms and circles of their several offices; and as they are below the notice of ministers, they live and die in court under all revolutions with great obsequiousness to those who are in any degree of favour or credit, and with rudeness or insolence to everybody else. Whence I have long concluded, that good manners are not a plant of the court growth: for if they were, those people who have understandings directly of a level for such acquirements, and who have served such long apprenticeships to nothing else, would certainly have picked them up. For as to the great officers, who attend the prince's person or councils, or preside in his family, they are a transient body, who have no better a title to good manners than their neighbours, nor will probably have recourse to gentlemen ushers for instruction. So that I know little to be learnt at court upon this head, except in the material circumstance of dress; wherein the authority of the maids of honour must indeed be allowed to be almost equal to that of a favourite actress.

I remember a passage my Lord Bolingbroke told me, that going to receive Prince Eugene of Savoy at his landing, in order to conduct him immediately to the Queen, the prince said, he was much concerned that he could not see her Majesty that night; for Monsieur Hoffman (who was then by) had assured his Highness that he could not be admitted into her presence with a tied-up periwig; that his equipage was not arrived; and that he had endeavoured in vain to borrow a long one among his valets and pages. My lord turned the matter into a jest, and brought the Prince to her Majesty; for which he was highly censured by the whole tribe of gentlemen ushers; among whom Monsieur Hoffman, an old dull resident of the Emperor's, had picked up this material point of ceremony; and which, I believe, was the best lesson he had learned in five-and-twenty years' residence.

I make a difference between good manners and good breeding; although, in order to vary my expression, I am sometimes forced to confound them. By the first, I only understand the art of remembering and applying certain settled forms of general behaviour. But good breeding is of a much larger extent; for besides an uncommon degree of literature sufficient to qualify a gentleman for reading a play, or a political pamphlet, it takes in a great compass of knowledge; no less than that of dancing, fighting, gaming, making the circle of Italy, riding the great horse, and speaking French; not to mention some other secondary, or subaltern accomplishments, which are more easily acquired. So that the difference between good breeding and good manners lies in this, that the former cannot be attained to by the best understandings, without study and labour; whereas a tolerable degree of reason will instruct us in every part of good manners, without other assistance.

I can think of nothing more useful upon this subject, than to point out some 15 particulars, wherein the very essentials of good manners are concerned, the neglect or perverting of which doth very much disturb the good commerce of the world, by introducing a traffic of mutual uneasiness in most companies.

First, a necessary part of good manners, is a punctual observance of time at our own dwellings, or those of others, or at third places; whether upon matter of civility, business, or diversion; which rule, though it be a plain dictate of common reason, yet the greatest minister I ever knew was the greatest trespasser against it; by which all his business doubled upon him, and placed him in a continual arrear. Upon which I often used to rally him, as deficient in point of good manners. I have known more than one ambassador, and secretary of state with a very moderate portion of intellectuals, execute their offices with good success and applause, by the mere force of exactness and regularity. If you duly observe time for the service of another, it doubles the obligation; if upon your own account, it would be manifest folly, as well as ingratitude, to neglect it. If both are concerned, to make your equal or inferior attend on you, to his own disadvantage, is pride and injustice.

Ignorance of forms cannot properly be styled ill manners; because forms are subject to frequent changes; and consequently, being not founded upon reason, are beneath a wise man's regard. Besides, they vary in every country; and after a short period of time, vary frequently in the same; so that a man who travels, must needs be at first a stranger to them in every court through which he passes; and perhaps at his return, as much a stranger in his own; and after all, they are easier to be remembered or forgotten than faces or names.

Indeed, among the many impertinencies that superficial young men bring with them from abroad, this bigotry of forms is one of the principal, and more prominent than the rest; who look upon them not only as points of importance; and are therefore zealous on all occasions to introduce and propagate the new forms and fashions they have brought back with them. So that, usually speaking, the worst bred person in the company is a young traveller just returned from abroad.

RIDERS TO THE SEA
A PLAY IN ONE ACT

John M. Synge

PERSONS IN THE PLAY

First performed at the Molesworth Hall, Dublin, February 25, 1904.
MAURYA (*an old woman*)
BARTLEY (*her son*)
CATHLEEN (*her daughter*)
NORA (*a younger daughter*)
MEN and WOMEN

SCENE. AN ISLAND OFF THE WEST OF IRELAND.

(*Cottage kitchen, with nets, oil-skins, spinning wheel, some new boards standing by the wall, etc. Cathleen, a girl of about twenty, finishes kneading cake, and puts it down in the pot-oven by the fire; then wipes her hands, and begins to spin at the wheel. Nora, a young girl, puts her head in at the door.*)

NORA (*in a low voice*). Where is she?

CATHLEEN. She's lying down, God help her, and may be sleeping, if she's able.

[*Nora comes in softly, and takes a bundle from under her shawl.*]

CATHLEEN (*spinning the wheel rapidly*). What is it you have?

NORA. The young priest is after bringing them. It's a shirt and a plain stocking were got off a drowned man in Donegal.

[*Cathleen stops her wheel with a sudden movement, and leans out to listen.*]

NORA. We're to find out if it's Michael's they are, some time herself will be down looking by the sea.

CATHLEEN. How would they be Michael's, Nora. How would he go the length of that way to the far north?

NORA. The young priest says he's known the like of it. "If it's Michael's they are," says he, "you can tell herself he's got a clean burial by the grace of God, and if they're not his, let no one say a word about them, for she'll be getting her death," says he, "with crying and lamenting."

[*The door which Nora half closed is blown open by a gust of wind.*]

CATHLEEN (*looking out anxiously*). Did you ask him would he stop Bartley going this day with the horses to the Galway fair?

NORA. "I won't stop him," says he, "but let you not be afraid. Herself does be saying prayers half through the night, and the Almighty God won't leave her destitute," says he, "with no son living."

CATHLEEN. Is the sea bad by the white rocks, Nora?

NORA. Middling bad, God help us. There's a great roaring in the west, and it's worse it'll be getting when the tide's turned to the wind.

[*She goes over to the table with the bundle.*]

Shall I open it now?

CATHLEEN. Maybe she'd wake up on us, and come in before we'd done. (*Coming to the table.*) It's a long time we'll be, and the two of us crying.

NORA (*goes to the inner door and listens*). She's moving about on the bed. She'll be coming in a minute.

CATHLEEN. Give me the ladder, and I'll put them up in the turf-loft, that way she won't know of them at all, and maybe when the tide turns she'll be going down to see would he be floating from the east.

[*They put the ladder against the gable of the chimney; Cathleen goes up a few steps and hides the bundle in the turf-loft. Maurya comes from the inner room.*]

MAURYA (*looking up at Cathleen and speaking querulously*). Isn't it turf enough you have for this day and evening?

CATHLEEN. There's a cake baking at the fire for a short space (*throwing down the turf*) and Bartley will want it when the tide turns if he goes to Connemara.

[*Nora picks up the turf and puts it round the pot-oven.*]

MAURYA (*sitting down on a stool at the fire*). He won't go this day with the wind rising from the south and west. He won't go this day, for the young priest will stop him surely.

NORA. He'll not stop him, mother, and I heard Eamon Simon and Stephen Pheety and Colum Shawn saying he would go.

CAT Where is he itself?

NORA. He went down to see would there be another boat sailing in the week, and I'm thinking it won't be long till he's here now, for the tide's turning at the green head, and the hooker's tacking from the east.

CATHLEEN. I hear some one passing the big stones.

NORA (*looking out*). He's coming now, and he in a hurry.

BARTLEY (*comes in and looks around the room. Speaking sadly and quietly*). Where is the bit of new rope, Cathleen, was bought in Connemara?

CATHLEEN (*coming down*). Give it to him, Nora; it's on a nail by the white boards. I hung it up this morning, for the pig with the black feet was eating it.

NORA (*giving him a rope*). Is that it, Bartley?

MAURYA. You'd do right to leave that rope, Bartley, hanging by the boards. (*Bartley takes the rope.*) It will be wanting in this place, I'm telling you, if Michael is washed up to-morrow morning, or the next morning, or any morning in the week, for it's a deep grave we'll make him by the grace of God.

BARTLEY (*beginning to work with the rope*). I've no halter the way I can ride down on the mare, and I must go now quickly. This is the one boat going for two weeks or beyond it, and the fair will be a good fair for horses I heard them saying below.

MAURYA. It's a hard thing they'll be saying below if the body is washed up and there's no man in it to make the coffin, and I after giving a big price for the finest white boards you'd find in Connemara.

[*She looks round at the boards.*]

BARTLEY. How would it be washed up, and we after looking each day for nine days, and a strong wind blowing a while back from the west and south?

MAURYA. If it wasn't found itself, that wind is raising the sea, and there was a star up against the moon, and it rising in the night. If it was a hundred horses, or a thousand horses you had itself, what is the price of a thousand horses against a son where there is one son only?

BARTLEY (*working at the halter, to Cathleen*). Let you go down each day, and see the sheep aren't jumping in on the rye, and if the jobber comes you can sell the pig with the black feet if there is a good price going.

MAURYA. How would the like of her get a good price for a pig?

BARTLEY (*to Cathleen*). If the west wind holds with the last bit of the moon let you and Nora get up weed enough for another cock for the kelp. It's hard set we'll be from this day with no one in it but one man to work.

MAURYA. It's hard set we'll be surely the day you're drownd'd with the rest. What way will I live and the girls with me, and I an old woman looking for the grave?

[Bartley lays down the halter, takes off his old coat, and puts on a newer one of the same flannel.]

BARTLEY (to Nora). Is she coming to the pier?

NORA (looking out). She's passing the green head and letting fall her sails.

BARTLEY (getting his purse and tobacco). I'll have half an hour to go down, and you'll see me coming again in two days, or in three days, or maybe in four days if the wind is bad.

MAURYA (turning round to the fire, and putting her shawl over her head). Isn't it a hard and cruel man won't hear a word from an old woman, and she holding him from the sea?

CATHLEEN. It's the life of a young man to be going on the sea, and who would listen to an old woman with one thing and she saying it over?

BARTLEY (taking the halter). I must go now quickly. I'll ride down on the red mare, and the gray pony'll run behind me. . . . The blessing of God on you.

[He goes out.]

MAURYA. (crying out as he is in the door). He's gone now, God spare us, and we'll not see him again. He's gone now, and when the black night is falling I'll have no son left me in the world.

CATHLEEN. Why wouldn't you give him your blessing and he looking round in the door? Isn't it sorrow enough is on every one in this house without your sending him out with an unlucky word behind him, and a hard word in his ear?

[Maurya takes up the tongs and begins raking the fire aimlessly without looking round.]

NORA (turning towards her). You're taking away the turf from the cake.

CATHLEEN (crying out). The Son of God forgive us, Nora, we're after forgetting his bit of bread.

[She comes over to the fire.]

NORA. And it's destroyed he'll be going till dark night, and he after eating nothing since the sun went up.

CATHLEEN (turning the cake out of the oven). It's destroyed he'll be, surely. There's no sense left on any person in a house where an old woman will be talking forever.

[Maurya sways herself on her stool.]

CATHLEEN (cutting off some of the bread and rolling it in a cloth; to Maurya). Let you go down now to the spring well and give him this and he passing. You'll see him then and the dark word will be broken, and you can say "God speed you," the way he'll be easy in his mind.

MAURYA (taking the bread). Will I be in it as soon as himself?

CATHLEEN. If you go now quickly.

MAURYA (standing up unsteadily). It's hard set I am to walk.

CATHLEEN (*looking at her anxiously*). Give her the stick, Nora, or maybe she'll slip on the big stones.

NORA. What stick?

CATHLEEN. The stick Michael brought from Connemara.

MAURYA (*taking a stick Nora gives her*). In the big world the old people do be leaving things after them for their sons and children, but in this place it is the young men do be leaving things for them that do be old.

[*She goes out slowly. Nora goes over to the ladder.*]

CATHLEEN. Wait, Nora, maybe she'd turn back quickly. She's that sorry, God help her, you wouldn't know the thing she'd do.

NORA. Is she gone round by the bush?

CATHLEEN (*looking out*). She's gone now. Throw it down quickly, for the Lord knows when she'll be out of it again.

NORA (*getting the bundle from the loft*). The young priest said he'd be passing to-morrow, and we might go down and speak to him below if it's Michael's they are surely.

CATHLEEN (*taking the bundle*). Did he say what way they were found?

NORA (*coming down*). "There were two men," says he, "and they rowing round with poteen before the cocks crowed, and the oar of one of them caught the body, and they passing the black cliffs of the north."

CATHLEEN (*trying to open the bundle*). Give me a knife, Nora, the string's perished with the salt water, and there's a black knot on it you wouldn't loosen in a week.

NORA (*giving her a knife*). I've heard tell it was a long way to Donegal.

CATHLEEN (*cutting the string*). It is surely. There was a man in here a while ago—the man sold us that knife—and he said if you set off walking from the rocks beyond, it would be seven days you'd be in Donegal.

NORA. And what time would a man take, and he floating?

[*Cathleen opens the bundle and takes out a bit of a stocking. They look at them eagerly.*]

CATHLEEN (*in a low voice*). The Lord spare us, Nora! isn't it a queer hard thing to say if it's his they are surely?

NORA. I'll get his shirt off the hook the way we can put the one flannel on the other. (*She looks through some clothes hanging in the corner.*) It's not with them, Cathleen, and where will it be?

CATHLEEN. I'm thinking Bartley put it on him in the morning, for his own shirt was heavy with the salt in it (*pointing to the corner*). There's a bit of a sleeve was of the same stuff. Give me that and it will do.

[*Nora brings it to her and they compare the flannel.*]

CATHLEEN. It's the same stuff, Nora; but if it is itself aren't there great rolls of it in the shops of Galway, and isn't it many another man may have a shirt of it as well as Michael himself?

NORA (*who has taken up the stocking and counted the stitches, crying out*). It's Michael, Cathleen, it's Michael; God spare his soul, and what will herself say when she hears this story, and Bartley on the sea?

CATHLEEN (taking the stocking). It's a plain stocking.

NORA. It's the second one of the third pair I knitted, and I put up three score stitches, and I dropped four of them.

CATHLEEN (counts the stitches). It's that number is in it (crying out). Ah, Nora, isn't it a bitter thing to think of him floating that way to the far north, and no one to keen him but the black hags that do be flying on the sea?

NORA (swinging herself round, and throwing out her arms on the clothes). And isn't it a pitiful thing when there is nothing left of a man who was a great rower and fisher, but a bit of an old shirt and a plain stocking?

CATHLEEN (after an instant). Tell me is herself coming, Nora? I hear a little sound on the path.

NORA (looking out). She is, Cathleen. She's coming up to the door.

CATHLEEN. Put these things away before she'll come in. Maybe it's easier she'll be after giving her blessing to Bartley, and we won't let on we've heard anything the time he's on the sea.

NORA (helping Cathleen to close the bundle). We'll put them here in the corner.

[They put them into a hole in the chimney corner. Cathleen goes back to the spinning-wheel.]

NORA. Will she see it was crying I was?

CATHLEEN. Keep your back to the door the way the light'll not be on you.

[Nora sits down at the chimney corner, with her back to the door. Maurya comes in very slowly, without looking at the girls, and goes over to her stool at the other side of the fire. The cloth with the bread is still in her hand. The girls look at each other, and Nora points to the bundle of bread.]

CATHLEEN (after spinning for a moment). You didn't give him his bit of bread?

[Maurya begins to keen softly, without turning round.]

CATHLEEN. Did you see him riding down?

[Maurya goes on keening.]

CATHLEEN (a little impatiently). God forgive you; isn't it a better thing to raise your voice and tell what you seen, than to be making lamentation for a thing that's done? Did you see Bartley, I'm saying to you.

MAURYA (with a weak voice). My heart's broken from this day.

CATHLEEN (as before). Did you see Bartley?

MAURYA. I seen the fearfulest thing.

CATHLEEN (leaves her wheel and looks out). God forgive you; he's riding the mare now over the green head, and the gray pony behind him.

MAURYA (starts, so that her shawl falls back from her head and shows her white tossed hair. With a frightened voice). The gray pony behind him.

CATHLEEN (coming to the fire). What is it ails you, at all?

MAURYA (speaking very slowly). I've seen the fearfulest thing any person has seen, since the day Bride Dara seen the dead man with the child in his arms.

CATHLEEN AND NORA. Uah.

[They crouch down in front of the old woman at the fire.]

NORA. Tell us what it is you seen.

MAURYA. I went down to the spring well, and I stood there saying a prayer to myself. Then Bartley came along, and he riding on the red mare with the gray pony behind him. *(She puts up her hands, as if to hide something from her eyes.)* The Son of God spare us, Nora!

CATHLEEN. What is it you seen.

MAURYA. I seen Michael himself.

CATHLEEN *(speaking softly)*. You did not, mother; It wasn't Michael you seen, for his body is after being found in the far north, and he's got a clean burial by the grace of God.

MAURYA *(a little defiantly)*. I'm after seeing him this day, and he riding and galloping. Bartley came first on the red mare; and I tried to say "God speed you," but something choked the words in my throat. He went by quickly; and "the blessing of God on you," says he, and I could say nothing. I looked up then, and I crying, at the gray pony, and there was Michael upon it—with fine clothes on him, and new shoes on his feet.

CATHLEEN *(begins to keen)*. It's destroyed we are from this day. It's destroyed, surely.

NORA. Didn't the young priest say the Almighty God wouldn't leave her destitute with no son living?

MAURYA *(in a low voice, but clearly)*. It's little the like of him knows of the sea. . . . Bartley will be lost now, and let you call in Eamon and make me a good coffin out of the white boards, for I won't live after them. I've had a husband, and a husband's father, and six sons in this house—six fine men, though it was a hard birth I had with every one of them and they coming to the world—and some of them were found and some of them were not found, but they're gone now the lot of them. . . . There were Stephen, and Shawn, were lost in the great wind, and found after in the Bay of Gregory of the Golden Mouth, and carried up the two of them on the one plank, and in by that door.

[She pauses for a moment, the girls start as if they heard something through the door that is half open behind them.]

NORA *(in a whisper)*. Did you hear that, Cathleen? Did you hear a noise in the north-east?

CATHLEEN *(in a whisper)*. There's some one after crying out by the seashore.

MAURYA *(continues without hearing anything)*. There was Sheamus and his father, and his own father again, were lost in a dark night, and not a stick or sign was seen of them when the sun went up. There was Patch after was drowned out of a curagh that turned over. I was sitting here with Bartley, and he a baby, lying on my two knees, and I seen two women, and three women, and four women coming in, and they crossing themselves, and not saying a word. I looked out then, and there were men coming after them, and they holding a thing in the half of a red sail, and water dripping out of it—it was a dry day, Nora—and leaving a track to the door.

[*She pauses again with her hand stretched out towards the door. It opens softly and old women begin to come in, crossing themselves on the threshold, and kneeling down in front of the stage with red petticoats over their heads.*]

MAURYA (*half in a dream, to Cathleen*). Is it Patch, or Michael, or what is it at all?

CATHLEEN. Michael is after being found in the far north, and when he is found there how could he be here in this place?

MAURYA. There does be a power of young men floating round in the sea, and what way would they know if it was Michael they had, or another man like him, for when a man is nine days in the sea, and the wind blowing, it's hard set his own mother would be to say what man was it.

CATHLEEN. It's Michael, God spare him, for they're after sending us a bit of his clothes from the far north.

[*She reaches out and hands Maurya the clothes that belonged to Michael. Maurya stands up slowly and takes them in her hands. Nora looks out.*]

NORA. They're carrying a thing among them and there's water dripping out of it and leaving a track by the big stones.

CATHLEEN (*in a whisper to the women who have come in*). Is it Bartley it is?

ONE OF THE WOMEN. It is surely, God rest his soul.

[*Two younger women come in and pull out the table. Then men carrying in the body of Bartley, laid on a plank, with a bit of sail over it, and lay it on the table.*]

CATHLEEN (*to the women, as they are doing so*). What way was he drowned?

ONE OF THE WOMEN. The gray pony knocked him into the sea, and he was washed out where there is a great surf on the white rocks.

[*Maurya has gone over and knelt down at the head of the table. The women are keening softly and swaying themselves with a slow movement. Cathleen and Nora kneel at the other end of the table. The men kneel near the door.*]

MAURYA (*raising her head and speaking as if she did not see the people around her*). They're all gone now, and there isn't anything more the sea can do to me. . . . I'll have no call now to be up crying and praying when the wind breaks from the south, and you can hear the surf is in the east, and the surf is in the west, making a great stir with the two noises, and they hitting one on the other. I'll have no call now to be going down and getting Holy Water in the dark nights after Samhain, and I won't care what way the sea is when the other women will be keening. (*To Nora.*) Give me the Holy Water, Nora, there's a small cup still on the dresser.

[*Nora gives it to her.*]

MAURYA (*drops Michael's clothes across Bartley's feet, and sprinkles the Holy Water over him*). It isn't that I haven't prayed for you, Bartley, to the Almighty God. It isn't that I haven't said prayers in the dark night till you wouldn't know what I'd be saying; but it's a great rest I'll have now, and it's time surely. It's a great rest I'll have now, and great sleeping in the long nights after Samhain, if it's only a bit of wet flour we do have to eat, and maybe a fish that would be stinking.

[*She kneels down again, crossing herself, and saying prayers under her breath.*]

CATHLEEN (to an old man). Maybe yourself and Eamon would make a coffin when the sun rises. We have fine white boards herself bought, God help her, thinking Michael would be found, and I have a new cake you can eat while you'll be working.

THE OLD MAN (looking at the boards). Are there nails with them?

CATHLEEN. There are not, Colum; we didn't think of the nails.

ANOTHER MAN. It's a great wonder she wouldn't think of the nails, and all the coffins she's seen made already.

CATHLEEN. It's getting old she is, and broken.

[Maurya stands up again very slowly and spreads out the pieces of Michael's clothes beside the body, sprinkling them with the last of the Holy Water.]

NORA (in a whisper to Cathleen). She's quiet now and easy; but the day Michael was drowned you could hear her crying out from this to the spring well. It's fonder she was of Michael, and would any one have thought that?

CATHLEEN (slowly and clearly). An old woman will be soon tired with anything she will do, and isn't it nine days herself is after crying and keening, and making great sorrow in the house?

MAURYA (puts the empty cup mouth downwards on the table, and lays her hands together on Bartley's feet). They're all together this time, and the end is come. May the Almighty God have mercy on Bartley's soul, and on Michael's soul, and on the souls of Sheamus and Patch, and Stephen and Shawn (bending her head); and may He have mercy on my soul, Nora, and on the soul of every one is left living in the world.

[She pauses, and the keen rises a little more loudly from the women, then sinks away.]

MAURYA (continuing). Michael has a clean burial in the far north, by the grace of Almighty God. Bartley will have a fine coffin out of the white boards, and a deep grave surely. What more can we want than that? No man at all can be living for ever, and we must be satisfied.

[She kneels down again and the curtain falls slowly.]

GROUP 2

EVERYDAY USE

Alice Walker

---

for your grandmama

I will wait for her in the yard that Maggie and I made so clean and wavy yesterday afternoon. A yard like this is more comfortable than most people know. It is not just a yard. It is like an extended living room. When the hard clay is swept clean as a floor and the fine sand around the edges lined with tiny, irregular grooves, anyone can come and sit and look up into the elm tree and wait for the breezes that never come inside the house.

Maggie will be nervous until after her sister goes: she will stand hopelessly in corners, homely and ashamed of the burn scars down her arms and legs, eyeing her sister with a mixture of envy and awe. She thinks her sister has held life always in the palm of her hand, that "no" is a word the world never learned to say to her.

You've no doubt seen those TV shows where the child who has "made it" is confronted, as a surprise, by her own mother and father tottering in weakly from backstage. (A pleasant surprise, of course. What would they do if parent and child came on the show only to curse out and insult each other?) On TV mother and father embrace and smile into each other's faces. Sometimes the mother and father weep, the child wraps them in her arms and leans across the table to tell how she would not have made it without their help. I have seen these programs.

Sometimes I dream a dream in which Dee and I are suddenly brought together on a TV program of this sort. Out of a dark and soft-seated limousine I am ushered into a bright room filled with many people. There I meet a smiling, gray, sporty man like Johnny Carson who shakes my hand and tells me what a fine girl I have. Then we are on the stage and Dee is embracing me with tears in her eyes. She pins on my dress a large orchid, even though she has told me once that she thinks orchids are tacky flowers.

In real life I am a large, big-boned woman with rough, man-working hands. In the winter I wear flannel nightgowns to bed and overalls during the day. I can kill and clean a hog as mercilessly as a man. My fat keeps me hot in zero weather. I can work outside all day, breaking ice to get water for washing: I can eat pork liver cooked over the open fire minutes after it comes steaming from the hog. One winter I knocked a bull calf straight in the brain between the eyes with a sledge hammer and had the meat hung up to chill before nightfall. But of course all this does not show on television. I am the way my daughter would want me to be: a hundred pounds lighter, my skin like an uncooked barley pancake. My hair glistens in the hot bright lights. Johnny Carson has much to do to keep up with my quick and witty tongue.

But that is a mistake. I know even before I wake up. Who ever knew a Johnson with a quick tongue? Who can even imagine me looking a strange white man in the eye? It seems to me I have talked to them always with one foot raised in flight, with my head turned in whichever way is farthest from them. Dee, though. She would always look anyone in the eye. Hesitation was no part of her nature.

"How do I look, Mama?" Maggie says, showing just enough of her thin body, enveloped in pink skirt and red blouse for me to know she's there, almost hidden by the door.

"Come out into the yard," I say.

Have you ever seen a lame animal, perhaps a dog run over by some careless person rich enough to own a car, sidle up to someone who is ignorant enough to be kind to him? That's the way my Maggie walks. She has been like this, chin on chest, eyes on ground, feet in shuffle, ever since the fire that burned the other house to the ground.

Dee is lighter than Maggie, with nicer hair and a fuller figure. She's a woman 10
now, though sometimes I forget. How long ago was it that the other house burned?
Ten, twelve years? Sometimes I can still hear the flames and feel Maggie's arms
sticking to me, her hair smoking, and her dress falling off her in little black papery
flakes. Her eyes seemed stretched open, blazed open by the flames reflected in
them. And Dee. I see her standing off under the sweet gum tree she used to dig gum
out of; a look of concentration on her face as she watched the last dingy gray board
of the house fall in toward the red-hot brick chimney. Why don't you do a dance
around the ashes? I'd wanted to ask her. She had hated the house that much.

I used to think she hated Maggie, too. But that was before we raised the money,
the church and me, to send her to Augusta to school. She used to read to us without
pity; forcing words, lies, other folks' habits, whole lives upon us two, sitting trapped
and ignorant underneath her voice. She washed us in a river of make-believe,
burned us with a lot of knowledge we didn't necessarily need to know. Pressed us to
her with the serious way she read, to shove us away at just the moment, like
dimwits, we seemed about to understand.

Dee wanted nice things. A yellow organdy dress to wear to her graduation from
high school; black pumps to match a green suit she'd made from an old suit somebody
gave me. She was determined to stare down any disaster in her efforts. Her eyelids
would not flicker for minutes at a time. Often I fought off the temptation to shake her.
At sixteen she had a style of her own: and she knew what style was.

I never had an education myself. After second grade the school was closed
down. Don't ask me why: in 1927 colored asked fewer questions than they do now.
Sometimes Maggie reads to me. She stumbles along good-naturedly but can't see
well. She knows she is not bright. Like good looks and money, quickness passed her
by. She will marry John Thomas (who has mossy teeth in an earnest face) and then
I'll be free to sit here and I guess just sing church songs to myself. Although I never
was a good singer. Never could carry a tune. I was always better at a man's job. I
used to love to milk till I was hooked in the side in '49. Cows are soothing and slow
and don't bother you, unless you try to milk them the wrong way.

I have deliberately turned my back on the house. It is three rooms, just like the
one that burned, except the roof is tin; they don't make shingle roofs any more. There
are no real windows, just some holes cut in the sides, like the portholes in a ship, but
not round and not square, with rawhide holding the shutters up on the outside. This
house is in a pasture, too, like the other one. No doubt when Dee sees it she will want
to tear it down. She wrote me once that no matter where we "choose" to live, she will
manage to come see us. But she will never bring her friends. Maggie and I thought
about this and Maggie asked me, "Mama, when did Dee ever *have* friends?"

She had a few. Furtive boys in pink shirts hanging about on wash-day after 15
school. Nervous girls who never laughed. Impressed with her they worshiped the
well-turned phrase, the cute shape, the scalding humor that erupted like bubbles in
lye. She read to them.

When she was courting Jimmy T she didn't have much time to pay to us, but
turned all her faultfinding power on him. He *flew* to marry a cheap city girl from a
family of ignorant flashy people. She hardly had time to recompose herself.

When she comes I will meet—but there they are!

Maggie attempts to make a dash for the house, in her shuffling way, but I stay her with my hand. "Come back here," I say. And she stops and tries to dig a well in the sand with her toe.

It is hard to see them clearly through the strong sun. But even the first glimpse of leg out of the car tells me it is Dee. Her feet were always neat-looking, as if God himself had shaped them with a certain style. From the other side of the car comes a short, stocky man. Hair is all over his head a foot long and hanging from his chin like a kinky mule tail. I hear Maggie suck in her breath. "Uhnnnh," is what it sounds like. Like when you see the wriggling end of a snake just in front of your foot on the road. "Uhnnnh."

Dee next. A dress down to the ground, in this hot weather. A dress so loud it 20 hurts my eyes. There are yellows and oranges enough to throw back the light of the sun. I feel my whole face warming from the heat waves it throws out. Earrings gold, too, and hanging down to her shoulders. Bracelets dangling and making noises when she moves her arm up to shake the folds of the dress out of her armpits. The dress is loose and flows, and as she walks closer, I like it. I hear Maggie go "Uhnnnh" again. It is her sister's hair. It stands straight up like the wool on a sheep. It is black as night and around the edges are two long pigtails that rope about like small lizards disappearing behind her ears.

"Wa-su-zo-Tean-o!" she says, coming on in that gliding way the dress makes her move. The short stocky fellow with the hair to his navel is all grinning and he follows up with "Asalamalakim, my mother and sister!" He moves to hug Maggie but she falls back, right up against the back of my chair. I feel her trembling there and when I look up I see the perspiration falling off her chin.

"Don't get up," says Dee. Since I am stout it takes something of a push. You can see me trying to move a second or two before I make it. She turns, showing white heels through her sandals, and goes back to the car. Out she peeks next with a Polaroid. She stoops down quickly and lines up picture after picture of me sitting there in front of the house with Maggie cowering behind me. She never takes a shot without making sure the house is included. When a cow comes nibbling around the edge of the yard she snaps it and me and Maggie *and* the house. Then she puts the Polaroid in the back seat of the car, and comes up and kisses me on the forehead.

Meanwhile Asalamalakim is going through motions with Maggie's hand. Maggie's hand is as limp as a fish, and probably as cold, despite the sweat, and she keeps trying to pull it back. It looks like Asalamalakim wants to shake hands but wants to do it fancy. Or maybe he don't know how people shake hands. Anyhow, he soon gives up on Maggie.

"Well," I say. "Dee."

"No, Mama," she says. "Not 'Dee.' Wangero Leewanika Kemanjo!" 25

"What happened to 'Dee'?" I wanted to know.

"She's dead," Wangero said. "I couldn't bear it any longer, being named after the people who oppress me."

"You know as well as me you was named after your aunt Dicie," I said. Dicie is my sister. She named Dee. We called her "Big Dee" after Dee was born.

"But who was *she* named after?" asked Wangero.

"Her mother," I said, and saw Wangero was getting tired. "That's about as far 30
as I can trace it," I said. Though, in fact, I probably could have carried it back
beyond the Civil War through the branches.

"Well," said Asalamalakim, "there you are."

"Uhnnnh." I heard Maggie say.

"There I was not," I said, "before 'Dicie' cropped up in our family, so why
should I try to trace it that far back?"

He just stood there grinning, looking down on me like somebody inspecting a
Model A car. Every once in a while he and Wangero sent eye signals over my head.

"How do you pronounce this name?" I asked.   35

"You don't have to call me by it if you don't want to," said Wangero.

"Why shouldn't I?" I asked. "If that's what you want us to call you, we'll call you."

"I know it might sound awkward at first," said Wangero.

"I'll get used to it," I said. "Ream it out again."

Well, soon we got the name out of the way. Asalamalakim had a name twice 40
as long and three times as hard. After I tripped over it two or three times he told
me to just call him Hakim-a-barber. I wanted to ask him was he a barber, but I didn't
really think he was, so I didn't ask.

"You must belong to those beef-cattle peoples down the road," I said. They
said "Asalamalakim" when they met you, too, but they didn't shake hands. Always
too busy: feeding the cattle, fixing the fences, putting up salt-lick shelters, throwing down hay. When the white folks poisoned some of the herd the men stayed up
all night with rifles in their hands. I walked a mile and a half just to see the sight.

Hakim-a-barber said, "I accept some of their doctrines, but farming and raising
cattle is not my style." (They didn't tell me, and I didn't ask, whether Wangero
[Dee] had really gone and married him.)

We sat down to eat and right away he said he didn't eat collards and pork was
unclean. Wangero, though, went on through the chitlins and corn bread, the greens
and everything else. She talked a blue streak over the sweet potatoes. Everything
delighted her. Even the fact that we still used the benches her daddy made for the
table when we couldn't afford to buy chairs.

"Oh, Mama!" she cried. Then turned to Hakim-a-barber. "I never knew how
lovely these benches are. You can feel the rump prints," she said, running her hands
underneath her and along the bench. Then she gave a sigh and her hand closed
over Grandma Dee's butter dish. "That's it!" she said. "I knew there was something
I wanted to ask you if I could have." She jumped up from the table and went over
in the corner where the churn stood, the milk in the clabber by now. She looked
at the churn and looked at it.

"This churn top is what I need," she said. "Didn't Uncle Buddy whittle it out 45
of a tree you all used to have?"

"Yes," I said.

"Uh huh," she said happily. "And I want the dasher, too."

"Uncle Buddy whittle that, too?" asked the barber. Dee (Wangero) looked up
at me.

"Aunt Dee's first husband whittled the dash," said Maggie so low you almost
couldn't hear her. "His name was Henry, but they called him Stash."

"Maggie's brain is like an elephant's," Wangero said, laughing. "I can use the churn top as a centerpiece for the alcove table," she said, sliding a plate over the churn, "and I'll think of something artistic to do with the dasher."

When she finished wrapping the dasher the handle stuck out. I took it for a moment in my hands. You didn't even have to look close to see where hands pushing the dasher up and down to make butter had left a kind of sink in the wood. In fact, there were a lot of small sinks; you could see where thumbs and fingers had sunk into the wood. It was beautiful light yellow wood, from a tree that grew in the yard where Big Dee and Stash had lived.

After dinner Dee (Wangero) went to the trunk at the foot of my bed and started rifling through it. Maggie hung back in the kitchen over the dishpan. Out came Wangero with two quilts. They had been pieced by Grandma Dee and then Big Dee and me had hung them on the quilt frames on the front porch and quilted them. One was in the Lone Star pattern. The other was Walk Around the Mountain. In both of them were scraps of dresses Grandma Dee had worn fifty and more years ago. Bits and pieces of Grandpa Jarrell's Paisley shirts. And one teeny faded blue piece, about the size of a penny matchbox, that was from Great Grandpa Ezra's uniform that he wore in the Civil War.

"Mama," Wangero said sweet as a bird. "Can I have these old quilts?"

I heard something fall in the kitchen, and a minute later the kitchen door slammed.

"Why don't you take one or two of the others?" I asked. "These old things was just done by me and Big Dee from some tops your grandma pieced before she died."

"No," said Wangero. "I don't want those. They are stitched around the borders by machine."

"That'll make them last better," I said.

"That's not the point," said Wangero. "These are all pieces of dresses Grandma used to wear. She did all this stitching by hand. Imagine!" She held the quilts securely in her arms, stroking them.

"Some of the pieces, like those lavender ones, come from old clothes her mother handed down to her," I said, moving up to touch the quilts. Dee (Wangero) moved back just enough so that I couldn't reach the quilts. They already belonged to her.

"Imagine!" she breathed again, clutching them closely to her bosom.

"The truth is," I said, "I promised to give them quilts to Maggie, for when she marries John Thomas."

She gasped like a bee had stung her.

"Maggie can't appreciate these quilts!" she said. "She'd probably be backward enough to put them to everyday use."

"I reckon she would," I said. "God knows I been saving 'em for long enough with nobody using 'em. I hope she will!" I didn't want to bring up how I had offered Dee (Wangero) a quilt when she went away to college. Then she had told me they were old-fashioned, out of style.

"But they're *priceless!*" she was saying now, furiously; for she has a temper. "Maggie would put them on the bed and in five years they'd be in rags. Less than that!"

"She can always make some more," I said. "Maggie knows how to quilt."

Dee (Wangero) looked at me with hatred. "You will not understand. The point is these quilts, *these* quilts!"

"Well," I said, stumped. "What would *you* do with them?"

"Hang them," she said. As if that was the only thing you *could* do with quilts.

Maggie by now was standing in the door. I could almost hear the sound her feet 70 made as they scraped over each other.

"She can have them, Mama," she said, like somebody used to never winning anything, or having anything reserved for her. "I can 'member Grandma Dee without the quilts."

I looked at her hard. She had filled her bottom lip with checkerberry snuff and it gave her face a kind of dopey, hangdog look. It was Grandma Dee and Big Dee who taught her how to quilt herself. She stood there with her scarred hands hidden in the folds of her skirt. She looked at her sister with something like fear but she wasn't mad at her. This was Maggie's portion. This was the way she knew God to work.

When I looked at her like that something hit me in the top of my head and ran down to the soles of my feet. Just like when I'm in church and the spirit of God touches me and I get happy and shout. I did something I never had done before: hugged Maggie to me, then dragged her on into the room, snatched the quilts out of Miss Wangero's hands and dumped them into Maggie's lap. Maggie just sat there on my bed with her mouth open.

"Take one or two of the others," I said to Dee.

But she turned without a word and went out to Hakim-a-barber. 75

"You just don't understand," she said, as Maggie and I came out to the car.

"What don't I understand?" I wanted to know.

"Your heritage," she said. And then she turned to Maggie, kissed her, and said, "You ought to try to make something of yourself, too, Maggie. It's really a new day for us. But from the way you and Mama still live you'd never know it."

She put on some sunglasses that hid everything above the tip of her nose and her chin.

Maggie smiled; maybe at the sunglasses. But a real smile, not scared. 80

After we watched the car dust settle I asked Maggie to bring me a dip of snuff. And then the two of us sat there just enjoying, until it was time to go in the house and go to bed.

SIGN FOR MY FATHER, WHO STRESSED THE BUNT

David Bottoms

On the rough diamond,
the hand-cut field below the dog lot and barn,
we rehearsed the strict technique

of bunting. I watched from the infield,
the mound, the backstop   5
as your left hand climbed the bat, your legs
and shoulders squared toward the pitcher.
You could drop it like a seed
down either base line. I admired your style,
but not enough to take my eyes off the bank   10
that served as our center-field fence.

Years passed, three leagues of organized ball,
no few lives. I could homer
into the garden beyond the bank,
into the left-field lot of Carmichael Motors,   15
and still you stressed the same technique,
the crouch and spring, the lead arm absorbing
just enough impact. That whole tiresome pitch
about basics never changing,
and I never learned what you were laying down.   20
Like a hand brushed across the bill of a cap,
let this be the sign
I'm getting a grip on the sacrifice.

PROFESSIONS FOR WOMEN

Virginia Woolf

When your secretary invited me to come here, she told me that your Society is
concerned with the employment of women and she suggested that I might tell you
something about my own professional experiences. It is true I am a woman; it is true I
am employed; but what professional experiences have I had? It is difficult to say. My
profession is literature; and in that profession there are fewer experiences for women
than in any other, with the exception of the stage—fewer, I mean, that are peculiar to
women. For the road was cut many years ago—by Fanny Burney, by Aphra Behn, by
Harriet Martineau, by Jane Austen, by George Eliot—many famous women, and
many more unknown and forgotten, have been before me, making the path smooth,
and regulating my steps. Thus, when I came to write, there were very few material
obstacles in my way. Writing was a reputable and harmless occupation. The family
peace was not broken by the scratching of a pen. No demand was made upon the
family purse. For ten and sixpence one can buy paper enough to write all the plays of
Shakespeare—if one has a mind that way. Pianos and models, Paris, Vienna and
Berlin, masters and mistresses, arc not needed by a writer. The cheapness of
writing paper is, of course, the reason why women have succeeded as writers
before they have succeeded in the other professions.

But to tell you my story—it is a simple one. You have only got to figure to yourselves a girl in a bedroom with a pen in her hand. She had only to move that pen from left to right—from ten o'clock to one. Then it occurred to her to do what is simple and cheap enough after all—to slip a few of those pages into an envelope, fix a penny stamp in the corner, and drop the envelope into the red box at the corner. It was thus that I became a journalist; and my effort was rewarded on the first day of the following month—a very glorious day it was for me—by a letter from an editor containing a cheque for one pound ten shillings and sixpence. But to show you how little I deserve to be called a professional woman, how little I know of the struggles and difficulties of such lives, I have to admit that instead of spending that sum upon bread and butter, rent, shoes and stockings, or butcher's bills, I went out and bought a cat—a beautiful cat, a Persian cat, which very soon involved me in bitter disputes with my neighbours.

What could be easier than to write articles and to buy Persian cats with the profits? But wait a moment. Articles have to be about something. Mine, I seem to remember, was about a novel by a famous man. And while I was writing this review, I discovered that if I were going to review books I should need to do battle with a certain phantom. And the phantom was a woman, and when I came to know her better I called her after the heroine of a famous poem, The Angel in the House. It was she who used to come between me and my paper when I was writing reviews. It was she who bothered me and wasted my time and so tormented me that at last I killed her. You who come of a younger and happier generation may not have heard of her—you may not know what I mean by the Angel in the House. I will describe her as shortly as I can. She was intensely sympathetic. She was immensely charming. She was utterly unselfish. She excelled in the difficult arts of family life. She sacrificed herself daily. If there was a chicken, she took the leg; if there was a draught she sat in it—in short she was so constituted that she never had a mind or a wish of her own, but preferred to sympathize always with the minds and wishes of others. Above all—I need not say it—she was pure. Her purity was supposed to be her chief beauty—her blushes, her great grace. In those days—the last of Queen Victoria—every house had its Angel. And when I came to write I encountered her with the very first words. The shadow of her wings fell on my page; I heard the rustling of her skirts in the room. Directly, that is to say, I took my pen in hand to review that novel by a famous man, she slipped behind me and whispered: "My dear, you are a young woman. You are writing about a book that has been written by a man. Be sympathetic; be tender; flatter; deceive; use all the arts and wiles of our sex. Never let anybody guess that you have a mind of your own. Above all, be pure." And she made as if to guide my pen. I now record the one act for which I take some credit to myself, though the credit rightly belongs to some excellent ancestors of mine who left me a certain sum of money—shall we say five hundred pounds a year?—so that it was not necessary for me to depend solely on charm for my living. I turned upon her and caught her by the throat. I did my best to kill her. My excuse, if I were to be had up in a court of law, would be that I acted in self-defence. Had I not killed her she would have killed me. She would have plucked the heart out of my writing. For, as I found, directly I put pen to paper, you cannot review even a novel without having a mind of your own, without expressing what you think to be the truth about human relations, morality, sex. And all these questions, according to the Angel in the House, cannot be dealt with freely and openly by women; they must charm, they must conciliate, they must—to put it bluntly—tell lies if they are to succeed. Thus, whenever I felt the shadow of her wing or the radiance of her halo upon my page, I took up the inkpot and flung it at her. She died hard. Her fictitious nature was of great assistance to her. It is far harder to kill a phantom than a reality. She was always creeping back when I though I had despatched her. Though I flatter myself that I killed her in the end, the struggle was severe; it took much time that had better have been spent upon learning Greek grammar; or in roaming the world in search of adventures. But it was a real experience; it was an experience that was bound to befall all women writers at that time. Killing the Angel in the House was part of the occupation of a woman writer.

But to continue my story. The Angel was dead; what then remained? You may say that what remained was a simple and common object—a young woman in a bedroom with an inkpot. In other words, now that she had rid herself of falsehood, that young woman had only to be herself. Ah, but what is "herself"? I mean, what is a woman? I assure you, I do not know. I do not believe that you know. I do not believe that anybody can know until she has expressed herself in all the arts and professions open to human skill. That indeed is one of the reasons why I have come here—out of respect for you, who are in process of showing us by your experiments what a woman is, who are in the process of providing us, by your failures and successes, with that extremely important piece of information.

But to continue the story of my professional experiences. I made one pound   5
ten and six by my first review; and I bought a Persian cat with the proceeds. Then I grew ambitious. A Persian cat is all very well, I said; but a Persian cat is not enough. I must have a motor car. And it was thus that I became a novelist—for it is a very strange thing that people will give you a motor car if you will tell them a story. It is a still stranger thing that there is nothing so delightful in the world as telling stories. It is far pleasanter than writing reviews of famous novels. And yet, if I am to obey your secretary and tell you my professional experiences as a novelist, I must tell you about a very strange experience that befell me as a novelist. And to understand it you must try first to imagine a novelist's state of mind. I hope I am not giving away professional secrets if I say that a novelist's chief desire is to be as unconscious as possible. He has to induce in himself a state of perpetual lethargy. He wants life to proceed with the utmost quiet and regularity. He wants to see the same faces, to read the same books, to do the same things day after day, month after month, while he is writing, so that nothing may break the illusion in which he is living—so that nothing may disturb or disquiet the mysterious nosings about, feelings round, darts, dashes and sudden discoveries of that very shy and illusive spirit, the imagination. I suspect that this state is the same both for men and women. Be that as it may, I want you to imagine me writing a novel in a state of trance. I want you to figure to yourselves a girl sitting with a pen in her hand, which for minutes, and indeed for hours, she never dips into the inkpot. The image that comes to my mind when I think of this girl is the image of a fisherman lying sunk in dreams on the verge of a deep lake with a rod held out over the water. She was

letting her imagination sweep unchecked round every rock and cranny of the world that lies submerged in the depths of our unconscious being. Now came the experience, the experience that I believe to be far commoner with women writers than with men. The line raced through the girl's fingers. Her imagination had rushed away. It had sought the pools, the depths, the dark places where the largest fish slumber. And then there was a smash. There was an explosion. There was foam and confusion. The imagination had dashed itself against something hard. The girl was roused from her dream. She was indeed in a state of the most acute and difficult distress. To speak without figure she had thought of something, something about the body, about the passions which it was unfitting for her as a woman to say. Men, her reason told her, would be shocked. The consciousness of what men will say of a woman who speaks the truth about her passions had roused her from her artist's state of unconsciousness. She could write no more. The trance was over. Her imagination could work no longer. This I believe to be a very common experience with women writers—they are impeded by the extreme conventionality of the other sex. For though men sensibly allow themselves great freedom in these respects, I doubt that they realize or can control the extreme severity with which they condemn such freedom in women.

These then were two very genuine experiences of my own. These were two of the adventures of my professional life. The first—killing the Angel in the House—I think I solved. She died. But the second, telling the truth about my own experiences as a body, I do not think I solved. I doubt that any woman has solved it yet. The obstacles against her are still immensely powerful—and yet they are very difficult to define. Outwardly, what is simpler than to write books? Outwardly, what obstacles are there for a woman rather than for a man? Inwardly, I think, the case is very different; she has still many ghosts to fight, many prejudices to overcome. Indeed it will be a long time still, I think, before a woman can sit down to write a book without finding a phantom to be slain, a rock to be dashed against. And if this is so in literature, the freest of all professions for women, how is it in the new professions which you are now for the first time entering?

Those are the questions that I should like, had I time, to ask you. And indeed, if I have laid stress upon these professional experiences of mind, it is because I believe that they are, though in different forms, yours also. Even when the path is nominally open—when there is nothing to prevent a woman from being a doctor, a lawyer, a civil servant—there are many phantoms and obstacles, as I believe, looming in her way. To discuss and define them is I think of great value and importance; for thus only can the labour be shared, the difficulties be solved. But besides this, it is necessary also to discuss the ends and the aims for which we are fighting, for which we are doing battle with these formidable obstacles. Those aims cannot be taken for granted; they must be perpetually questioned and examined. The whole position, as I see it—here in this hall surrounded by women practising for the first time in history I know not how many different professions—is one of extraordinary interest and importance. You have won rooms of your own in the house hitherto exclusively owned by men. You are able, though not without great labour and effort, to pay the rent. You are earning your five hundred pounds a year. But this freedom is only a beginning; the room is your own, but it is still bare. It has to be furnished; it has to be decorated; it has to be shared. How are you going to furnish it, how are you going to decorate it? With whom are you going to share it, and upon what terms? These, I think, are questions of the utmost importance and interest. For the first time in history you are able to ask them; for the first time you are able to decide for yourselves what the answers should be. Willingly would I stay and discuss those questions and answers—but not tonight. My time is up; and I must cease.

AM I BLUE?

Beth Henley

CHARACTERS
JOHN POLK, seventeen
ASHBE, sixteen
HILDA, a waitress, thirty-five
STREET PEOPLE: Barker, Whore, Bum, Clareece

SCENE: A BAR, THE STREET, THE LIVING ROOM OF A RUN-DOWN APARTMENT.
TIME: FALL 1968

The scene opens on a street in the New Orleans French Quarter on a rainy, blue bourbon night. Various people—a whore, a bum, street barker, Clareece—appear and disappear along the street. The scene then focuses on a bar where a piano is heard from the back room playing softly and indistinctly "Am I Blue?" The lights go up on John Polk, who sits alone at a table. He is seventeen, a bit overweight and awkward. He wears nice clothes, perhaps a navy sweater with large white monograms. His navy raincoat is slung over an empty chair. While drinking John Polk concentrates on the red and black card that he holds in his hand. As soon as the scene is established, Ashbe enters from the street. She is sixteen, wears a flowered plastic raincoat, a white plastic rain cap, red galoshes, a butterfly barrette, and jeweled cat-eye glasses. She is carrying a bag full of stolen goods. Her hair is very curly. Ashbe makes her way cautiously to John Polk's table. As he sees her coming, he puts the card into his pocket. She sits in the empty chair and pulls his raincoat over her head.

JOHN POLK (*looks up at her—then down into his glass*): What are you doing hiding under my raincoat? You're getting all wet.
ASHBE: Well, I'm very sorry, but after all it is a raincoat. (*He tries to pull off coat.*) It was rude of me I know, but look I just don't want them to recognize me.
JOHN POLK (*looking about*): Who to recognize you?
ASHBE: Well, I stole these two ash trays from the Screw Inn, ya know right down the street. (*She pulls out two glass commercial ash trays from her white plastic bag.*) Anyway, I'm scared the manager saw me. They'll be after me I'm afraid.

JOHN POLK: Well, they should be. Look, do you mind giving me back my raincoat? I don't want to be found protecting any thief.

ASHBE (coming out from under coat): Thief—would you call Robin Hood a thief?

JOHN POLK: Christ.

ASHBE (back under coat): No, you wouldn't. He was valiant—all the time stealing from the rich and giving to the poor.

JOHN POLK: But your case isn't exactly the same, is it? You're stealing from some crummy little bar and keeping the ash trays for yourself. Now give me back my coat.

ASHBE (throws coat at him): Sure, take your old coat. I suppose I should have explained—about Miss Marcey. (Silence.) Miss Marcey, this cute old lady with a little hump on her back. I always see her in her sun hat and blue print dress. Miss Marcey lives in the apartment building next to ours. I leave all the stolen goods, as gifts on her front steps.

JOHN POLK: Are you one of those kleptomaniacs? (He starts checking his wallet.)

ASHBE: You mean when people all the time steal and they can't help it?

JOHN POLK: Yeah.

ASHBE: Oh, no. I'm not a bit careless. Take my job tonight, my very first night job, if you want to know. Anyway, I've been planning it for two months, trying to decipher which bar most deserved to be stolen from. I finally decided on the Screw Inn. Mainly because of the way they're so mean to Mr. Groves. He works at the magazine rack at Diver's Drugstore and is really very sweet, but he has a drinking problem. I don't think that's fair to be mean to people simply because they have a drinking problem—and, well, anyway, you see I'm not just stealing for personal gain. I mean, I don't even smoke.

JOHN POLK: Yeah, well, most infants don't, but then again, most infants don't hang around bars.

ASHBE: I don't see why not, Toulouse-Lautrec did.

JOHN POLK: They'd throw me out.

ASHBE: Oh, they throw me out too, but I don't accept defeat. (Slowly moves into him.) Why it's the very same thing with my pickpocketing.

John Polk sneers, turns away.

ASHBE: It's a very hard art to master. Why every time I've done it, I've been caught.

JOHN POLK: That's all I need, is to have some slum kid tell me how good it is to steal. Everybody knows it's not.

ASHBE (about his drink): That looks good. What is it?

JOHN POLK: Hey, would you mind leaving me alone—I just wanted to be alone.

ASHBE: Okay. I'm sorry. How about if I'm quiet?

John Polk shrugs. He sips drink, looks around, catches her eye, she smiles and sighs.

ASHBE: I was just looking at your pin. What fraternity are you in?

JOIIN POLK: S.A.E.

ASHBE: Is it a good fraternity?

JOHN POLK: Sure, it's the greatest.

ASHBE: I bet you have lots of friends.

JOHN POLK: Tons.

ASHBE: Are you being serious?

JOHN POLK: Yes.

ASHBE: Hmm. Do they have parties and all that?

JOHN POLK: Yeah, lots of parties, booze, honking horns, it's exactly what you would expect.

ASHBE: I wouldn't expect anything. Why did you join?

JOHN POLK: I don't know. Well, my brother . . . I guess it was my brother . . . he told me how great it was, how the fraternity was supposed to get you dates, make you study, solve all your problems.

ASHBE: Gee, does it?

JOHN POLK: Doesn't help you study.

ASHBE: How about dates? Do they get you a lot of dates?

JOHN POLK: Some.

ASHBE: What were the girls like?

JOHN POLK: I don't know—they were like girls.

ASHBE: Did you have a good time?

JOHN POLK: I had a pretty good time.

ASHBE: Did you make love to any of them?

JOHN POLK (to self): Oh, Christ . . .

ASHBE: I'm sorry . . . I just figured that's why you had the appointment with the whore . . . cause you didn't have anyone else . . . to make love to.

JOHN POLK: How did you know I had the, ah, the appointment?

ASHBE: I saw you put the red card in your pocket when I came up. Those red cards are pretty familiar around here. The house is only about a block or so away. It's one of the best though, really very plush. Only two murders and a knifing in its whole history. Do you go there often?

JOHN POLK: Yeah, I like to give myself a treat.

ASHBE: Who do you have?

JOHN POLK: What do you mean?

ASHBE: I mean which girl. (John Polk gazes into his drink.) Look, I just thought I might know her is all.

JOHN POLK: Know her, ah, how would you know her?

ASHBE: Well, some of the girls from my high school go there to work when they get out.

JOHN POLK: G.G., her name is G.G.

ASHBE: G.G. . . . Hmm, well, how does she look?

JOHN POLK: I don't know.

ASHBE: Oh, you've never been with her before?

JOHN POLK: No.

ASHBE (confidentially): Are you one of those kinds that likes a lot of variety?

JOHN POLK: Variety? Sure, I guess I like variety.

ASHBE: Oh, yes, now I remember.

JOHN POLK: What?

ASHBE: G.G., that's just her working name. Her real name is Myrtle Reims, she's Kay Reims' older sister. Kay is in my grade at school.

JOHN POLK: Myrtle? Her name is Myrtle?

ASHBE: I never liked the name either.

JOHN POLK: Myrtle, oh, Christ. Is she pretty?

ASHBE (matter of fact): Pretty, no she's not real pretty.

JOHN POLK: What does she look like?

ASHBE: Let's see . . . she's, ah, well, Myrtle had acne and there are a few scars left. It's not bad. I think they sort of give her character. Her hair's red, only I don't think it's really red. It sort of fizzles out all over her head. She's got a pretty good figure . . . big top . . . but the rest of her is kind of skinny.

JOHN POLK: I wonder if she has a good personality.

ASHBE: Well, she was a senior when I was a freshman; so I never really knew her. I remember she used to paint her finger nails lots of different colors . . . pink, orange, purple. I don't know, but she kind of scares me. About the only time I ever saw her true personality was around a year ago. I was over at Kay's making a health poster for school. Anyway, Myrtle comes busting in, screaming about how she can't find her spangled bra anywhere. Kay and I just sat on the floor cutting pictures of food out of magazines while she was storming about slamming drawers and swearing. Finally, she found it. It was pretty garish—red with black and gold sequined G's on each cup. That's how I remember the name—G.G.

As Ashbe illustrates the placement of the G's, she spots Hilda, the waitress, approaching. Ashbe pulls the raincoat over her head and hides on the floor. Hilda enters through the beaded curtains spilling her tray. Hilda is a woman of few words.

HILDA: Shit, damn curtain, Nuther drink?

JOHN POLK: Mam?

HILDA (points to drink): Vodka coke?

JOHN POLK: No, thank you. I'm not quite finished yet.

HILDA: Napkin's clean.

Ashbe pulls her bag off the table. Hilda looks at Ashbe then to John Polk. She walks around the table, as Ashbe is crawling along the floor to escape. Ashbe runs into Hilda's toes.

ASHBE: Are those real gold?

HILDA: You again. Out.

ASHBE: She wants me to leave. Why should a paying customer leave? (Back to Hilda.) Now I'll have a mint julep and easy on the mint.

HILDA: This pre-teen with you?

JOHN POLK: Well, I . . . No . . . I . . .

HILDA: I.D.'s.

ASHBE: Certainly, I always try to cooperate with the management.

HILDA (looking at John Polk's): I.D., 11-12-50. Date: 11-11-68.

JOHN POLK: Yes, but . . . well, 11-12 is less than two hours away.

HILDA: Back in two hours.

ASHBE: I seem to have left my identification in my gold lamé bag.

HILDA: Well, boo-hoo. (Motions for Ashbe to leave with a minimum of effort. She goes back to table.) No tip.

ASHBE: You didn't tip her?

JOHN POLK: I figured the drinks were so expensive . . . I just didn't . . .

HILDA: No tip!

JOHN POLK: Look, Miss, I'm sorry. (*Going through his pockets.*) Here would you like a . . . a nickel . . . wait, wait, here's a quarter.

HILDA: Just move ass, sonny. You too, Barbie.

ASHBE: Ugh, I hate public rudeness. I'm sure I'll refrain from ever coming here again.

HILDA: Think I'll go in the back room and cry.

Ashbe and John Polk exit. Hilda picks up tray and exits through the curtain, tripping again.

HILDA: Shit, Damn curtain.

Ashbe and John Polk are now standing outside under the awning of the bar.

ASHBE: Gee, I didn't know it was your birthday tomorrow. Happy birthday! Don't be mad. I thought you were at least twenty-one, really.

JOHN POLK: It's o.k. Forget it.

As they begin walking, various blues are heard coming from the near-by bars.

ASHBE: It's raining.

JOHN POLK: I know.

ASHBE: Are you going over to the house now?

JOHN POLK: No, not till twelve.

ASHBE: Yeah, the red and black cards—they mean all night. Midnight till morning.

At this point a street barker beckons the couple into his establishment. Perhaps he is accompanied by a whore.

BARKER: Hey mister, bring your baby on in, buy her a few drinks, maybe tonight ya get lucky.

ASHBE: Keep walking.

JOHN POLK: What's wrong with the place?

ASHBE: The drinks are watery rot gut, and the show girls are boys . . .

BARKER: Up yours, punk!

JOHN POLK (*who has now sat down on a street bench*): Look, just tell me where a cheap bar is. I've got to stay drunk, but I just don't have much money left.

ASHBE: Yikes, there aren't too many cheap bars around here, and a lot of them check I.D.'s.

JOHN POLK: Well, do you know of any that don't?

ASHBE: No, not for sure.

JOHN POLK: Oh, God, I need to get drunk.

ASHBE: Aren't you?

JOHN POLK: Some, but I'm losing ground fast.

By this time a bum who has been traveling drunkenly down the street falls near the couple and begins throwing up.

ASHBE: Oh, I know! You can come to my apartment. It's just down the block. We keep one bottle of rum around. I'll serve you a grand drink, three or four if you like.

JOHN POLK (*fretfully*): No, thanks.

ASHBE: But look, we're getting all wet.

JOHN POLK: Sober too, wet and sober.

ASHBE: Oh, come on! Rain's blurring my glasses.

JOHN POLK: Well, how about your parents? What would they say?

ASHBE: Daddy's out of town and Mama lives in Atlanta; so I'm sure they won't mind. I think we have some cute, little marshmallows. (*Pulling on him.*) Won't you really come?

JOHN POLK: You've probably got some gang of muggers waiting to kill me. Oh, all right . . . what the hell, let's go.

ASHBE: Hurrah! Come on. It's this way. (*She starts across the stage, stops, and picks up an old hat.*) Hey, look at this hat. Isn't it something! Here, wear it to keep off the rain.

JOHN POLK (*throwing hat back onto street*): No, thanks, you don't know who's worn it before.

ASHBE: (*picking hat back up*): That makes it all the more exciting. Maybe it was a butcher's who slaughtered his wife or a silver pirate with a black bird on his throat. Who do you guess?

JOHN POLK: I don't know. Anyway what's the good of guessing? I mean you'll never really know.

ASHBE: (*trying the hat on*): Yeah, probably not.

At this point Ashbe and John Polk reach the front door.

ASHBE: Here we are.

Ashbe begins fumbling for her key. Clareece, a teeny-bopper, walks up to John Polk.

CLAREECE: Hey, man, got any spare change?

JOHN POLK (*looking through his pockets*): Let me see . . . I . . .

ASHBE: (*Coming up between them, giving Clareece a shove*): Beat it, Clareece. He's my company.

CLAREECE (*walks away and sneers*): Oh, shove it, Frizzels.

ASHBE: A lot of jerks live around here. Come on in.

She opens the door. Lights go up on the living room of a run-down apartment in a run-down apartment house. Besides being merely run-down the room is a malicious pig sty with colors, paper hats, paper dolls, masks, torn up stuffed animals, dead flowers and leaves, dress-up clothes, etc., thrown all about.

My bones are cold. Do you want a towel to dry off?

JOHN POLK: Yes, thank you.

ASHBE: (*she picks up a towel off the floor and tosses it to him*): Here. (*He begins drying off, as she takes off her rain things; then she begins raking things off the sofa.*) Please do sit down. (*He sits.*) I'm sorry the place is disheveled, but my father's been out of town. I always try to pick up and all before he gets in. Of course, he's pretty used to messes. My mother never was too good at keeping things clean.

JOHN POLK: When's he coming back?

ASHBE: Sunday, I believe. Oh, I've been meaning to say . . .

JOHN POLK: What?

ASHBE: My name's Ashbe Williams.

JOHN POLK: Ashbe?

ASHBE: Yeah, Ashbe.

JOHN POLK: My name's John Polk Richards.

ASHBE: John Polk? They call you John Polk?

JOHN POLK: It's family.

ASHBE: (putting on socks): These are my favorite socks, the red furry ones. Well, here's some books and magazines to look at while I fix you something to drink. What do you want in your rum?

JOHN POLK: Coke's fine.

ASHBE: I'll see if we have any. I think I'll take some hot Kool-Aid myself.

She exits to the kitchen.

JOHN POLK: Hot Kool-Aid?

ASHBE: It's just Kool-Aid that's been heated, like hot chocolate or hot tea.

JOHN POLK: Sounds great.

ASHBE: Well, I'm used to it. You get so much for your dime, it makes it worth your while. I don't buy presweetened, of course, it's better to sugar your own.

JOHN POLK: I remember once I threw up on a lot of grape Kool-Aid when I was a kid. I've hated it ever since. Hey, would you check on the time?

ASHBE: (she enters carrying a tray with several bottles of food coloring, a bottle of rum, and a huge glass): I'm sorry we don't have Coke. I wonder if rum and Kool-Aid is good? Oh, we don't have a clock either.

She pours a large amount of rum into the large glass.

JOHN POLK: I'll just have it with water then.

ASHBE: (she finds an almost empty glass of water somewhere in the room and dumps it in with the rum): Would you like food coloring in the water? It makes a drink all the more aesthetic. Of course, some people don't care for aesthetics.

JOHN POLK: No, thank you, just plain water.

ASHBE: Are you sure? The taste is entirely the same. I put it in all my water.

JOHN POLK: Well . . .

ASHBE: What color do you want?

JOHN POLK: I don't know.

ASHBE: What's your favorite color?

JOHN POLK: Blue, I guess.

She puts a few blue drops into the glass. As she has nothing to stir with, she blows into the glass turning the water blue.

JOHN POLK: Thanks.

ASHBE: (exits. She screams from the kitchen): Come on, say come on, cat, eat your fresh, good milk.

JOHN POLK: You have a cat?

ASHBE: No.

JOHN POLK: Oh.

ASHBE: (she enters carrying a tray with a cup of hot Kool-Aid and Cheerios and colored marshmallows): Here are some Cheerios and some cute, little, colored marshmallows to eat with your drink.

JOHN POLK: Thanks.

ASHBE: I one time smashed all the big white marshmallows in the plastic bag at the grocery store.

JOHN POLK: Why did you do that?

ASHBE: I was angry. Do you like ceramics?

JOHN POLK: Yes.

ASHBE: My mother makes them. It's sort of her hobby. She is very talented.

JOHN POLK: My mother never does anything. Well, I guess she can shuffle the bridge deck okay.

ASHBE: Actually, my mother is a dancer. She teaches at a school in Atlanta. She's really very talented.

JOHN POLK (indicates ceramics): She must be to do all these.

ASHBE: Well, Madeline, my older sister, did the blue one. Madeline gets to live with Mama.

JOHN POLK: And you live with your father.

ASHBE: Yeah, but I get to go visit them sometimes.

JOHN POLK: You do ceramics too?

ASHBE: No, I never learned . . . but I have this great potholder set. (Gets up to show him.) See, I make lots of multicolored potholders and send them to Mama and Madeline. I also make paper hats. (Gets material to show him.) I guess they're more creative, but making potholders is more relaxing. Here would you like to make a hat?

JOHN POLK: I don't know, I'm a little drunk.

ASHBE: It's not hard a bit. (Hands him material.) Just draw a real pretty design on the paper. It really doesn't have to be pretty, just whatever you want.

JOHN POLK: It's kind of you to give my creative drives such freedom.

ASHBE: Ha, ha, ha. I'll work on my potholder set a bit.

JOHN POLK: What time is it? I've really got to check on the time.

ASHBE: I know. I'll call the operator.

She goes to the phone.

JOHN POLK: How do you get along without a clock?

ASHBE: Well, I've been late for school a lot. Daddy has a watch. It's 11:03.

JOHN POLK: I've got a while yet. (Ashbe twirls back to her chair, drops, and sighs.) Are you a dancer, too?

ASHBE: (delighted): I can't dance a bit, really. I practice a lot is all, at home in the afternoon. I imagine you go to a lot of dances.

JOHN POLK: Not really, I'm a terrible dancer. I usually get bored or drunk.

ASHBE: You probably drink too much.

JOHN POLK: No, it's just since I've come to college. All you do there is drink more beer and write more papers.

ASHBE: What are you studying for to be?

JOHN POLK: I don't know.

ASHBE: Why don't you become a rancher?

JOHN POLK: Dad wants me to help run his soybean farm.

ASHBE: Soybean farm. Yikes, that's really something. Where is it?

JOHN POLK: Well, I live in the Delta, Hollybluff, Mississippi. Anyway, Dad feels I should go to business school first; you know, so I'll become, well, management-minded. Pass the blue.

ASHBE: Is that what you really want to do?

JOHN POLK: I don't know. It would probably be as good as anything else I could do. Dad makes good money. He can take vacations whenever he wants. Sure it'll be a ball.

ASHBE: I'd hate to be management-minded. (John Polk shrugs.) I don't mean to hurt your feelings, but I would really hate to be a management mind. (She starts walking on her knees, twisting her fists in front of her eyes, and making clicking sounds as a management mind would make.)

JOHN POLK: Cut it out. Just forget it. The farm could burn down, and I wouldn't even have to think about it.

ASHBE: (after a pause): Well, what do you want to talk about?

JOHN POLK: I don't know.

ASHBE: When was the last dance you went to?

JOHN POLK: Dances. That's a great subject. Let's see, oh, I don't really remember—it was probably some blind date. God, I hate dates.

ASHBE: Why?

JOHN POLK: Well, they always say they don't eat popcorn, and they wind up eating all of yours.

ASHBE: You mean, you hate dates just because they eat your popcorn? Don't you think that's kind of stingy?

JOHN POLK: It's the principle of the thing. Why can't they just say, yes, I'd like some popcorn when you ask them. But, no, they're always so damn coy.

ASHBE: I'd tell my date if I wanted popcorn. I'm not that immature.

JOHN POLK: Anyway, it's not only the popcorn. It's a lot of little things. I've finished coloring. What do I do now?

ASHBE: Now you have to fold it. Here . . . like this. (She explains the process with relish.) Say, that's really something.

JOHN POLK: It's kind of funny looking. (Putting the hat on.) Yeah, I like it, but you could never wear it anywhere.

ASHBE: Well, like what anyway?

JOHN POLK: Huh?

ASHBE: The things dates do to you that you don't like, the little things.

JOHN POLK: Oh, well, just the way, they wear those false eyelashes and put their hand on your knee when you're trying to parallel park, and keep on giggling and going off to the bathroom with their girl friends. It's obvious they don't want to go out with me. They just want to go out so they can wear their new clothes and won't have to sit on their ass in the dormitory. They never want to go out with me. I can never even talk to them.

ASHBE: Well, you can talk to me, and I'm a girl.

JOHN POLK: Well, I'm really kind of drunk, and you're a stranger . . . well, I probably wouldn't be able to talk to you tomorrow. That makes a difference.

ASHBE: Maybe it does. (*A bit of a pause and when extremely pleased by the idea she says.*) You know we're alike because I don't like dances either.

JOHN POLK: I thought you said you practiced . . . in the afternoons.

ASHBE: Well, I like dancing. I just don't like dances. At least not like . . . well, not like the one our school was having tonight . . . they're so corny.

JOHN POLK: Yeah, most dances are.

ASHBE: All they serve is potato chips and fruit punch, and then this stupid baby band plays and everybody dances around thinking they're so hot. I frankly wouldn't dance there. I would prefer to wait till I am invited to an exclusive hall. It doesn't really matter which ball, just one where they have huge, golden chandeliers and silver fountains, and serve delicacies of all sorts and bubble blue champagne. I'll arrive in a pink silk cape. (*Laughing.*) I want to dance in pink!

JOHN POLK: You're mixed up. You're probably one of those people that live in a fantasy world.

ASHBE: I do not. I accept reality as well as anyone. Anyway you can talk to me, remember. I know what you mean by the kind of girls it's hard to talk to. There are girls a lot that way in the small clique at my school. Really tacky and mean. They expect everyone to be as stylish as they are, and they won't even speak to you in the hall. I don't mind if they don't speak to me, but I really love the orphans, and it hurts my feelings when they are so mean to them.

JOHN POLK: What do you mean—they're mean to the "orpheens?" (*Giggles to himself at the wordplay.*)

ASHBE: Oh, well they sometimes snicker at the orphans' dresses. The orphans usually have hand-me-down, drab, ugly dresses. Once Shelly Maxwell wouldn't let Glinda borrow her pencil, even though she has two. It hurt her feelings.

JOHN POLK: Are you best friends with these orphans?

ASHBE: I hardly know them at all. They're really shy. I just like them a lot. They're the reason I put spells on the girls in the clique.

JOHN POLK: Spells, what do you mean, witch spells?

ASHBE: Witch spells? Not really, mostly just voodoo.

JOHN POLK: Are you kidding? Do you really do voodoo?

ASHBE: Sure here I'll show you my doll. (*Goes to get doll, comes back with straw voodoo doll. Her air as she returns is one of frightening mystery.*) I know a lot about the subject. Cora, she used to wash dishes in the Moonlight Cafe, told me all about voodoo. She's a real expert on the subject, went to all the meetings and everything. Once she caused a man's throat to rot away and turn almost totally black. She's moved to Chicago now.

JOHN POLK: It doesn't really work. Does it?

ASHBE: Well, not always. The thing about voodoo is that both parties have to believe in it for it to work.

JOHN POLK: Do the girls in school believe in it?

ASHBE: Not really, I don't think. That's where my main problem comes in. I have to make the clique believe in it, yet I have to be very subtle. Mainly, I give reports in English class or Speech.

JOHN POLK: Reports?

ASHBE: On voodoo.

JOHN POLK: That's really kind of sick, you know.

ASHBE: Not really. I don't cast spells that'll do any real harm. Mainly, jut the kind of thing to make them think . . . to keep them on their toes. (*Blue-drink intoxication begins to take over and John Polk begins laughing.*) What's so funny.

JOHN POLK: Nothing. I was just thinking what a mean little person you are.

ASHBE: Mean! I'm not mean a bit.

JOHN POLK: Yes, you are mean . . . (*picking up color*) . . . and green too.

ASHBE: Green?

JOHN POLK: Yes, green with envy of those other girls; so you plan all those mean little tricks.

ASHBE: Envious of those other girls, that stupid, close-minded little clique!

JOHN POLK: Green as this marshmallow. (*Eats marshmallow.*)

ASHBE: You think I want to be in some group . . . a sheep like you? A little sheep like you that does everything when he's supposed to do it!

JOHN POLK: Me a sheep . . . I do what I want!

ASHBE: Ha! I've known you for an hour and already I see you for the sheep you are!

JOHN POLK: Don't take your green meanness out on me.

ASHBE: Not only are you a sheep, you are a NORMAL sheep. Give me back my colors! (*Begins snatching colors away.*)

JOHN POLK (*pushing colors at her*): Green and mean! Green and mean! Green and mean!

ASHBE (*throwing marshmallows at him*): That's the reason you're going to manage your mind. And dates . . . you go out on dates merely because it's expected of you even though you have a terrible time. That's the reason you go to the whorehouse to prove you're a normal man. Well, you're much too normal for me.

JOHN POLK: Infant bitch. You think you're really cute.

ASHBE: That really wasn't food coloring in your drink, it was poison! (*She laughs, he picks up his coat to go, and she stops throwing marshmallows at him.*) Are you going? I was only kidding. For Christ's sake, it wasn't really poison. Come on, don't go. Can't you take a little friendly criticism?

JOHN POLK: Look, did you have to bother me tonight? I had enough problems without . . .

Phone rings. Both look at phone, it rings for the third time. He stands undecided.

ASHBE: Look, wait, we'll make it up. (*She goes to answer phone.*) Hello . . . Daddy. How are you? . . . I'm fine . . . Dad, you sound funny . . . What? . . . Come on, Daddy, you know she's not here. (*Pause.*) Look, I told you I wouldn't call anymore. You got her number in Atlanta. (*Pause, as she sinks to the floor.*) Why have you started again? . . . Don't say that. I can tell it. I can. Hey, I have to go to bed now, I don't want to talk anymore, okay? (*Hangs up phone, then softly to self.*) Goddamnit.

JOHN POLK (*he has heard the conversation and is taking off his coat*): Hey, Ashbe . . . (*She looks at him blankly, her mind far away.*) You want to talk?

ASHBE: No. (*Slight pause.*) Why don't you look at my shell collection? I have this special shell collection. (*She shows him collection.*)

JOHN POLK: They're beautiful, I've never seen colors like this. (*Ashbe is silent, he continues to himself.*) I used to go to Biloxi a lot when I was a kid . . . One time my brother and I, we camped out on the beach. The sky was purple, I remember it was really purple. We ate pork and beans out of a can. I'd always kinda wanted to do that. Every night for about a week after I got home, I dreamt about these waves foaming over my head and face. It was funny. Did you find these shells or buy them?

ASHBE: Some I found, some I bought. I've been trying to decipher their meaning. Here, listen, do you hear that?

JOHN POLK: Yes.

ASHBE: That's the soul of the sea. (*She listens.*) I'm pretty sure it's the soul of the sea. Just imagine when I decipher the language. I'll know all the secrets of the world.

JOHN POLK: Yeah, probably you will. (*Looking at the shell.*) You know, you were right.

ASHBE: What do you mean?

JOHN POLK: About me, you were right. I am a sheep, a normal one. I've been trying to get out of it, but now I'm as big a sheep as ever.

ASHBE: Oh, it doesn't matter. You're company. It was rude of me to say.

JOHN POLK: No, because it was true. I really didn't want to go into a fraternity, I didn't even want to go to college, and I sure as hell don't want to go back to Hollybluff and work the soybean farm till I'm eighty.

ASHBE: I still say you could work on a ranch.

JOHN POLK: I don't know. I wanted to be a minister or something good, but I don't even know if I believe in God.

ASHBE: Yeah.

JOHN POLK: I never used to worry about being a failure. Now I think about it all the time. It's just I need to do something that's . . . fulfilling.

ASHBE: Fulfilling, yes, I see what you mean. Well, how about college? Isn't it fulfilling? I mean, you take all those wonderful classes, and you have all your very good friends.

JOHN POLK: Friends, yeah, I have some friends.

ASHBE: What do you mean?

JOHN POLK: Nothing . . . well, I do mean something. What the hell, let me try to explain. You see it was my "friends," the fraternity guys that set me up with G.G., excuse me, Myrtle, as a gift for my eighteenth birthday.

ASHBE: You mean, you didn't want the appointment?

JOHN POLK: No, I didn't want it. Hey, ah, where did my blue drink go?

ASHBE (*as she hands him the drink*): They probably thought you really wanted to go.

JOHN POLK: Yeah, I'm sure they gave a damn what I wanted. They never even asked me. Hell, I would have told them a handkerchief, a pair of argyle socks, but, no, they have to get me a whore just because it's a cool-ass thing to do. They make me sick. I couldn't even stay at the party they gave. All the sweaty T-shirts, and moron sex stories . . . I just couldn't take it.

ASHBE: Is that why you were at the Blue Angel so early?

JOHN POLK: Yeah, I needed to get drunk, but not with them. They're such creeps.

ASHBE: Gosh, so you really don't want to go to Myrtle's?

JOHN POLK: No, I guess not.

ASHBE: Then are you going?

JOHN POLK (*pause*): Yes.

ASHBE: That's wrong. You shouldn't go just to please them.

JOHN POLK: Oh, that's not the point anymore, maybe at first it was, but it's not anymore. Now I have to go for myself . . . to prove to myself that I'm not afraid.

ASHBE: Afraid? (*Slowly, as she begins to grasp his meaning.*) You mean, you've never slept with a girl before?

JOHN POLK: Well, I've never been in love.

ASHBE (*in amazement*): You're a virgin?

JOHN POLK: Oh, God.

ASHBE: No, don't feel bad, I am too.

JOHN POLK: I thought I should be in love . . .

ASHBE: Well, you're certainly not in love with Myrtle. I mean, you haven't even met her.

JOHN POLK: I know, but, God, I thought maybe I'd never fall in love. What then? You should experience everything . . . shouldn't you? Oh, what's it matter, everything's so screwed.

ASHBE: Screwed? Yeah, I guess it is. I mean, I always thought it would be fun to have a lot of friends who gave parties and go to dances all dressed up. Like the dance tonight . . . it might have been fun.

JOHN POLK: Well, why didn't you go?

ASHBE: I don't know. I'm not sure it would have been fun. Anyway, you can't go . . . alone.

JOHN POLK: Oh, you need a date?

ASHBE: Yeah, or something.

JOHN POLK: Say, Ashbe, ya wanna dance here?

ASHBE: No, I think we'd better discuss your dilemma.

JOHN POLK: What dilemma?

ASHBE: Myrtle. It doesn't seem right you should . . .

JOHN POLK: Let's forget Myrtle for now. I've got a while yet. Here have some more of this blue-moon drink.

ASHBE: You're only trying to escape through artificial means.

JOHN POLK: Yeah, you got it. Now come on. Would you like to dance? Hey, you said you liked to dance.

ASHBE: You're being ridiculous.

JOHN POLK (*winking at her*): Dance?

ASHBE: John Polk, I just thought . . .

JOHN POLK: Hmm?

ASHBE: How to solve your problem . . .

JOHN POLK: Well . . .

ASHBE: Make love to me!

JOHN POLK: What?!

ASHBE: It all seems logical to me. It would prove you weren't scared, and you wouldn't be doing it just to impress others.

JOHN POLK: Look, I . . . I mean, I hardly know you . . .

ASHBE: But we've talked. It's better this way, really. I won't be so apt to point out your mistakes.

JOHN POLK: I'd feel great, stripping a twelve-year-old of her virginity.

ASHBE: I'm sixteen! Anyway, I'd be stripping you of yours just as well. I'll go put on some Tiger Claw perfume. (*She runs out.*)

JOHN POLK: Hey, come back! Tiger Claw perfume, Christ.

ASHBE (*entering*): I think one should have different scents for different moods.

JOHN POLK: Hey, stop spraying that! You know I'm not going to . . . well, you'd get neurotic, or pregnant, or some damn thing. Stop spraying, will you!

ASHBE: Pregnant? You really think I could get pregnant?

JOHN POLK: Sure, it'd be a delightful possibility.

ASHBE: I really wouldn't be bad. Maybe I would get to go to Tokyo for an abortion. I've never been to the Orient.

JOHN POLK: Sure getting cut on is always a real treat.

ASHBE: Anyway, I might just want to have my dear baby. I could move to Atlanta with Mama and Madeline. It'd be wonderful fun. Why I could take him to the supermarket, put him in one of those little baby seats to stroll him about. I'd buy peach baby food and feed it to him with a tiny golden spoon. Why I could take colored pictures of him and send them to you through the mail. Come on . . . (*Starts putting pillows onto the couch.*) Well, I guess you should kiss me for a start. It's only etiquette, everyone begins with it.

JOHN POLK: I don't think I could even kiss you with a clear conscience. I mean, you're so small with those little cat-eye glasses and curly hair . . . I couldn't even kiss you.

ASHBE: You couldn't even kiss me? I can't help it if I have to wear glasses. I got the prettiest ones I could find.

JOHN POLK: Your glasses are fine. Let's forget it, okay?

ASHBE: I know, my lips are too purple, but if I eat carrots, the dye'll come off and they'll be orange.

JOHN POLK: I didn't say anything about your lips being too purple.

ASHBE: Well, what is it? You're just plain chicken, I suppose . . .

JOHN POLK: Sure, right, I'm chicken, totally chicken. Let's forget it. I don't know how, but, somehow, this is probably all my fault.

ASHBE: You're darn right it's all your fault! I want to have my dear baby or at least get to Japan. I'm so sick of school I could smash every marshmallow in sight! (*She starts smashing.*) Go on to your skinny pimple whore. I hope the skinny whore laughs in your face, which she probably will because you have an easy face to laugh in.

JOHN POLK: You're absolutely right, she'll probably hoot and howl her damn fizzle red head off. Maybe you can wait outside the door and hear her, give you lots of pleasure, you sadistic, little thief.

ASHBE: Thief! Was Robin Hood . . . Oh, what's wrong with this world? I just wasn't made for it, is all. I've probably been put in the wrong world, I can see that now.

JOHN POLK: You're fine in this world.

ASHBE: Sure, everyone just views me as an undesirable lump.

JOHN POLK: Who?

ASHBE: You, for one.

JOHN POLK (*pause*): You mean because I wouldn't make love to you?

ASHBE: It seems clear to me.

JOHN POLK: But you're wrong, you know.

ASHBE (*to self, softly*): Don't pity me.

JOHN POLK: The reason I wouldn't wasn't that . . . it's just that . . . well, I like you too much to.

ASHBE: You like me?

JOHN POLK: Undesirable lump, Jesus. Your cheeks they're . . . they're . . .

ASHBE: My cheeks? They're what?

JOHN POLK: They're rosy.

ASHBE: My cheeks are rosy?

JOHN POLK: Yeah, your cheeks, they're really rosy.

ASHBE: Well, they're natural, you know. Say, would you like to dance?

JOHN POLK: Yes.

ASHBE: I'll turn on the radio. (*She turns on radio. Ethel Waters is heard singing "Honey in the Honeycomb." Ashbe begins snapping her fingers.*) Yikes, let's jazz it out.

They dance.

JOHN POLK: Hey, I'm not good or anything . . .

ASHBE: John Polk.

JOHN POLK: Yeah?

ASHBE: Baby, I think you dance fine!

They dance on laughing, saying what they want till end of song. Then a radio announcer comes on and says the 12:00 news will be in five minutes. Billie Holiday or Terry Pierce, begins singing, "Am I Blue?"

JOHN POLK: Dance?

ASHBE: News in five minutes.

JOHN POLK: Yeah.

ASHBE: That means five minutes till midnight.

JOHN POLK: Yeah, I know.

ASHBE: Then you're not . . .

JOHN POLK: Ashbe, I've never danced all night. Wouldn't it be something to . . . to dance all night and watch the rats come out of the gutter?

ASHBE: Rats?

JOHN POLK: Don't they come out at night? I hear New Orleans has lots of rats.

ASHBE: Yeah, yeah, it's got lots of rats.

JOHN POLK: Then let's dance all night and wait for them to come out.

ASHBE: All right . . . but, but how about our feet?

JOHN POLK: Feet?

ASHBE: They'll hurt.

JOHN POLK: Yeah.

ASHBE (*smiling*): Okay, then let's dance.

> *He takes her hand, and they dance as lights black out and the music soars and continues to play.*

End

Appendix A
Collaborative Projects

If you recall reading the Preface and the first chapter of this book, you'll probably also recall being aware that there are three authors—this book is itself a collaborative project. In fact, if you look at the covers of your textbooks, you'll notice that many are written by two or more authors. Occasionally you too may be called upon to compose a collaborative presentation. Although such a project may be quite different from anything you've done before, it need not be intimidating. After all, you've been working collaboratively on informal interpretations already; a collaborative project is a natural extension of that process. Through your responses to literary works—from active reading through research—you have discovered that literature is not written in a vacuum. Your group work has also taught you that readers rarely approach literature in isolation. It is only natural, then, to sometimes extend the collaborative process to include the formal presentation itself.

Perhaps the most important thing to remember when embarking on a collaborative project is that you are no longer responsible only for your own work: you are part of a team, and your contribution will affect other students as well as yourself. Often that sense of responsibility to others results in a greater effort on everyone's part. The rewards of composing a worthwhile collaborative project are great—often greater than the rewards of composing an individual project, because the sense of accomplishment is shared.

If you find yourself facing a collaborative assignment, you should be confident in knowing that you are familiar with the most important parts of collaboration: sharing your individual responses with others and attempting to come to a consensus in a group. This appendix, then, will focus primarily on the "nuts and bolts" of formal presentations. There are many ways of going about preparing a collaborative project (a good deal depends on the nature of the project), but some general guidelines can help you work through the logistics. To work most effectively, you'll want to consider three things: choosing groups, choosing a topic, and preparing the presentation.

CHOOSING GROUPS

Occasionally instructors will assign students to groups, but more often they will ask students to choose their own groups. If you are given the option of choosing groups, consider *interest, compatibility,* and *availability.* If you have worked with a number of different groups as you discussed the literature, you should have a sense of different students' interests. The advantage of *common interest* is obvious: your preparations should go more smoothly and your presentation should be more coherent if everyone in the group shares a similar perspective. Groups should be *compatible* because each member will be responsible to the entire group, and because the group will be working together for a length of time. Sometimes, however, when group members share a common interest and seem compatible, they tend to overlook the problems that arise when not all members are available at the same times. Even though *availability* has little to do with the substance of a project, difficulties with scheduling can frustrate a group's efforts. Your attention and energy should be directed toward working through your project, not toward finding a time when everyone can meet. Thus it's important to find a group whose schedules allow for common meeting times.

CHOOSING TOPICS

Occasionally instructors will assign topics, in which case a group can simply decide between several choices. (See Appendix B for information on working with assigned topics.) But even in such situations, the group will have to decide on a focus for the topic. Suppose, for example, that your instructor would like groups to make biographical presentations on authors studied in class. Your group chooses Susan Glaspell. In journals and small group discussion a little biographical information has emerged, but nobody in the group knows much about her life. It will be up to the group, then, to do some preliminary research to determine the focus of the report. Was her home life such an influence on her work that you wish to focus on that? Is the work so autobiographical that you want to use it as your focus? Were outside political and social influences important enough to focus on? Such questions should be considered early in the process, so that the topic is as clearly focused as possible before the group begins working in earnest.

PREPARING THE PRESENTATION

Early Stages

One of the great advantages of working in a collaborative classroom is that even before you begin working on a project, you have a good deal of information already—in the form of annotated texts, journals, and notes from group discussions, class discussions, and research. As the members of your group share this material, you should develop a sense of the direction you'd like to follow, both as individuals and as a group. One member, for example, might pay a good deal of attention to the setting in Glaspell's play;

that member might explore setting in other works, comparing them and considering Glaspell's reasons for choosing such settings. Another group member might seem quite interested in the injustices of the men, ranging from John Wright's smothering of his wife's spirit to the Sheriff's and the Attorney's dismissal of women's concerns as "trifles." That member might explore Glaspell's life and work with an eye toward determining a pattern of such portrayals, or uncovering a cause for the author's preoccupation with such a theme. If group members pursue initial research based on their own interests, the entire group will benefit.

Although group members will be working individually throughout the initial stages of preparation, it's important to remember that the project is a *group* project. At regular meetings members should share experiences, keeping the group up-to-date on their progress. It's almost inevitable that someone will discover early on either that there isn't enough material available to pursue a specific interest, or that the direction he or she is taking is inconsistent with the focus of the report. Suppose, for example, that your group has decided to focus on how Susan Glaspell's relationships influenced her work. One group member has chosen to explore setting in her work, and discovers that Glaspell's choice of setting doesn't seem relevant to her life; rather, setting differs from work to work. The entire group will have to decide how to deal with this obstacle—perhaps by broadening the focus of the entire presentation or by helping the group member find another, more profitable, focus for his or her individual research. Such obstacles occur, of course, in individual presentations as well, but the nature of a collaborative presentation demands that the group determine what should be done to overcome the obstacle.

Meetings should also allow the group to see the entire presentation taking shape. Sometimes when individual members encounter surprises in their preparation, those surprises actually help the group. A member exploring Glaspell's home life, for example, might come across a connection to a woman suffrage group—something that the group had not considered in its early shaping of the topic. Such a connection, however, may well help establish a social as well as a personal grounding for Glaspell's work.

Drafting

At first the idea of drafting a multiple-authored presentation may seem intimidating; after all, the idea of drafting their own papers intimidates many students. But in fact, if the group has been sharing material throughout the early stages of preparation, drafting should go smoothly. As each member shares with the group his or her material, the overall presentation will begin to take shape. A meeting at which the group does nothing but talk about how each member's contribution will fit into the presentation can be very helpful, even before members begin drafting their own sections of the presentation. As members discover how their sections fit together, they'll be able to begin drafting with a clear sense of overall purpose. Subsequent meetings can focus on fine-tuning the content and organization of individual sections, on developing transitions between sections, and on composing an introduction and a conclusion. Finally, the members of the group who are best at editing can review the entire presentation for grammar, spelling, and mechanics.

A Note on Style

As coauthors of this book, we are well aware of the need to make the entire piece sound like it's being spoken in the same voice. That's something you'll want to be aware of as well. The best way to accomplish this unity of voice is to make sure that each member of the group reads every other member's work—and comments on it. If you find another member's expressions overly formal, for example, you must say so. Perhaps the group will decide that the presentation should be this formal (thereby necessitating some changes in your section), or they may decide that the writer of the formal section should revise. *What* the group decides is less important than the fact *that* it decides—as a group—how the presentation will be made. You'll probably discover, in any case, that working on the same presentation for some length of time makes you subtly aware of the other "voices" in the group. That awareness usually leads to easy accommodation, and a unified voice for the presentation.

ORAL REPORTS

Not all presentations are presented in written form. If your instructor asks for an oral presentation, you'll follow essentially the same process outlined previously. When it comes time to draft individual sections, however, you should focus more on the impact of the spoken word than on the written word. An oral presentation, for example, is easier to follow if there aren't too many long, complex sentences. Informational footnotes can also be distracting in an oral presentation. And, of course, each member of the group must practice delivering the presentation. Practice sessions will help you work out the amount of time each section takes, the transitions between sections, the tone and level of voice necessary to keep the audience's attention, and other such matters. You may also decide to provide handouts for your audience—an outline of the presentation, perhaps, or photographs of relevant characters. The most important thing to remember in an oral presentation is that you don't get a second chance to capture your audience's attention; thus anything you can do to enhance your presentation will usually be worthwhile.

CONCLUSIONS

Preparing and presenting a collaborative report can be a rewarding experience, even more rewarding than making an individual presentation. The commitment of a group to a single project enhances the significance of the project and provides the authors with invaluable experience in negotiating meaning. If you remember that the collaborative presentation is simply a logical extension of the collaborative learning process, you should have no trouble adapting to its particular demands.

Appendix B
Essay Assignments

Throughout this book we have elaborated upon ways in which readers can generate their own responses to literature. Occasionally, however, you will find yourself faced with a specific essay assignment—perhaps even an exam question—that on the surface may not seem related to the material in your journals and group discussions. In fact, your previous work has prepared you better than you may think to respond to such assignments. Your journal entries and group discussions may not have focused specifically on issues addressed in a given essay assignment, but you have been practicing a method of making meaning from literature, a method that will serve you well in responding to assigned topics as well as in generating your own topics. Furthermore, the writing process outlined in Chapters 6 and 7 can be adapted to fit both essay assignments and essay examinations. In addition, the strategies outlined here should help you work within the constraints of both writing situations.

THE ESSAY ASSIGNMENT

An instructor who prepares an essay assignment is, in effect, entering the conversation begun with your active reading—entering at a much later stage in the meaning-making process. If you consider the assignment as you would a question posed by a group member, or even posed by yourself in your journal, you should be able to adapt the process you have practiced throughout this book to the task at hand. The instructor's assignment is presenting you with an alternative perspective from which to view the literary work. Suppose, for example, that small group and class discussions of "The Story of an Hour" have focused on the emergence of Mrs. Mallard's sense of freedom, the irony of her death, and the position of women at the time. Suddenly you find yourself faced with the following question:

> In "The Story of an Hour," Mrs. Mallard's awakening takes place in a closed room, but is heavily influenced by the view from the window. Analyze the setting of the story, focusing on the significance of closed spaces and the natural world.

Although the class has never discussed setting at any length, you may well find references to setting in your annotations, your journal, or your notes on group discussions. If you treat this question as though it were introduced in a group discussion, you should be able to work your way through to a response. If your instructor asks that you generate ideas for the assignment collaboratively, you will follow the same practice in responding to the assignment that you would use when responding to your own questions and observations. You will write journal entries on the assignment, discuss the assignment with members of your group, and perhaps even discuss your draft with members of the group. If you are asked to develop your essay on your own, you should be able to internalize the conversation that has been taking place in groups and in class discussions. Even if there are no references to setting in your notes, the collaborative process will have prepared you to return to the literary work to continue the conversation from a new perspective.

THE ESSAY EXAMINATION

Like other essay assignments designed by instructors, essay exams provide you with the focus (and usually the organizational strategy) you'll use in composing your response to a literary work. Unlike out-of-class essays, however, essay exams require you to compose your response in one sitting, usually without consulting other students. If you have practiced responding to literature through active reading, journals, and group discussion, you should be able to adapt your composing process to suit the needs and time constraints of the essay exam. What follows are some strategies for responding to essay questions.

Strategies for Taking Essay Exams

- Preparing for the Test—Reviewing Texts, Journals, and Notes from Group Discussions
- Looking for Key Words in the Question
- Responding to the Question in One or Two Sentences
- Outlining Your Response
- Composing/Revising/Editing All at Once
- Reviewing Your Response

Preparing for the Test—Reviewing Texts, Journals, Notes from Group Discussions

Even though you probably don't know ahead of time precisely what the essay question will be, you are familiar with the direction taken by class discussion prior to the exam. By reviewing your journal entries and your notes from group and class discussions, you can refresh your memory of the literary works under consideration. Pay specific attention to unresolved issues: frequently instructors in collaborative classrooms use the essay exam to test your strategies for responding to literature, so they focus on an issue that arose in class discussion but on which the class never reached consensus. The instructor may also ask you to pursue further an issue that was discussed at some length. In either case, a review of your journals and notes will get your mind working, asking new questions about the work, resolving some issues, and generally providing you with a foundation on which to build a response.

Looking for Key Words in the Question

A well constructed essay question will include key words that direct students to a focus and an organizing strategy. Pay careful attention to terms such as those found in Chapters 9 and 10 (*explication, analysis, evaluation*), as well as to hints regarding possible organizing strategies (comparison/contrast, classification).

Responding to the Question in One or Two Sentences

Since the person designing the essay question has in mind a focus for the response, it's wise to try to find that focus before you begin to write. Sometimes in an exam situation, there's the temptation to use a "shotgun approach"—spraying the paper with pellets representing everything you can think of, hoping that one idea will hit the target. The result of such an approach is an unfocused, confusing essay—and usually a poor grade. In order to maintain your focus, a profitable strategy to use is to respond to the question in one or two sentences, using that response as a focal point for the development of the essay. You need not even use the short response as part of your essay, but the *idea* will help you keep on track.

Outlining Your Response

Some writers can't even begin to compose a draft until they have outlined their ideas; others can't compose an outline until they have completed a draft. When writing outside class, you have the luxury of following your own individual writing process. But when your composing process must be compressed into an hour or less, it's usually helpful to follow generally accepted strategies. One of those strategies is the outline. It's not necessary to construct an elaborate outline before drafting a response to an essay question, but it is helpful to jot down several words or sentences that cover each section of your response. When time is short and the pressure is on, it's easy to forget a key element of your response. If you've outlined the response before beginning, then you'll be less likely to omit something important as you develop your essay.

Composing/Revising/Editing All at Once

Very few students work fast enough to be able to write a draft, revise and edit it, and prepare a final copy in the time allotted for an essay question. Thus it's necessary to develop strategies for integrating drafting, revising, and editing into one compact process. Different writers use variations of this strategy: Some write a few sentences, stop and check the sentences for coherence and general correctness, and then move on. Others revise and edit paragraph by paragraph (or section by section). Some writers compose the entire essay before revising. Unless you find that a specific strategy works for you, it's probably most profitable to use the paragraph-by-paragraph method. This method allows you to focus on a small section while keeping the main idea of the paper in mind. Working with a few sentences at a time can be useful for editing (checking for correctness), but revising for content and organization is far more important, especially when working under time constraints. Writing the entire essay first, of course, would be the ideal way to keep the main idea in mind while revising. But you may find, after writing the entire essay, that one section really isn't relevant to the assignment. If that section comes early in or midway through the paper, you'll face some major revisions complicated by time constraints. If you check each section as you write it, on the other hand, you'll be able to identify digressions before you've moved too far in an unprofitable direction.

Reviewing Your Response

You will find yourself much more comfortable and confident upon leaving an exam if you've had time to review your response fully before turning in your paper. When you feel that your essay is complete, reread it from beginning to end, asking yourself the following questions:

Content/Organization
- Is my main idea clearly stated early in the essay?
- Does each paragraph cover one element of my main idea?
- Does each paragraph build on the preceding paragraphs and lead to the subsequent paragraphs?
- Does my concluding paragraph effectively end the essay?

Constraints of the Question
- Have I responded specifically to the question?
- Have I complied with the requirements of the question (e.g., examples, quotations, etc.)

Style/Mechanics (if time permits)
- Are my sentences varied in length and type?
- Is my vocabulary precise and vivid?
- Is my grammar, punctuation, and spelling correct?

This checklist may seem rather mechanical to you, especially if you have developed your own unique way of responding to literature. It seems to turn a creative process into a "paint-by-numbers" exercise. While on the surface that criticism may be valid, you should remember that the essay examination poses specific problems that don't exist for out-of-class essays, especially essays whose main ideas have been developed by the writers themselves. The nature of the essay exam, like the nature of the research paper, necessitates adhering to certain conventions. If you can work within these constraints, you have surely mastered the process discussed in the rest of this book.

Another problem arises when you consider mechanical issues—especially spelling—in an essay exam. While you are usually expected to display mastery of standard written English in an essay exam, you can't be expected to produce the kind of polished product you'd produce for an out-of-class essay. Most instructors understand this and don't require perfection in essay exams. Of course, errors and awkward passages distract readers, and the fewer of these interfering with your presentation, the better. However, even the most nearly perfect grammatical presentation, spelled impeccably, is worthless unless it has something to say. You should certainly keep correctness in mind, but don't equate a correct paper with a good, solid essay. If time constraints prevent you from revising and editing thoroughly, it's wiser to focus your attention on the revising—a well-thought-out presentation with a few errors is far more valuable than a correct presentation with serious content problems.

CONCLUSIONS

Essay assignments and essay exams need not strike fear into the hearts of students. In the collaborative classroom you have learned to make your own meaning from a text; thus you are in a far better position to respond to such assignments than is a student in a traditional lecture class. Furthermore, the challenge of adding yet another voice to the conversation and of exploring the literary work from yet another perspective can be exhilarating. If you remember that the interpretations that arose in class were generated by *your* thinking process, then you should face essay assignments and exams with well grounded confidence.

Appendix C
Glossary of Literary Terms

Throughout this book, we have used literary terms with which you may not be entirely familiar. What follows are brief explanations of those terms and others you are likely to encounter in an introductory study of literature. You will find these explanations useful when the context in which a term appears does not make the term's meaning entirely clear to you. This glossary does not repeat terms that are discussed in detail in the book itself, nor does it pretend to be an exhaustive list of terms used in literary criticism. For a complete glossary of literary terms, see

> Holman, C. Hugh, and William Harmon. A *Handbook to Literature*. 5th. ed. New York: Macmillan, 1986.

Allegory A literary work with two meanings: a literal, surface meaning, and a parallel meaning, which is usually symbolic.

Alliteration The repetition of initial consonant sounds in words that appear close together.

Allusion A reference to a person, place, event, or era that exists outside the literary work.

Ambiguity A deliberate use of language that can have several different meanings.

Anecdote A brief story within a longer work, intended to illustrate a specific point or idea.

Antagonist A character whose actions oppose those of the protagonist.

Anticlimax A conclusion that is considerably less important or meaningful than expected, a "let-down."

Antihero A main character whose attributes are not admirable.

Archetype Symbols that represent universally accepted truths. Archetypes can be characters, places, or events.

Atmosphere The aura, or emotional impact of a literary work.

Climax The high point in the plot of a narrative.

Comedy A narrative with a happy ending (*not* necessarily funny).

Conflict The struggle between the protagonist and antagonistic forces in a narrative.

Critical approaches Sometimes referred to as **schools of literary criticism,** systems of belief about literature and the world that form the basis of the way scholars look at (or approach) literary works. The following are some popular approaches:

Archetypal criticism   searches for universal patterns in literary works, such as the notions of life being cyclical (birth, death, rebirth), the journey from innocence to experience, the scapegoat who takes away a civilization's ills, etc.

Biographical criticism   uncovers significant events in the author's life in his or her text.

Deconstructionism   seizes upon the critic's delight in the endless web of possibilities a work contains, constantly exposing gaps and thus revealing a text's instability.

Feminist criticism   examines the portrayal of women in a work, considers the special contribution of women to literature, and seeks out feminine images and language in a work.

Formalist or new criticism   focuses attention on the work of literature as a unified whole, without considering the author's state of mind, history, politics, or economics.

Historical criticism   places literature in the context of its writer's times.

Semiotic/structural criticism   examines the shape or picture of a work (semiotics) as well as its motifs and patterns (structuralism).

New historicism   looks at literature as a window to the past—a source of insight into the writer's times—rather than the reverse.

Psychological criticism   (based on Freud's famous *Oedipal complex*) analyzes the author's motivation for writing, the reader's various motivations for his or her interpretations, and the motivations of the characters in a text.

Reader-response criticism   considers the text created anew each time a reader approaches it.

Sociological criticism   looks to uncover the economic and political ramifications of a work of literature.

Drama   Literature written to be performed, consisting primarily of dialogue. Can be written in either prose or poetry.

Epigraph   A quotation designed to introduce a theme; it appears at the beginning of an entire work or a section of a work (see the Preface of this book).

Epilogue   A closing piece in a literary work, usually adding more information or commentary on the action.

Epiphany   A moment of enlightenment for a character.

Essay   A brief, nonfiction work of literature, usually focusing on one subject or theme.

Fiction   A narrative recounting events that are not based on fact.

Genre   A type of literature, e.g., fiction , essay, poetry, and drama.

Imagery   Language that appeals to any of the senses.

Irony   A situation in which words or events mean the opposite of what they are expected to mean.

Meter   Patterns of rhythm in poetry.

Motif   An idea or theme that recurs throughout a literary work.

Narrative In fiction, drama, or poetry, a recounting of events.

Nonfiction Prose based on fact.

Persona The narrator of a work, not always representative of the writer.

Personification The attribution of human qualities to animals or things.

Poetry Literature in which the rhythm of the language is a primary feature. (Poems do not have to rhyme.)

Point of view The perspective from which a narrative is related.

Plot The arrangement of events in a narrative.

Prose Literature presented in ordinary, spoken language—as opposed to the rhythmic language of poetry.

Protagonist The main character in a story, one with whom the audience usually identifies.

Rhyme scheme The pattern of rhyme in a poem.

Rhythm The pattern of sounds in a poem.

Scene In drama, an episode or small division of the action.

Setting The general environment—including time, place, and culture—in which a literary work takes place.

Stage directions The dramatists explanations for layout of the stage, expressions on characters' faces, and movement of characters.

Stanza A group of lines forming one unit of a poem (similar to a paragraph in prose).

Symbol A person, an object, or an event that stands for something beyond its literal meaning.

Theme The main ideas that permeate a literary work.

Tone The writer's attitude toward the subject, the characters, and the audience.

Tragedy A narrative in which the main character is destroyed.

Verse A single line of poetry.

Index

Formal presentations. *See*
Presentations, formal
Format, references/bibliography,
170–171
Free verse, 190
Frost, Robert: "Mending Wall,"
136–137
student presentation,
explication, 134–136
Frost, Robert: "The Tuft of
Flowers," 5–7
interpretation of, 9–12
sample discussion, 7–9

General Periodicals Index, 65
Glaspell, Susan: *Trifles,*
68–77
annotation sample, 28–34
character analysis, 140
evaluation, example of,
148–151
point of view, analysis of,
142–143
setting analysis, 141–142
student discussion, 79–81
student samples, 77–79
symbols, analysis of, 143–144
theme, analysis of, 145–146
Group discussion
double-entry journal checklist,
44
"Polygamy," 91–94
reviewing for essay
examination, 248–249
"The Story of an Hour," 84–87
and topic development for
formal presentation,
103–104
"To the Ladies," 96–98
"Trifles," 79–81
Group exploration process,
49–57
classroom discussion, 56–57
environment, 50–51

focus/determination of issues,
53–54
preparation for, 51–52
student role, 50
teacher role, 49
topics, isolation of, 54–56
Groups, choosing, 242–243

*Harvard Guide to American
History,* 64
Henley, Beth: *Am I Blue?*
226–241
Historical context
proposition development for
formal presentation,
106–107
reference books, 64
Hopkins, Gerard Manley: "I
awake and feel the fell of
dark," 27–28
Humanities reference books,
63–64

Ibsen, Henrik: *A Doll's House,*
188
Images
commenting on language,
20
student comments, 34
Improvisation, 100
Inductive reasoning, 113,
115–117
Informal comments, "To the
Ladies," 98
Informal research
student sample, 81
"The Story of an Hour,"
87–88
In medias res story development,
183, 184–186
Integration of quotations into
text, 158–162
*International Cyclopedia of Music
and Musicians,* 64

New Testament, 25
New York Times Index, 65

Onomatopoeia, 186
Open-ended questions, 2–3
Oral reports, 245
Order of importance, 118
Organization of essay test
responses, 250
Organization of formal
presentations, 118–126
comparison/contrast, 124–126
derivative organization,
chronological, 118,
121–122
derivative organization, spatial,
118, 119–121
order of importance, 122–124
Outlining essay test responses,
249–250
*Oxford Companion to American
Literature,* 63
*Oxford Companion to English
Literature,* 63

Paraphrase/paraphrasing, 155
and plagiarism, 165–166
Parenthetical documentation of
references, 168
Parenthetical references, 162
Passive reading, 13
Peer review
descriptive, 127
formal presentations, 126–130
judgmental, 130
mechanisms of, 129–130
reading aloud, 127
technical, 128–129
written, 126
Personal story development,
180–188
Philosophy reference books, 63
Phrases, quotation of, 160
Plath, Sylvia: "Metaphors," 191

Poetry writing, 190, 191–193
Point of view, analysis of, 142–143
Political context, research
sources, 62–63
Preliminary reading, 15–16
Premeditation, 100
Presentations, formal
audience, 110–117
choosing groups, 242–243
choosing topics, 243
drafting presentations, 244–245
oral reports, 245
organization of, 118–126
peer review, 126–130
reference to sources (*see*
Reference to sources)
thesis development, 106–110
topics, 102–106
Presentations, types of
analysis of character, 139–141
analysis of language, 144–145
analysis of point of view,
142–143
analysis of setting, 141–142
analysis of symbols, 143–144
analysis of theme, 145–146
drama, 193, 194–197
evaluation, 146–151
explication, 132–138
personal stories, 180–188
poetry, 190, 191–193
short story, 197, 198–201
Primary source, 153
Primary source introduction,
reference to, 170
Prior knowledge, 15–16
Proposition development for
formal presentation,
106–110
Punctuation
and plagiarism, 166
of quotations, 161–162
Pynchon, Thomas: *The Crying of
Lot 49,* 24–25

Credits continued

Carvainis Agency, Inc.; p. 223, "Professions for Women" in *The Death of a Moth and Other* Essays by Virginia Woolf, copyright 1942 by Harcourt Brace Jovanovich, Inc. and renewed 1970 by Marjorie T. Parsons, Executrix, reprinted by permission of the publisher; p. 226, © Copyright, 1982, by Beth Henley. CAUTION: Professionals and amateurs are hereby warned that AM I BLUE is subject to a royalty. It is fully protected under the copyright laws of the United States of America, and of all countries covered by the International Copyright Union (including the Dominion of Canada and the rest of the British Commonwealth), and of all countries covered by the Pan-American Copyright Convention and the Universal Copyright Convention, and of all countries with which the United States has reciprocal copyright relations. All rights, including professional, amateur, motion picture, recitation, lecturing, public reading, radio broadcasting, television, video or sound taping, all other forms of mechanical or electronic reproduction, such as information storage and retrieval systems, and the rights of translation into foreign languages, are strictly reserved. Particular emphasis is laid upon the question of readings, permission for which must be secured from the author's agent in writing. All inquiries concerning rights (other than amateur rights) should be addressed to Gilbert Parker, c/o William Morris Agency, Inc., 1350 Avenue of the Americas, New York, N.Y. 10019. Stock and amateur production rights in AM I BLUE are controlled exclusively by the DRAMATISTS PLAY SERVICE, INC., 440 Park Avenue South, New York, N.Y. 10016. No amateur performance of the play may be given without obtaining in advance the written permission of the DRAMATISTS PLAY SERVICE, INC., and paying the requisite fee.

NEW HANOVER COUNTY PUBLIC LIBRARY
201 Chestnut Street
Wilmington, N.C. 28401

GAYLORD S